To Ken & Joy Woods,

with best wishes

from their long-lost-

cousin,

Eric Quayle

Zennor
Cornwall.

30th March, 1972.

Ballantyne the Brave

R.M.Ballantyne.

Eric Quayle

Ballantyne the Brave

A VICTORIAN WRITER AND HIS FAMILY

RUPERT HART-DAVIS
1-3 Upper James Street London
1967

Printed in Great Britain by
Western Printing Services Ltd, Bristol

To my wife
Jean

Illustrations

To the Hesitating Purchaser

If sailor tales to sailor tunes,
Storm and adventure, heat and cold,
If schooners, islands, and maroons
And Buccaneers and buried Gold,
And all the old romance, retold
Exactly in the ancient way,
Can please, as me they pleased of old,
The wiser youngsters of to-day:

—So be it, and fall on! If not,
If studious youth no longer crave,
His ancient appetites forgot,
Kingston, or Ballantyne the brave,
Or Cooper of the wood and wave:
So be it, also! And may I
And all my pirates share the grave
Where these and their creations lie!

*Verses written by Robert Louis Stevenson
which appear at the front of the first
edition of* TREASURE ISLAND.

Preface

WHEN THE NEWS OF THE DEATH of R. M. Ballantyne reached England from Rome in 1894, it was received with dismay by the many thousands of readers to whom his books had brought countless hours of silent enjoyment. Led by the boys of Harrow School, a movement immediately started which had as its objective the collection of sufficient funds to raise a lasting monument to his name, with the result that, within a few months, over six hundred pounds had been received by the organisers, mostly in hard-won pennies and sixpences from the pockets of the young. Such a spontaneous gesture by the impecunious schoolboys of Victoria's Britain to perpetuate an author's name is without precedent to the present day, and gives us a clear indication of the esteem in which he was held by the young men of the latter half of the nineteenth century.

Robert Michael Ballantyne was born only ten years after the Battle of Waterloo, but his youngest child, now in her eighty-sixth year, survives happily at a Kentish farm, busily enjoying an active old age. Throughout the years Miss Isobel Ballantyne carefully preserved the family archive of letters, faded photographs, notebooks, manuscripts and drawings of her internationally famous father, twice saving them from certain destruction during wartime salvage drives, besides keeping the vast assortment of papers safe from the dispersing hands of dealers and disinterested relations. I therefore tender to Miss Ballantyne my sincere thanks, for without her guardianship there can be little doubt that documents that have been of inestimable value in piecing together the disjointed fragments of this troubled family history would have inevitably been scattered and lost.

This unexpected discovery of the family papers, locked in a battered tin trunk where they had lain concealed for more than seventy years, has enabled me to uncover a great number of hitherto unknown facts regarding book production in the nineteenth century, especially those works written for the juvenile market and the vast field covered by adventure tales for boys. Discoveries have been made which show that Ballantyne, whose family had been utterly ruined by their association with Sir Walter Scott, was himself the victim of greedy and unscrupulous publishers, who paid him a mere fraction of their true value for stories that became the undisputed best-sellers of their day in the juvenile market.

Not only was Ballantyne one of the romantic figures of literature in the later Victorian era; he was also a pioneer of the straightforward adventure story set in a factual background. He was one of the first to let the youthful characters of his books fend for themselves in the plots he created, without the curbing hands and interfering restrictions of dreary chaperones, or the sententious comments of pious uncles and straitlaced moralising aunts with which earlier authors invariably stuffed their tales. Time has withered his popularity, but a number of his titles are still in print today, well over a hundred years since they first appeared. Stories he wrote with a quill pen back in the 1850's are now being read by the fifth generation of young men to hold a book of his in the glow of a bedside lamp—as their candle and gas-lit predecessors did before them.

But despite the pleasure his tales brought to those of us who grew up reading *The Coral Island*, *Martin Rattler*, *The Young Fur Traders*, *Ungava*, or, in our nursery days, *The Three Little Kittens*, to say nothing of the rest of his host of adventure books, this prolific writer has been almost completely ignored by biographers and students of literature. Except for a few paragraphs in *The Dictionary of National Biography*, silence shrouds the memory of the author about whom J. M. Barrie wrote:[1] 'Ballantyne was for long my man, and I used to study a column of the *Spectator* about forthcoming books, waiting for his next, as if for the pit door to open. I think I looked upon him as the author of the "Hundred Best Books," and wondered why that list ever needed to be the subject of controversy.'

These are some of the reasons that have influenced me in my decision to write the biography of R. M. Ballantyne: the unexpected twists to the story of a most interesting life having made the task well worth while.

[1] From the de luxe edition of *The Coral Island*, published by James Nisbet & Company, London, 1913.

I take this opportunity of thanking the many friends and advisers who have contributed to the making of this biography, especially Miss E. M. Mein, of Edinburgh, whose painstaking researches North of the Border have saved me a number of long journeys to Edinburgh; Percival Hinton, Esq., of Sutton Coldfield, who encouraged me to undertake this task and whose expert knowledge of bibliographical detail has been invaluable; Mr. and Mrs. Ian Smith, the present occupiers of Walton Hall, Kelso, for their hospitality and advice regarding the early history of the house; and all my friendly rivals amongst the collectors of first editions of English juvenile literature who have oft-times informed me of volumes I should otherwise have sought in vain.

To these, and many other friends, societies and institutions, I acknowledge my indebtedness.

Sutton Coldfield,   ERIC QUAYLE
Warwickshire.
1967

Chapter One

IT IS SELDOM one meets a man who has not, in his youth, read
at least one of Ballantyne's adventure tales. To most of the fathers
and grandfathers of today there must still cling around the name
of this nineteenth-century author the golden fragrance of the
enchanted coral islands of their youth, when the smallest backyard or tiniest patch of threadbare lawn seemed wider than the
Seven Seas, and the whole bright, inviting world appeared to
pipe and shrill with impatient adventure—just waiting for a boy
to cut the strings.

To the young men who were his contemporaries in the latter
half of Victoria's reign, he was a well-loved and respected household name; an author whose books could be relied upon to stir
romance and danger into the humdrum affairs of everyday life
and whose stories never failed to tingle with the steel of dramatic
suspense and the bloodthirsty incidents so beloved by boys of all
ages. To these young men he was a figure larger than life-size;
a bearded, romantic-looking hero from the wilds of Hudson Bay,
and a man whose tales they could relive—shipwrecked in suburban gardens; marooned on muddy backyard islands; or while they
retreated before overwhelming odds—badly wounded, but still
fighting bravely—up the attic stairs. Ballantyne had been far-
sighted enough to make all his heroes boys, and the young heroes
who read his books, steeped in the dreams he conjured, became
themselves the intrepid explorers, the castaways and hunters,
with which he peopled his tales. To them, this was the author
whose stories dissolved the drab monotony of reality into a
pirate world of treasure chests and buccaneers, Redskins and
grizzly bears, and a hundred hair's-breadth escapes from fates too
horrible to contemplate. He had gained the distinction of being
identified in the minds of his young followers with the bravest
deeds performed by the manly characters in the fictional tales he
wrote; and his photographs, which showed him as a handsome,
bearded figure, with the shoulder-length hair of a typical North
American trapper, complete with long-barrelled gun and

powder-horn across his knees, went far to confirm this impression.

This was the image of the author which Ballantyne, through the stories he wrote, created in the minds of his readers; a picture of a tough, resolute pioneer, bred in a school of merchant adventurers, who served God and his country strong in the unshakable conviction of the righteousness and justice of the British cause; the type of Empire builder he hoped to become in reality if only fortune came his way. But events were to shatter the dreams and aspirations of the eager young man from the backwoods of Rupert's Land, long before the closing scenes of the drama were reached in an apartment house in Rome.

Ballantyne's childhood was clouded by the atmosphere of continual financial distress in which his parents struggled to rear and educate their children. To understand the sequence of events which led to the ruin of the boy's father and uncle we must start the story in the middle of the eighteenth century, when Robert Michael's paternal grandfather, John Ballantyne, established himself as a general merchant in the Border town of Kelso in Roxburghshire. He worked hard and the business prospered, and, by 1780, his shop had become the largest in the town, standing on the corner of the main square in a spot now occupied by the Linen Bank of Scotland. It was a store in which, according to the advertisements that appeared in the local papers at the time, one could buy everything from 'Taplin's Genuine Horse Medicine,' to 'The Very Latest London Fashions in Millinery,' these last-mentioned feminine garments being dispensed by his bustling little wife, Jean, whose hands must have already been fully occupied with the task of rearing their three young sons.

These brown-haired, good-looking boys, James, John and Alexander, all artistic and musical by nature and seeming anything but the sons of a provincial grocer, were later destined to have their fortunes intimately entwined with those of Sir Walter Scott; the eldest, James, as the printer of his works, while John was for many years his publisher. This association was ultimately to prove the ruin of the entire Ballantyne family.

The youngest of the trio, Alexander Thomson Ballantyne, the

father of R. M. Ballantyne, was born on 28th April, 1776, and, like his elder brothers, attended Kelso Grammar School for several years. From the age of fourteen he worked in his father's general store, but soon came to hate the life of a grocer and provision merchant and begged his parents to set him free to indulge his passion for music and the arts. He was described[1] as being a youth of only slight build, his deep brown eyes being set in a thin, aquiline face, the nose long and slightly hooked, while his hair was brushed back and gathered loosely at the back in a style fashionable at that period. His hands were remembered for the long sensitive fingers, which are said to have looked far more suitable to the handling of some fine *objet d'art* than the sacks of oats and sides of bacon which his father kept in stock.

As a boy he proved himself an extremely gifted musician, and, for a twenty-first birthday present, his father bought him a Stradivarius violin for the then princely sum of forty-five guineas, and sent him to London for tuition. He returned, to be acknowledged after a few years as one of the finest amateur violinists in the whole of Scotland, and an adept performer of the small flageolet or 'penny whistle' as he called it. In *Memoirs of a Long Life* by Surgeon-General W. C. Maclean,[2] the doctor tells of the pleasure he had in being acquainted with the youngest of the Ballantyne brothers:

> He was a man of quiet and retired habits, with a large fund of Scottish humour; devoted to music and an accomplished performer on the violin. To hear him play Scottish airs was a thing to be remembered. He used to charm his friends with what he called his 'Penny Whistle,' and on this little instrument he played native airs with astonishing sweetness and expression, extracting from this unpromising source, tones that surprised and delighted his hearers. I remember dining with a small party, of whom Mr. Alexander Ballantyne was one, at the house of Mr. Playfair. Before the guests went to a concert by the greatest violin player of the

[1] These details are quoted from a written description of her parents by Mary Ballantyne, their eldest daughter.
[2] Published in Edinburgh in 1895.

age, perhaps of any age, Mr. Ballantyne, at Mr. Playfair's request, delighted the company by playing first on the penny whistle, and afterwards on his violin. From Mr. Ballantyne's charming music we adjourned to the Assembly Rooms to a Paganini concert . . . Of this I am sure, not a few of our party were not ashamed to confess that they derived more pleasure and real musical enjoyment from Alexander Ballantyne's refined and tasteful playing of the simple airs of Scotland, than from listening to the diabolical 'tricks' of probably the greatest master of the violin the world has ever seen.

His exquisite mastery of the violin and the easy-going good-humour he invariably displayed brought him many friends amongst the famous in Scottish society, and, thanks to an intro-duction from his brother James, who had attended school with Walter Scott, he quickly became one of the author's special favourites. It was Scott who dubbed him 'Sandy' for reasons that are now obscure, and that nickname stuck to Alexander Ballantyne for the rest of his life.[1]

James Ballantyne had originally been trained as a solicitor, but in 1797, with financial help from his father, he had become the proprietor of *The Kelso Mail*, a Tory newspaper which proved remarkably successful in the early years of its life, quickly oust-ing its only local rival, *The British Chronicle*, which the land-owners and gentry of the neighbourhood refused to support because of its radical views. As a boy, Scott had become one of James's closest friends at Kelso Grammar School, which the bud-ding author had attended for a few hours each day during his summer vacations from Edinburgh, and in later life, as a none too successful young lawyer, he still paid frequent visits to the Border town to stay with his uncle at Rosebank Cottage. It was on one of these visits that he called at James's printing office to supply his friend with a few paragraphs on some legal question of the day, and he suggested to Ballantyne before leaving that he ought to keep his types in play during the part of the week when

[1] Scott always wrote the name as 'Sandie,' but I have adopted the family spelling of the nickname.

4

they were idle by obtaining some booksellers' work. James was never one to let the grass grow under his feet, and before long, with Scott's encouragement and help, he had developed the book-printing side of the business to a point where he had more work than his presses could cope with. The high quality of his printing quickly brought him more than local fame and, in 1802, Scott having advanced five hundred pounds in consideration of a part-nership, the Ballantyne Press, as it later came to be called, moved to Edinburgh.

Sandy Ballantyne stayed on in Kelso as manager of the *Kelso Mail*, taking over the editorship from his brother James in 1806,[1] and on the 24th November of the following year, having bought and furnished a small house, he married Miss Anne Randall Scott Grant, 'a lass wi' a lang pedigree' who could trace her ancestry back to the Earls of Seaforth and Cromartie. The pair seemed to have been eminently suited to one another, and from the time of their wedding their marriage proved a very happy one. They settled contentedly in Belmount Place, Kelso, in a tiny villa surrounded by an old-fashioned cottage garden where the new Mrs. Ballantyne used to pass many of her leisure hours. Randall (she never used the name Anne) was the daughter of Dr. Robert Grant and Mary Howard of Inverness, members of a well-known Scottish family who were considerably higher in the social scale than the Ballantynes, and at whose large country house Sandy had often taken part in the musical evenings so beloved by Georgian middle-class society.

In later years, Randall liked to confess to her children that she had fallen in love with their handsome father at their first meet-ing, and Ballantyne must himself have been greatly impressed by this slim and beautiful girl of nineteen, with her fresh complexion, oval face and deep blue eyes. Her brown hair, held in place with a silken band, she wore parted in the middle, with ringlets at her ears and on her forehead, and this style exactly suited her slightly haughty, aristocratic face with its impeccably straight Grecian nose and well-shaped little mouth. Sandy was soon deeply in love with this attractive young creature ten years his junior, and it is

---

[1] Sandy later purchased the newspaper from his brother with the help of the dowry his wife brought him on their marriage.

noticeable with what affection he mentions her in his diary and letters right up to the time of his death.

Before many years had passed they were the parents of a rapidly growing family of children, and only the death of his brother John in 1821, and the start of what was to prove a slow but progressive decline in the circulation of the *Kelso Mail*, marred what was otherwise a serene and happy period in their lives. By 1822 the Ballantyne brood comprised five daughters and two sons, one other child having died in infancy. Their ages ranged from six months to ten years and it was not long before the small villa in Belmount Place became too overcrowded for Randall's peace of mind. Shortly before his death at the age of forty-seven, John Ballantyne had begun building Walton Hall in Kelso, an imposing house not far from the junction of the rivers Tweed and Teviot, and one which he hoped to use as a country seat for the fishing and hunting parties in which he delighted. But consumption of the lungs, helped by a life of almost continual dissipation, cut short his career before the building was half finished. Sandy was already looking for a larger home and he took the opportunity which the death of his brother afforded to acquire the land and complete the house for his own use, with the result that in the autumn of 1822, having furnished the interior and landscaped the garden, Randall and he moved into their grand new home with their seven children.

There followed two years which Sandy and his wife looked on as amongst the happiest of their life. His brother James had for some time commissioned him to copy out the sheets of manuscript of the astoundingly successful series of novels and romances which were now flowing from the prolific pen of Sir Walter Scott.[1] The author had a rooted objection to acknowledging that he was the writer of any of his fictional prose works (although he displayed no such reluctance with regard to his poetry), being convinced that to be known as a novelist conflicted with his status as laird of Abbotsford, the imposing country house on whose lands and build-ings he was expending immense sums every year; and that the legal position he occupied as Clerk to the Court of Session, and his

---

[1] On the 30th March, 1820, Scott was created a baronet by the Prince Regent.

rank as Sheriff of Selkirkshire, were not to be identified as being in the hands of a writer of romantic fiction. He preferred to remain as 'The Great Unknown,' as the literary critics of the day had dubbed the mysterious author of the Waverley Novels, with the result that his manuscripts were all painstakingly copied out by Sandy before being handed to the typesetters at his brother's printing office in Paul's Works in Edinburgh. Ballantyne treated this task as one of the greatest of honours, and in the long hours when he was locked alone in the tiny parlour in Belmount Place, and later at Walton Hall, Randall enforced a strict rule that he was not to be disturbed on any account by either the children or his friends.

This work brought him into frequent contact with Scott and some of the members of his circle of friends, and, as Kelso was conveniently situated between Abbotsford and Berwick-upon-Tweed, there were occasions when the author called at Walton Hall on his way to the coast and the south. For miles around the house was known for the concerts which Sandy arranged at the weekends; concerts in which his friends and neighbours joined and in which the host's exquisitely toned violin played a leading part.

During the day any guests staying at the Hall could use the beautiful garden which sloped gently down to the banks of the Tweed. There was a small summer-house at the lawn's edge, dubbed the 'Cigarium' by the writer 'Christopher North,' and here Ballantyne's friends, who included some of the most famous names in music and literature of the day, could sit talking to their host and smoke the cigars which Randall did not permit indoors. On the one occasion when Scott stayed overnight, she came down early to prepare breakfast, and was amazed to see him standing before the shrubs on the terrace, fencing and weaving with his walking stick and muttering to himself as he twirled it around. He confessed to the family during the meal that he had been rehearsing a duel, and when Sandy came to transcribe the manuscript he found that the scene had been incorporated in the second chapter of *Quentin Durward*.

Professor John Wilson, who wrote under the name of 'Christopher North,' was a frequent visitor to the Hall and was a great favourite with Ballantyne's two young sons. At the age of eight,

7

when on his way to school in Kelso, James (named after his uncle) once met the tall, broad-shouldered, fearless-looking man, striding along to the river:

How well we remember the day when we played truant to go fishing with him. It was in Roxburghshire, at the junction of the Teviot and the Tweed. The morning was exquisite —one of those mornings when it is a sin to send boys to school to sit dismally on a form all day until the sun is near to going down.

We were trudging our way 'unwillingly to school,' when the Professor came round the corner, stepping out at a swinging pace with his fishing-rod over his shoulder and his son trotting behind him. We gazed wistfully, and the son beckoned us to come on.

'What's the use?' said we, 'we have not a halfpenny to pay the toll of the bridge.' 'Never mind,' whispered he, looking towards his father with a glance of complacent admiration, 'he always carries halfpence; and he never thinks how many go through the toll along with him.'

There was hope in this. We pitched our satchel behind a wall, and walked close by the side of our friend, trying to look as like an unquestionable member of the party as possible. At the toll-bar the Professor tendered a penny for himself and son. The toll-keeper grumbled 'Ain't there three?' and the Professor looked back and caught our intent gaze. A slight smile lightened his face as he fumbled in his pocket for another halfpenny—and we passed through the mystic barrier of the toll-bar.

At the mouth of the Teviot, where it joins the Tweed, there is an island, formed by the Teviot itself and by a mill-leat. You reach the island by crossing the mill-leat on the top of the flood-gate—and then you are in fairy-land. The long grass is filled with forget-me-nots, and, on the margin of the water, with the noble broad-leaved tussilago. How we loved that tussilago! The Professor took no note of it—at all events he made no remark. On he stalked, fitting on his flies to the end of his line; and, to our utter astonishment, he made no pause when he reached the water. In he walked, shoes, stockings and all. The affair of the halfpenny at the toll-bar made us aware that he was a great man—but we now regarded him as a hero. Such an utter casting off of the fear of mothers, nursemaids and washerwomen, it had never entered our minds to conceive—as that evinced in his walking into the Teviot as boldly as he had walked through the town.

Fair Tweed and Teviot! Does the sun ever shine as brightly there as it used sometimes to do?[1]

The financial storm that was gathering around Scott and the Ballantyne brothers had not yet broken when Sandy moved into the Hall, but even so, increasing expenses and money difficulties, due mainly to all his spare capital being locked up in the Ballantyne Press, coupled with the continuing decline in the status of the *Kelso Mail*, made it impossible after less than two years for the family to continue the upkeep of the place. Only the glorious summers of 1823 and 1824 were spent there, and many years later their daughter Mary looked back wistfully to those halcyon days when she wrote:

After a long summer's day fishing in the Tweed, Professor Wilson and my father came in to join their other friends for supper which was eaten in the room with the large bay-window overlooking the river. The Professor, who was 'Christopher North' the well known writer, was called on for a song and he responded by singing 'Auld Lang Syne' but with his own words!

'And ever o'er sweet Walton Hall
May summer's sun still shine,
And still may meeting friends recall
The days of Auld Lang Syne.

And ever may yon beautious wreath[2]
In heavenly fragrance twine,

[1] From the *Benares Magazine*, August 1850.
[2] As he reached this line 'he pointed to the wee bairns that had just come in to say goodnight' according to a guest, Miss M. Wilson, who wrote down the words as the Professor sang them.

And still the opening blossoms breath
O'er the buds o' Auld Lang Syne.

Yet sitting here a pensive tear
Will mingle with our wine,
For him[1] whom a' our hearts hold dear
In the days o' Auld Lang Syne.

But life is like our own sweet Tweed,
Made up o' shade and shine,
And time will heal the wounds that bleed
For friends o' Auld Lang Syne.

But, unfortunately for the Ballantynes, the summer's sun did
not shine for long and that autumn Professor Wilson wrote:

And sweet Walton Hall, art thou too silent? But the kind
hearts that beat there are happy still, although removed for a
time from the murmurs of that little fountain well. The
Cigarium is smokeless now and desolate, and the beautiful
leopard curtains shade windows that look not out upon the
woods of Fleurs.[2] Yet we do not despair, before our locks
are thin, to see our good friends seated there once more,
when, to the tune of the matchless violin (matchless in the
hands of our dear S.B.) we shall sing together, as of yore:

'Then gie's your hand, my trusty fier,
And surely I'll gie mine,
And we'll tak a cup of kindness yet,
For the sake o' Auld Lang Syne.'

But, beneath the original of these words, there is written in
Alexander Ballantyne's hand:

'NO, my dear Professor—NEVER!'
A.B. Nov. 1837.

The bitterness of that added line can still be felt. For, as the
years passed and the little capital he had left gradually dwindled,

[1] This was a reference to John Ballantyne, who had planned the house
but did not live to see it completed.
[2] Fleurs (or Floors, as it is now called) is the residence of the Duke of
Roxburgh and can be seen from the windows of Walton Hall.

his hopes of ever returning to that happy house slowly faded, but his love of Kelso and its rivers, and the home he built there, remained with him to the end.

Faced with the failure of all his efforts to revive the flagging circulation of the *Kelso Mail*, Sandy was at last forced to accept the offer of editorship[1] of the *Edinburgh Weekly Journal* made to him two years previously by his brother, James. In August 1824, sorrowfully and with many regrets, the family left the town by stage coach for Edinburgh, where they had taken a small house at 25 Comley Bank. In a few months, due to the good offices of their old friend Professor Wilson, who lived near by, they were able to rent 25 Ann Street, a house situated in the most fashionable area of the town, and it was here, on the 24th April, 1825, that Randall's ninth child, a boy, was born. Robert Michael Ballantyne had arrived.

[1] Although James Ballantyne's name continued to appear as the editor of the paper until his death in 1833, the actual task of editorship was undertaken by Alexander from September 1824 onwards.

Chapter Two

WITH THE OTHER SEVEN CHILDREN already in possession, the modestly sized house in Ann Street must have been crowded before baby Bob arrived, but with his mother's tender care, he survived the squash and at the age of five was described by his Aunt Hunter,[1] as being 'a handsome wee laddie but onco' mischievous and has clean broke my Argand lamp!'

Once, obstinately determined to return at all costs to the arms of his beloved Mamma, who had cruelly left him at her sister-in-law's for a few days while she visited friends in Aberdeen, he had waited until he had been carefully dressed in his Sunday best and told to walk the few yards to the Sabbath School, at which he did not arrive, having beetled, short-legged, in the opposite direction as fast as he could go. For some time he was not missed, but when, after several hours, he had still not returned, a frantic search was organised in which the whole street, plus his relations and the police, all took part. It was after midnight when at last he was found, stained, dirty and fast asleep, curled up at the bottom of a stairwell, having walked many wandering miles through the crooked streets of Edinburgh in a tearful but resolute attempt to get back to his own home.

The early years of Robert Michael's boyhood were spent in an atmosphere of continual financial strain for his parents, but he said he remembered nothing of this and that his only recollections of the period were of the candle-lit musical evenings, on which occasions he was sometimes allowed proudly to resin his father's bow; and of having to sing with his ten-year-old sister, Randall Hunter, a duet, in the course of which he skipped a verse, confusion reigned, and the two of them fled in tears from the room. The sticks of rhubarb and saucers of sugar which were to have been their prize for singing to the company were later brought up to the miserable little boy and girl by their mother, who dried their tears and soothed their wounded hearts. They dearly loved their beautiful Mamma, and she was a devoted mother to all her children.

[1] Mrs. Ballantyne's sister.

Bob could recall the country holidays he spent with his sisters at friends' houses in the Highlands, and the long days fishing with his father and brothers on the Tweed at Kelso. He was seven when he was first taken by his father and Professor Wilson for a morning's fishing, both the men being dressed in the tall beaver hats and gilt-buttoned tail-coats fashionably worn in those days by gentlemen indulging in sport. The Professor, having watched the runny-nosed and soon dirty-faced little lad as he excitedly peered at the float his father had made for him, later sent Mrs. Ballantyne an account of how he viewed her young son's first catch, a tale which, although apocryphal in the sense that it had been written before the event took place, so exactly described Bob's demeanour as to delight the family, but left the hero of the piece completely unmoved:[1]

There the new-breeched little urchin stood on the low bridge of the little bit burnie! And with crooked pin, baited with one unwrithing ring of dead worm, and attached to a yarn thread—for he has not yet got into hair, and is years off gut—his rod nothing more than a mere hazel wand—there he stood in mute, deep, earnest, passionate, heart-mind-and-soul engrossing hope of catching a minnow or a beardie! When he got a tug his face went flushed and pale by turns, but he at last had strength, in the agitation of his fear and joy, to pull in the monster, and with a mighty heave he whapped him right over his head far and away, among the gowans and the greensward—a fish a quarter of an ounce in weight, and, at the very least, two inches long! Off he flew to his father, holding the fish aloft in both hands, still fearful of its escape, his eyes brightening at the first blush of cold blood on his small, fishy-fumy fingers. He carried about with him, upstairs and downstairs, his prey

[1] Wilson later used this scene in *The Recreations of Christopher North*, which appeared in three volumes in 1842. My copy, which belonged to the Ballantyne family, has a pencilled note in his sister Mary's hand 'Bob's first catch—Kelso, 1832, which the Professor wrote for mother.' But the story had first appeared in September 1828 in *Blackwood's Magazine*, when Bob was only three. Wilson probably thought the description so apt in the present case that he rewrote the tale in similar, although not identical form, and sent it to Randall.

upon a plate; he would not wash his hands before dinner and exulted in the silver scales adhering to the thumbnail that scooped the pin out of the baggy's maw—and that night, 'cabin'd, cribb'd, confined,' he was overheard murmuring in his sleep as he lived his infant dreams.

Sandy Ballantyne must have needed the occasional relief of a weekend's fishing, for the worry of the years immediately after Bob's birth drove him to the edge of despair. His eldest daughter, Mary, remembered coming downstairs when she was about four-teen, and seeing her father slumped, ashen faced, in his chair, a crumpled newspaper at his feet, while her mother, as pale as death herself, was comforting her man with words only a wife can use when the one she loves has been badly hurt.

This was the morning in January 1826, when the news of the financial ruin of Sir Walter Scott, and that of the Ballantyne Press, of which Sandy's brother, James, was part owner and in which all his own spare capital was invested, first broke upon an astonished world. Despite the large sums which Scott earned from his writing, these had proved quite inadequate to finance his immense purchases of land to surround his country estate at Abbotsford, and to pay for the building and upkeep of so palatial an establishment. He had therefore drawn increasing amounts from the printing business in which he was a partner, the insol-vency of the firm being concealed by a complicated system of accommodation bills and other credit-raising manipulations. James had been powerless to halt these raids on the company's capital, for his illustrious partner had invested far more in the business than he had, and in fact was the owner of the Ballantyne Press in all but name. And the fact that he insisted to his pub-lishers that all his books should be printed there, and induced many of his literary friends to do likewise, made his position even more powerful. But when the true extent of the company's deficiency became apparent, debts of immense proportions were revealed.

The catastrophe which finally overwhelmed them was of a magnitude which swept aside all thoughts of rescue, leaving the Ballantynes stunned, bewildered and with no hopes of relief. In a letter to his friend, Stephen Barber, dated 26th April, 1819,[1] nearly seven years before the débâcle, Sir Walter revealed that he had already spent over £35,000 on land at Abbotsford, and in the years succeeding this date his expenditure had continued unabated. The outlay on the building and its contents, plus the landscaping of its immediate gardens, has been conservatively estimated at a further £76,000,[2] and the fact that Scott acknowledged liabilities of nearly £127,000 in 1826, gives support to the fact that his spending on the mansion and its estate must have been immense.

It was the failure of Hurst, Robinson & Company, the London agents of Archibald Constable & Company, whom they dragged down with them, which toppled the whole edifice of I.O.U.s and promises-to-pay behind which the partners of James Ballantyne & Company had sheltered. The printing company had issued counter bills for many of the bills of exchange signed on their behalf by Constable & Company for literary work and printing, and these now amounted to tens of thousands of pounds, all of which were in circulation. The inability of Constable to meet his obligations instantly precipitated Sir Walter Scott and the Ballantynes into the pit as well, although they needed only the slightest push to topple, as the massive drawings of the senior partner had rendered them hopelessly insolvent. In a few weeks the full extent of the financial disaster became apparent. The total liabilities of Archibald Constable & Company amounted to about £256,000; that of Hurst, Robinson & Company, with whom their fortunes were inextricably mixed, to another £300,000; while Scott discovered that he must find nearly £117,000 to pay his creditors, and this still left a mortgage of £10,000 secured on the estate of Abbotsford.

Sandy's first thought was of finding a house in France and taking the family to live cheaply abroad, thereby escaping the more extreme consequences of the failure, the sounds of which

[1] Extracts from this letter of Scott's are quoted in Catalogue 899, issued by Messrs. Maggs Bros. Ltd., London, the antiquarian booksellers. Unfortunately, enquiries have failed to trace the present whereabouts of this letter.
[2] *The Ballantyne Press and Its Founders.* Edinburgh, 1909.

were for months rumbling and rolling through the courts of Edinburgh and London. When he finally perceived the shocking extent of the damage, it is little wonder that, having been sucked into the vortex and whirled into a cloud of worry and anxiety on a scale he had never imagined possible, he should have entreated news of any continental cottage, house, or hiding place, where the family could rest in peaceful poverty. But before any firm plan for flight could be formulated, the pressing attentions of his creditors forced him and his family to leave Ann Street, and they thankfully accepted an offer to share the home of their friends, the Cowans, who lived near by in the Canongate.[1]

Archibald Constable & Company were declared bankrupt and ultimately paid a total of two shillings and ninepence in the pound. Hurst, Robinson & Company were even deeper in debt and a sale of their assets resulted in a total payment of only one shilling and threepence in the pound, thus spreading ruin through the ranks of scores of their small creditors and dragging down many other firms of seemingly sound financial standing. Many of the copyrights of Scott's novels which Constable owned were disposed of at a fraction of their true value, and there is no doubt that had the sale of these valuable properties not been forced through in haste by anxious creditors, the Edinburgh publishing company would have been in a position to make a payment considerably larger than two shillings and ninepence.

Whatever blame Scott may deserve for saddling James Ballantyne & Company with such a huge load of debt, his actions after the crash were selfless and little short of heroic. He resolved not to become a bankrupt, perhaps paying only pence in the pound and escaping his true responsibilities, but made a solemn declaration to carry on his literary work solely for the benefit of those to whom he owed money. On 24th January, 1826, he wrote in his journal:

> If I am hard pressed, and measures used against me, I must use all means of legal defence, and subscribe myself bankrupt in a petition for sequestration. It is the course I

---

[1] Mr. David Cowan and his wife, who lived in the Regent Moray's House, Canongate. He was a partner in the Edinburgh paper-making firm of Cowan & Company.

would have advised a client to take, and would have the effect of saving my land, which is secured by my son's contract of marriage. I might save my library, etc. by assistance of friends, and bid my creditors defiance. But for this I would, in a court of honour, deserve to lose my spurs.

No, if they permit me, I will be their vassal for life, and dig in the mine of my imagination to find diamonds (or what may sell for such), to make good my engagements, not to enrich myself.

Scott's obvious sincerity of purpose and the fact that his bankruptcy would have been considered as little short of a national disaster, caused most of his creditors to stay their hands, and a crowded meeting unanimously agreed to the setting up of a trust fund by means of which he might be enabled to pay off his debts by sustained literary exertions. Some idea of the high esteem in which the author was held in all walks of life is conveyed by the Earl of Dudley when the news of the crash reached him at Brighton:

'Scott ruined!' he cried. 'The author of *Waverley* ruined! Good God, let every man to whom he has given months of delight give him a sixpence, and he will rise tomorrow morning richer than Rothschild!'[1]

But for James Ballantyne there was no escape. His house[2] was sold by auction and all he had of value was sequestrated to pay his debts, the trustees of the fund allowing him to keep only his household furniture and personal effects. Bob Ballantyne's father fared little better. He was innocent of any pecuniary guile and had taken no part in the financial intrigues in which his brother and Sir Walter had become involved, but he was deeply identified with James and his misfortunes by reason of the money he had recently invested in the printing business and its sister company which produced the *Edinburgh Weekly Journal*. After moving to the capital he had sold the *Kelso Mail* for £1,600, investing nearly

[1] Lockhart's *Life of Scott*, vol. VI, p. 309.
[2] 3 Heriot Row, Edinburgh. It realised £2,700 but one thousand pounds of this amount was needed to pay off the mortgage (*Ballantyne-Humbug Handled* by J. G. Lockhart).

the whole of this sum in shares in the Edinburgh newspaper, whose fortunes were indissolubly linked with that of the Ballantyne Press. As part-owner of the paper he thus found himself liable for a share of its debts instead of the steadily increasing profits he had hoped for.

But the private trust fund which the creditors had set up to enable Scott to pay off his debts was also of some benefit to James and Sandy—the axes were blunted to some extent and the air of Edinburgh became a little more salubrious—but both their pride and their pockets suffered in no small degree. Sandy's standard of living declined abruptly; the nursemaid who looked after the children was dismissed, and practically all of his assets, including, of course, his remaining property in Kelso, were sold at forced prices. The printing firm of James Ballantyne & Company was permitted by the trust to continue to trade, with James demoted to the position of manager instead of partner, but Sir Walter's interest in the business was terminated. Both the Ballantynes were able to retain their personal household effects, but the shame he felt at the scandal had a crushing effect on the spirit of the younger brother from which he never fully recovered, and the melancholy sight of James's house being auctioned brought him to tears in the street.

The months passed slowly as they strove to keep their heads above water, and only the news that the creditors had decided to allow him to resume the management of the *Edinburgh Weekly Journal* persuaded Sandy to renounce, for the present, any plans for making a home abroad. James received four hundred and the younger brother only two hundred pounds a year for their salaries as managers and neither now had any other resources.

Troubles seldom come singly and in April one of Randall's little girls, Christina Hogarth, died suddenly at the age of seven. 'A delightful sunny child,' is set against her name in the family Bible in her mother's hand, and her loss must have plunged an already miserable family deeper into gloom. With her husband's income so drastically reduced, Randall, with eight mouths to feed, was careful to watch every penny, and from being able to command the week's provisions with a lofty indifference to the minutiae of coppers, she was reduced to haggling with the tradesmen and walking miles in search of the cheapest supplies. For two years they had to exist in this fashion, her husband's income from the newspaper being barely sufficient to clothe and feed them and pay the small rent which they insisted the Cowans should receive, and his beloved Stradivarius violin was sold with the rest of their hidden treasures.[1] But at last news came from Abbotsford that gave Sandy cause for hope that the low-water mark in the level of their fortunes had perhaps been passed, for Sir Walter had intimated that he would soon have such tidings for the trustees as would gladden the heart of the most flinty creditor in Scotland.

At first Ballantyne hardly dared mention to Randall that relief might be on the way, but finally the day came when he broke the news to the family that Scott, by prodigious exertions and at great cost to his health, had earned nearly forty thousand pounds in only two years[2] and this sum had been made over to the trustees of the fund. The unbelievably large amount which the author had raised by his pen made possible a first payment of six shillings in the pound towards the extinction of the debt, his creditors unanimously passing a vote of thanks for the indefatigable industry which had achieved so much on their behalf. Impressed and more than a little astonished, these gentlemen now awaited sanguinely the outcome of his further efforts, with the result that the pressure on the Ballantynes eased appreciably. Sandy was permitted to draw a larger salary from the *Weekly Journal*, plus a little from the Ballantyne Press for the assistance he now gave his brother, and for the first time since the crash he began to discern a lighter horizon and a gleam of hope. The new year of 1828 dawned after a Hogmanay warmed with a fresh spirit of optimism and the hand-clasping cheer of brothers who believed that the worst of their penance might already have been performed.

Within a few months Sandy had rented a house at 20 Fettes Row, and that spring, complete with young Bob and the rest of

[1] According to a letter found in Sandy's papers, his violin was offered to a London dealer for twenty-five pounds.

[2] Scott received £8,228 for *Woodstock*, which appeared in three volumes in 1826; £18,000 for the nine-volume *Life of Napoleon*, published in 1827; and about £12,000 for the six-volume edition of his *Miscellaneous Prose Works* also published in 1827.

the children, the family moved into a home of their own once more. The continuing excellence of the products of the Ballantyne Press, and the often beautiful examples of typography which it produced, still brought them many customers and gradually retrieved most of the clients who had earlier deserted them. Under James's management, and with the Abbotsford wound finally staunched, the business started to prosper. By an arrangement with the trustees, Alexander Cowan (the owner of Cowan and Company, the Edinburgh paper-makers, from whom James had for years bought his supplies) purchased the printing house, complete with its type and machinery and the rest of the stock-in-trade, for the sum of ten thousand pounds on behalf of its present manager, James Ballantyne. This capital sum was to be repaid with interest from the profits of the press over a period of several years, and there were certain provisos attaching to the loan: the paper the press used was to be obtained only from Cowan & Company, and assurances of the continuing goodwill of Sir Walter Scott towards the firm in regard to the printing of his works were sought and obtained. James grasped with both hands this chance of eventually becoming independent, and the trustees were happy to be able to dispose of the company for a lump sum of such generous proportions, the debts at the time of the bankruptcy being a separate obligation for which Scott remained responsible. Soon after these arrangements were completed, James admitted his younger brother into partnership, Sandy relinquishing his post with the *Weekly Journal* in order to devote all his time to the affairs of the printing house.

With the children growing rapidly and the demands of the family increasing every year, he worked hard and successfully in his new job, spending most of his time reading and correcting the proofs of the newspapers, magazines and books which formed the bulk of their printing turnover; he often arrived home after midnight, tired 'and near blind with the print, the bairns long since abed and Mrs. B. asleep in her chair from waiting.'[1]

In 1829 their last child was born, a pretty little daughter for whom they chose the name Williamina. By this time Mary, their eldest girl, was a capable young lady of seventeen, and her brother

[1] An entry in Sandy Ballantyne's diary, in April 1829.

James, only a year her junior, had become a youth of studious and scholarly expression, seldom seen when not buried in a book on the most abstruse and learned subjects. He was now studying at the East India College in Hertfordshire, attempting to master the tortuous oriental languages in which, in a few years, he became a fluent expert.

Their second son, John, was only fourteen—a slightly built, pale little lad, thin-faced and large-eyed, nervous in company, being more often than not tongue-tied and embarrassed if addressed by anybody other than a member of the family. However, the style and technical skill he was displaying in the pictures he loved to paint were delighting his parents, and somehow Sandy scraped together enough money to have him specially trained in art, entering him as a student at the Royal Institution, where he stayed for three years. Jane, Madalina, Randall Hunter (named after her mother), young Bob, aged four and already proving a handful of mischief, plus the new baby girl; this must together have made a lively household, but they had a home full of warmth and affection despite the shortage of ready money, and Randall cherished and loved them all. She was herself a water-colour painter of more than average amateur ability, and from her Bob acquired much of his own skill with brush and pencil, a talent which stood him in good stead when he came to illustrate the books he wrote. Poetry, literature and the arts occupied the family's leisure time, and the musical evenings continued—but with the wining and dining on a very attenuated scale.

Notwithstanding his own troubles and privations, Sandy's mastery of the violin (though no longer a Stradivarius) brought solace and pleasure to his many friends, and Scott especially appreciated his fine playing, inviting him to Abbotsford for many of the more important dinner parties. He mentioned Ballantyne in his journal on many occasions, and in 1827 he wrote:

'We heard Sandy's violin after dinner:
    'Whose touch harmonious can remove,
    The pangs of guilty power and hopeless love.'
I do not understand or care about fine music; but there is something in his violin that goes straight to the heart.

Writing to his eldest son, James, in 1831, his father told him of his last meeting with Sir Walter Scott:

Edinburgh, 26th October, 1831

Dear James,

Paganini, the greatest of violinists, is here at present, delighting us to the very spinal marrow. Last night Mama, Mary, John and Jane and I, all went to his concert and were all of us extatified. You don't know his powers, sir, having heard him only once!

John and I went to Abbotsford and were most kindly received. We partook of Sir Walter's last dinner, it may be, in that beautiful spot. He left it next morning. John took 'The Great Unknown,' a picture of a warrior listening to his mistress playing the lute—Sir Walter was extremely pleased with it, as also were Miss Scott and Lockhart. We caught a dish of trout for dinner.

Sir Walter was full of fun and mirth; but his health has received a rude, rude shock! He wrote me a note which says, 'I would I could insure our meeting again in life.' He harped once or twice on Smollett and Richardson having gone abroad for the recovery of their health and dying there. He took John over all the house and showed him all his curiosities, with millions of anecdotes relating to them. At length we parted.

Mary will write soon, as John, I fancy, *will not.*

Thine,

A. Ballantyne.

Few could have worked as hard as Scott in his effort to pay off his massive debts, and at the same time maintain a social calendar as full as the laird of Abbotsford. Many were the crowded house parties at which he had presided as host, where his friends from the literary and art world mingled with the nobility and gentry from the surrounding shires, spending the daylight hours in hunting or shooting expeditions, or fishing in the Tweed as it flowed past the garden's edge. The wining and dining and the nocturnal suppers ending in the wee small hours were returned in similar fashion by many of his wealthy acquaintances, and much time he could ill afford was spent travelling on horseback, or in his well-appointed carriage, to accept a weekend's hospitality at some nobleman's country seat or at the home of one of his numerous friends.

The bride which he had made of a society whose dining tables groaned beneath the weight of a hundred temptations to human weakness, had long since begun to take toll of his virility, and coupled with the many calls made on his time by his political activities and his duties at the Scottish Bar, where he still held the position of Clerk to the Court of Session, and the sustained driving of his pen in every spare minute he could snatch for writing—the pressure of these and other activities had chipped remorselessly away at his strong and vigorous constitution until his health had become seriously undermined. Before leaving on the trip which Sandy mentions in his letter, Sir Walter had already suffered two strokes, the last of which had for a time impaired his speech and caused some degree of paralysis, and the journey abroad was made in the hope that a change of climate might help him to recuperate. But on the evening of the 9th June, 1832, while at a small town on the Rhine, he suffered a near-fatal attack of cerebral haemorrhage and was brought back to his beloved Abbotsford.

His death on the 21st September, 1832, was mourned throughout the land. Almost every newspaper in Scotland, and many in England, appeared with black edges on the day they announced the event, and, with hardly an exception, they spoke of the grief felt at the passing of the Wizard of the North. The train of carriages at his funeral extended for over a mile and every village was crowded with black-clothed country folk paying their last respects as the hearse passed on its way to Dryburgh for the interment.

Less than six months after Scott's death, the massive debts he had striven so hard to wipe out were cleared for ever by a settlement with the creditors. The principal of the debt then amounted to £54,000, but against this there was a life insurance policy of £22,000, plus about £2,000 in the trust fund, and Robert Cadell, who was then his publisher, advanced the balance of £30,000 upon the security of the copyrights, thus enabling the author's children to sponge clean the slate as their father had tried so hard to do. The debt to Cadell was finally discharged in 1847, when the publisher accepted both the remaining copyright of the works and the copyright of J. G. Lockhart's *Life of Sir Walter Scott, Bart*, which had appeared in seven volumes during 1837/8. By these means was Abbotsford at last freed from the debts of its founder.

James Ballantyne did not long survive his illustrious patron, and on the 16th January, 1833, after a painful illness,[1] his body was laid to rest near that of his brother John in Canongate Church-yard, Edinburgh. Sandy then found himself the sole survivor of the trio of brothers, who, but a few years since, had looked to a future bright with promise, but whose families had now been scattered by the winds of ill-fortune.

By this time he had managed to secure his release from any further claims by his creditors, and even if the prospect before him held out little hope of an affluent old age, he could at least hold his head high in the town with the knowledge that he owed not any man. The children were growing and Bob Ballantyne had already survived chicken-pox and mumps and a mild attack of measles. Randall had become reconciled in some degree to their more lowly status in society—her husband left every morning for the office and returned as regularly every night—and family life had settled into an even tenor in which scrimping and saving came to be accepted as part of their normal existence.

In the spring of 1835, they were able to cut expenses by sharing a house at 60, Cumberland Street with Randall's widowed sister Madalina, and it was here that Bob reached his tenth birthday. The only schooling the boy had so far received was from his mother and sisters; he could read and write and knew a little of mathematics—but for the rest, what he had learned was self-taught. Near to his present home was Edinburgh Academy, a school for boys which Sir Walter Scott had helped to found in 1824. Both Bob's elder brothers had been pupils from the opening day, the studious and hard-working James for three years, and

[1] He died following the perforation of a stomach ulcer.

John, who admitted to being a hopeless scholar, for nearly four.[1]

It was here that Bob obtained his only regular schooling, attending the Academy for two years as a pupil in Mr. Ferguson's class.[2] His career was undistinguished, his name never appearing amongst those of the ten top boys in his form at any of the prize-givings, but this is hardly surprising when one considers that he had not attended a junior school and was thrown amidst boys whose education was already well advanced. In the sports field he fared little better and he evinced no interest in games at any period of his life. His boyhood passions were angling, hunting and bird's nesting, and from eight years of age he took every opportunity to disappear, rod in hand and catapult in pocket, accompanied by his brother John or one of the neighbours' children, returning for supper, grimed and hungry, but usually elated, proudly carrying the dejected trophies of a hard day's sport.

An almost total disregard for the suffering of wild creatures is evidenced in many of the books he wrote in later life, and in this respect he is as guilty as the other children's authors of the period, whose heroes had a propensity to shoot on sight any animal or bird which happened to cross their paths. Bob Ballantyne was reared in an age in which the cruelty of children to animals, both domestic and wild, was tolerated with amusement by many of their elders, and the hanging of a cat, stoning of a cockerel, or an organised dog fight to the death, were some of the milder excesses practised for fun by the youths of the district. Few things swarmed the streets with children more quickly than the savagery of a fight between dogs trained for slaughter. Even the respectable Professor Wilson, when challenged by a half-drunken carrier to match his dog 'Fro' against the carter's mastiff, could not resist the temptation to slip loose the chain and goad his dog. His account of the ensuing battle, in which his powers of description appear heightened by the excitement he felt, pictures the sort of scene that Bob and his companions must have witnessed on many occasions:

[1] The eldest brother, James, was brilliant at languages and classical subjects and earned a scholarship to Haileybury School, which he attended from 1829 to 1832.

[2] *Edinburgh Academy Register*, p. 81, published by T. & A. Constable, 1914.

We let Fro engage in a pitched battle with a mastiff victorious in fifty fights—a famous shanker—and a throttler beyond compare. It was indeed a bloody business—now growling along the glawr of the road—a hairy hurricane—now snorting in the suffocating ditch—now fair play on the clean and clear crown of the causey—now rolling over and over through a chance open white gate, into a cottage garden—now separated by choking them both with a cord—now brought out again with savage and fiery eyes to the scratch, on a green plat round the sign-board swinging tree in the middle of the village—auld women in their mutches crying out, 'Shame! whare's the minister?'—young women with combs in their pretty heads, blinking with pale and almost weeping faces from low lintelled doors—children crowding for sight and safety on the louping-on stane—and loud cries ever and anon at each turn and eddy of the fight, of 'Well done, Fro, well done, Fro—see how he worries his windpipe,—well done, Fro!' for Fro was the delight of the whole parish, and the honour of all its inhabitants, male and female, was felt to be staked on the issue—while at intervals was heard the harsh hoarse voices of the carrier and his compeers, cursing and swearing in triumph in a many-oathed language peculiar to the race that drive the broad-wheeled waggons with the high canvas roofs, as the might of Teeger prevailed, and the indomitable Fro seemed to be on his last legs beneath a grip of the jugular, and then stretched motionless and passive—in defeat or death. A mere ruse to recover wind.

Like unshorn Sampson starting from his sleep, and snapping like fired flax the vain bands of the Philistines, Fro whawmled Teeger off, and twisting round his head in spite of the grip on the jugular, the skin stretching and giving way in a ghastly but unfelt wound, he suddenly seized with all his tusks his antagonist's eye, and bit it clean out of its socket. A yowl of unendurable pain—spouting of blood—sickness—swooning—tumbling over—and death. His last fight is over! His remaining eye glazed—his protruding tongue bitten in anguish by his own grinding teeth—his massy hind legs stretched out with a kick like a horse—his short tail stiffens—he is laid out a grim corpse—flung into a cart tied behind the waggon—and off to the tan-yard.[1]

When the dust had settled and the front doors had closed, the children would resume their hop-scotch and the games abandoned for the gore of the fight, but the impression such ferocities must have scored on young minds, and the effect of seeing respected adults screaming for the kill, can be easily imagined. Witnessing similar scenes, young Bob Ballantyne no doubt shouted as loud as the rest of the boys, and one has only to read passages in *The Gorilla Hunters*, *The World of Ice*, or indeed any of his books in which wild animals are encountered, to see that he had come to have little sympathy for the sufferings of creatures who found themselves at the mercy of man.

When the new term started at the Edinburgh Academy in January, 1838, Robert Michael Ballantyne's name was not amongst the list of scholars—his father had been unable to find sufficient money to pay any further school fees. But, on his mother's insistence, the boy continued to receive instruction every morning from either herself or one of his elder sisters. The girls took turns at seeing that their young brother did not escape before his tasks were completed, and this procedure was followed, with time off for the holidays, until the lad reached an age when he was considered old enough to make his own way in the world.

His father's main source of income was now derived from his share of the profits of the *Edinburgh Weekly Journal*, plus a small retainer he drew from the printing firm, now renamed simply Ballantyne & Company. His late brother James's son was now in command, and having received a controlling interest in the firm under the will of his father, had gradually been successful in easing out his Uncle Sandy until he occupied only a position as proof-reader. His papers show that at this time his income never exceeded four hundred pounds a year, but as the elder sons were now both working, the family's finances gradually improved.

By 1841, James had published no fewer than eight books and

[1] *The Recreations of Christopher North*, by Professor John Wilson, 3 vols., Edinburgh, 1842.

pamphlets on the foreign-language subjects in which he specialised, and in addition had successfully started a class for pupils who
wished to learn the tongues of the East. His brother John was
carving a career in London as a portrait painter and commanding
up to thirty guineas for a picture. As for young Bob—well he was
now sixteen, and one morning, at the breakfast table, his father
lowered his newspaper and said,[1]

'Bob—have you thought what you want to make of yourself,
sir?'

'No, father.'

'Then how would you like to go into the service of the Hudson's
Bay Company and perhaps discover the North-West Passage?'

'I should like it very much, father.'

'Then that's settled then.'

And on the thirty-first day of May, 1841, an agreement was
signed between 'Robert Michael Ballantyne of the City of
Edinburgh, on the one hand, and the Governor and Company of
Adventurers of England, Trading into Hudson's Bay, on the
other, whereby the said Robert Michael Ballantyne agreed to
become an apprentice clerk of the Company, for a period of not
less than five years, at a starting salary of twenty pounds a year.'

For Bob—the die was cast.

[1] *Personal Reminiscences in Book-Making*, by R. M. Ballantyne (1893).

Chapter Three

HE WAS NOW a good-looking, stalwart young man, spoilt by his sisters and idolised by his mother—'My own exquisite Bob,' as she called him in her letters. The females of the family plunged gladly into the weeks of excitement, shopping and buying the kit for his new life in Canada; making him stand to be measured for a long-coated suit, complete with double-breasted waistcoat; sit while they pulled on the thick woollen stockings his mother had knitted, or tried his new peaked cap; extracting from him promises of unfailing vigilance against insidious chills and draughts. On the day of departure Sandy came aboard the ship, and, amidst the tears of the females, solemnly shook hands with the son he was never to see again.

But there was no sorrow for Bob, as his description of his emotions on learning that he was to leave Edinburgh for the wilds of Rupert's Land show clearly.[1]

I was thrown into a state of ecstatic joy by the arrival of the letter appointing me to the enviable situation of apprentice clerk in the services of the Honourable Hudson's Bay Company. To describe the immense extent to which I expanded, both mentally and bodily, upon the receipt of this letter, is impossible; it is sufficient to know that from that moment I fancied myself a complete man-of-business, and treated my old companions with the condescending suavity of one who knows that he is talking to his inferiors.

A few days after, however, my pride was brought very low indeed, as I lay tossing in my berth on the tumbling waves of the German Ocean, eschewing breakfast as a dangerous meal, and looking upon dinner with a species of horror utterly incomprehensible by those who have not experienced an attack of sea-sickness. Miseries of this description, fortunately, do not last long. In a couple of days we got into the comparatively still waters of the Thames; and I, with a host of pale-

[1] *Hudson's Bay*, by R. M. Ballantyne, Edinburgh, 1848.

faced young ladies, and cadaverous-looking young men, emerged for the first time from the interior of the ship, to behold the beauties and wonders of the great metropolis, as we glided slowly up the crowded river.

Final tearful farewells were taken of his mother and the sisters who had travelled down with him from Edinburgh, and of his brother John, with whom he stayed for the few days he spent in London. With the family at last left behind he boarded the Company ship *Prince Rupert* at Gravesend.

I stood (having parted from all my friends) contemplating the boats and crowds of shipping that passed continually before me, and thinking how soon I was to leave the scenes to which I had been so long accustomed, for a far distant land.

I was a boy, however, and this I think is equivalent to saying that I did not sorrow long, . . . So, my spirits began to rise, and, when the cry arose on deck that the steamer containing the committee of the Honourable Hudson's Bay Company was in sight, I sprang to the companion-ladder in a state of mind, if not happy, at least as nearly so as, under the circumstances, could be expected.

It is the custom of the directors of the Hudson's Bay Company to give a public dinner to the officers of their ships upon the eve of their departure from Gravesend; and ere the gentlemen of the committee left the vessel, one of them invited the captain and the officers to attend, and, to my astonishment and delight, also begged me to honour them with my company. I accepted the invitation with extreme politeness . . .

The dinner, like other public dinners, was as good and substantial as a lavish expenditure of cash could make it . . . Nothing intelligible, however, was to be heard, except when a sudden lull in the noise gave a bald-headed old gentleman, near the head of the table, the opportunity of drinking the health of a red-faced old gentleman near the foot, upon whom he bestowed an amount of flattery perfectly bewildering; and, after making the red-faced gentleman writhe for half an hour in a fever of modesty, sat down amid thunders of applause. The red-faced gentleman, now having become purple with excitement, then rose, and during a solemn silence, delivered himself of a speech to the effect that the day then passing, was certainly the happiest in his mortal career, and that he felt quite faint with the load of honour thrown upon his willing shoulders.

Within a few hours of setting sail on 6th June, 1841, Bob was once again in the grip of sea-sickness and it was six days before he could leave his bunk; but by the time they reached the harbour of Stornaway in the Isle of Lewis, he had regained his sea-legs and was eating ravenously.

The *Prince Rupert* was a three-masted sailing ship and considered fast, but, even with favourable winds, it was about six weeks before land was again sighted. He soon settled down with the other young apprentices and within a few weeks he was writing in his journal:

For my part, I had become a sailor, and could ascend and descend easily to the truck without creeping through the 'lubber's hole.' I shall not forget the first time I attempted this: our youngest apprentice had challenged me to try it, so up we went together—he on the fore and I on the main mast. The tops were gained easily, and we even made two or three steps up the top-mast shrouds with affected indifference; but alas! our courage was failing—at least mine was— very fast. However, we gained the cross-trees pretty well, and then sat down for a little to recover breath. The top-gallant-mast still reared its taper form high above me, and the worst was yet to come. The top-gallant shrouds had no rattlins on them, so I was obliged to shin up; and as I worked my way up the two small ropes, the tenacity with which I gripped them was fearful. At last I reached the top, and with my feet on the small collar which fastens the ropes to the mast, and my arms circling the mast itself—for nothing but a bare pole, crossed by the royal-yard, now rose above me —I glanced upwards.

After taking a long breath, and screwing up my courage, I slowly shinned up the slender pole, and, standing on the royal-yard, laid my hands upon the truck. After a time I became accustomed to it, and thought nothing of taking an airing on the royal-yard after breakfast.

About the 5th or 6th of August, the captain said we must be near land. The deep-sea lead was rigged and a sharp look-out kept, but no land appeared. At last, one fine day, while at the mast-head, I saw something like land on the horizon, and told them so on deck. They saw it too, but gave me no answer. Soon a hurried order to 'Dowse top-gallant-sails and reef top-sails,' made me slide down rather hastily from my elevated position. I had scarcely gained the deck, when a squall, the severest we had yet encountered, struck the ship, laying her almost on her beam ends; and the sea, which had been nearly calm a few minutes before, foamed and hissed like a seething cauldron, and became white as snow. This, I believe, was what sailors call a 'white squall.' It was as short as it was severe, and great was our relief when the ship retained her natural position in the water.

Next day we saw land in earnest, and in the afternoon anchored in 'Five Fathoms Hole,' after passing in safety a sand-bar which renders the entrance into the roadstead rather difficult. Here, then, for the first time I beheld the shores of Hudson's Bay.

In the year 1669, a Company had been formed in London, under the direction of Prince Rupert, for the purpose of prosecuting the fur-trade in the regions surrounding Hudson Bay. This Company obtained a charter from Charles II, granting to them and their successors, under the name of 'The Governor and Company of Adventurers Trading into Hudson's Bay,' the sole right of trading in all the country watered by rivers flowing into Hudson Bay. The charter also authorised them to build and fit out men-of-war, establish forts, prevent any other company from carrying on trade with the natives in their territories, and required that they should do all in their power to promote discovery.

Armed with these powers the Company was not long in establishing a strong and well-armed fort near the head of James Bay, the commander and his men having as their first objective the complete subjection of the Indian tribes who inhabited that part of the country. The ruthlessness and enterprise of these early pioneers quickly yielded results and valuable furs and other goods brought in by the defeated Indians were soon being despatched to London in ever increasing quantities. The newly found wealth and growing power of the London boardroom enabled a network of similar forts and posts to be set up, and, as the years passed, the influence of the Hudson's Bay Company and the British flag spread far beyond the territory granted by the original charter.

The Red Indian tribes proved a delightful source of expendable slave labour, the braves being willing to work for months on end in the worst of weather as hunters and trappers, often bringing in furs worth hundreds of pounds which they were then permitted to exchange in the Company's stores for a handful of the cheapest products of British industry. The commodity these unwashed and evil-smelling natives sought above all others, and one which their white masters were only too willing to supply in exchange for hard-won pelts and skins, was quart bottles of firewater, their particularly vicious brand of rot-gut whisky. They worked for this as for nothing else, but the constant thinning of the ranks of the most skilful of the Indian trappers by knife and axe fights during frequent drunken orgies, in which whole tribes often indulged, started to prove bad for business. Restrictions were imposed on the amount of alcoholic drink that could be supplied to an Indian at any one time, but this rule was relaxed in districts where American companies were in competition for the furs the trappers had to barter. Here it was made plain that business considerations were to override all moral objections to the supply of liquor.

York Factory was the principal depot for the Northern Department, this being one of the four sections into which the territory had been divided for administrative purposes. The fort, as all the Company's establishments in Indian territory were called, was situated on the banks of the Hayes River, about five miles from where it joined the waters of Hudson Bay. This important trading post covered about seven acres, all of which were enclosed inside a high stockade of pointed stakes which gave shelter to the

33

rough-hewn wooden houses and other buildings. Before the massive gates of the stockade stood a relic of its troubled past in the shape of four large brass field-pieces, now only used for firing salutes to herald the arrival of a ship. Their under-carriages were warped and rotten, making it impossible to load them with a full charge of powder and shot. But they looked most impressive on first sight to new arrivals from the mother country, conjuring up pictures of Indian raids and bloody battles with the Redskins in years gone by.

The trading post boasted a population of between thirty and forty workpeople of one kind and another, mostly Scottish Highlanders and Orkneymen who had been agricultural labourers before joining the service. These dour, taciturn, weather-beaten men composed about seventy-five per cent of the total employees, as they did at the majority of other posts; the Scottish winters they had endured and the long hours they had spent minding stock on wind-swept mountain-sides back home made them ideal types for the conditions met with in Rupert's Land. The rest of the men were French-Canadians and half-caste Indians, leavened with a sprinkling of Irishmen plus an Englishman or two. The chief trader, or Chief Factor to give him his official name, was the man in charge of the post, and at the time of Ballantyne's stay this role was occupied by a Mr. James Hargrave. The appointment of Chief Factor was one of the most highly paid and keenly sought after ranks in the Company, a post which carried with it the responsibility of administering an area considerably larger than the whole of Wales. But with it also went many lucrative perquisites that usually enabled the fortunate occupant of the office to retire at the end of his term of service a moderately wealthy man.

One could probably best gain some idea of the vastness of the Hudson's Bay Company's sparsely populated territory if one imagined for a moment that the British Isles had become converted into a wilderness of forest and prairie and had been planted in the middle of Rupert's Land. An area this size would have in it only three trading posts: one at Land's End, one in Wales, and another in the Highlands of Scotland. Outside this area the rest of the posts administered by the Company would be scattered in much the same proportion over the rolling leagues of seemingly endless prairie, mountains, rivers, lakes and forest. When Ballantyne entered the Company's service, Sir George Simpson had been Governor of the Hudson's Bay Company territory for some years, the posts under his command then extending from the Atlantic to the shores of the Pacific Ocean, and from within the Arctic Circle to the northern boundaries of the United States of America.

From York Factory the whole of the supplies for the posts in the Northern Departments were issued. Throughout the short summer period of about four months there occurred the continual bustle of loading and unloading the arriving and departing canoes, and this activity, after a long and dreary winter during which new faces were seldom if ever seen, helped to make life a little more tolerable to the permanent staff. Letters from home were received only twice a year and the arrival of the ship from England, loaded with stores and personal luxuries for men whose supplies of tobacco and other comforts never seemed to last from one ship's call to the next, always resulted in the greatest excitement and never failed to raise a welcoming cheer as the white sails were sighted far out in the bay. Thus it was that Bob and his companions, after being forced to spend a cramped and sleepless night in a rowing boat on the mud flats, due to missing the incoming tide, were greeted on their arrival like long-lost friends. When they finally landed at the tiny wooden wharf they were pounced on by the more exuberant of the waiting crowd and lifted shoulder high before being set down to make their way, stiff-legged, unshaven and smiling embarrassedly, through the gates of the stockade and into the log-built houses which were to be their new home.

In his first letter to his family, written the day after his arrival, a somewhat bewildered young Ballantyne acquainted his father and mother with the news that he was now safe and well at his destination.

I am still more than a little confused by my being on dry land once again, but thank God for seeing me safe here after the perils of the Atlantic crossing. Mr. James Hargrave, the

Chief Factor in charge, received us very kindly, and introduced us to some of the gentlemen standing beside him on the wharf, although the noise and hand-shaking were such that I can recall none of their names with certainty.

Mr. Charles, who accompanied me on the voyage, being himself a Chief Factor, was taken by Mr. Hargrave into his own house, while we apprentice clerks went to the commissioned gentlemen's house—or, as the young gentlemen call it—Bachelors' Hall. There we were told to make ourselves at home. Soon afterwards there were assembled inside, the accountant, five clerks, the postmaster, and one or two others. Most of them were smoking, all of them were talking, and a pretty considerable noise they made. Bachelors' Hall seems worthy of its name, being a place that would kill any woman, so full is it of smoke, noise and confusion.

He was not to endure these conditions for very long, for about ten days later, on Tuesday, 31st August, 1841, the Chief Factor wrote in the *York Factory Journal*:

> Heavy clouds, but fair weather: wind from north to east. In the afternoon the 4 Portage La Loche Boats started for Red River with Cargoes of 50 pieces each and the following passengers:
>> The Rev. A. Cowley & wife,
>> The Rev. John Roberts,
>> John Charles Esqre.
>> Mr. R. Ballantyne, clerk
> all for Red River: also 6 Tradesmen and laborers for the same place, and 10 Sloopers & laborers for Norway House. . . .[1]

The Portage la Loche, as it was called, usually consisted of from four to eight boats, specially adapted for inland travelling where the navigation was obstructed by rapids, waterfalls and whirlpools, to surmount which boats and cargoes were carried overland by the crews. These carrying places, sometimes several miles in length, were termed portages, and between York

[1] Hudson's Bay Company archives B.239/a/154.

Factory and Red River there were upwards of thirty-six of varying difficulty and distance.

Bob must certainly have had a sudden and arduous dose of hard work, what with paddling steadily for many hours during the day, at times helping to drag the heavily loaded canoes up the steep river banks and over rocks and gullies to the next stretch of smooth water, plus the frequent forays he was expected to make into the woods in search of game to supplement their food supply. The rapids were numerous and sometimes extremely dangerous, and, with the current against them, the boats had often to be pushed up river, yard by yard, with the help of long poles, sometimes for many weary miles at a stretch, so that, when they finally landed at Red River Settlement nearly a month later, it was a far tougher and more wiry youngster that arrived than the one who had light-heartedly boarded the *Prince Rupert* some four months before.

The boat in which he travelled was 'long, broad and shallow, capable of carrying forty hundredweight and nine men, besides three or four passengers, with provisions for themselves and the crew. It did not, I suppose, draw more than three feet of water when loaded, perhaps less, and moreover was very light for its size. The cargoe consisted of bales, being the goods intended for Red River sale-room and trading shop. A rude mast and tattered sail lay along the seats, ready for instant use, should a favourable breeze spring up; but this seldom occurred . . .'[1]

With the ready adaptability of youth, he quickly accepted the tough new regimen and before many days had passed gained the reputation of being a lad who never complained of the privations of the journey, roughing it as well as men who had spent years in the wilds and eating food that would have turned the stomachs of his young companions back home in Scotland. Writing a letter to his family describing the first night's camp on the journey, he was careful to reassure his mother by glossing over the hardships and difficulties of the trip:

We encamped upon a rough gravelly piece of ground as there was no better in the neighbourhood; so that my first night

[1] *Hudson's Bay*, by R. M. Ballantyne, Edinburgh, 1848.

in the woods did not hold out the prospect of being a very agreeable one. The huge log fires, however, soon blazed cheerfully, casting a ruddy glow upon the surrounding foliage and the wild, uncouth figures of the voyageurs, who, with their long dark hair hanging in luxuriant masses over their bronzed faces, sat or reclined round the fires, smoking their pipes and chatting with as much carelessness and good-humour, as if the long and arduous journey before them never once entered their minds. . . When I was called to supper, I began to think that if all the travelling in Hudson's Bay was like this, a voyage of discovery to the North Pole would be a pleasure trip!

Supper was soon disposed of, and having warmed ourselves at the fire, we spread our blankets over an oiled cloth, and lay lovingly down together; Mr. Charles to snore vociferously and I to dream of home.

The trade then carried on by the Company was in fur pelts of all kinds, oil, dried and salted fish, feathers, quills, etc., and such varied items as walrus ivory, swanskins and castoreum, to obtain which latter commodity thousands of unfortunate beavers lost their groin sacs.

But by far the most profitable business was obtained from the furs which the Indian trappers brought into the posts every summer. The new fashion at home of wearing silk top-hats had killed the trade in beaver skins to a great extent, but fox, wolf, seal and bear skins were eagerly sought, together with lynx, marten, musquash, buffalo and deer. In the early 1840's, the most valuable pelt was that of the black fox, the silver fox not fetching nearly so high a price, and single skins of the black variety brought up to thirty guineas in the British market. The smaller animals were usually caught by baiting the concealed jaws of steel or heavy wooden traps, while the deer and buffaloes were shot or snared in their hundreds, or run down by hunters mounted on swift little Indian ponies.

Money was of little value in the wilds, most trade with the Indians being carried on by a system of barter, using a standard of value called a 'castor.' On arriving at a fort, sometimes after a canoe journey lasting many weeks, the Indian hunter would take his bundle of furs to the trading room, where the Company trader would examine them as to quality and separate the pelts into their different types. When this scrutiny was completed the trapper would be told that he had earned perhaps sixty or seventy castors, and the clerk would hand him this number of small, carved pieces of wood. Whether the unfortunate Indian received the true worth of his furs or not, he could have little say in the matter, the next trading post being perhaps two hundred or more miles away and owned by the same Company; to argue was of little avail once the trader had made his decision, but the Hudson's Bay Company was careful to pay the natives roughly the same amount throughout its territories, each type of skin having a set value in castors, and any variations being governed by the size and quality of the pelts. Needless to say, the standard value for a skin was set by the Company, and the natives were forced to accept without question the scale of payment imposed. For an Indian to be branded as a trouble-maker and barred from trading was often akin to a sentence of death by starvation in the next hard winter, a fate even the most intrepid young brave did not court lightly.

Having obtained these small, specially shaped pieces of wood, the Indian and his squaw would then look round the bales of cloth, powder-horns, guns, blankets, knives, etc., with which the shop was filled, and perhaps select a blanket, for which he would hand back six castors, and then a hatchet for a further two; proceeding in this way until all his wooden cash was expended. The value of a castor was about eighteen pence at the time of Ballantyne's employment in the service.

An Indian trapper could make from fifty to two hundred castors in a winter's hunt, depending on the number of traps he was able to set and the frequency of his visits to the snares, but luck always played a large part in determining the number of pelts obtained. The highest value that Bob saw an Indian receive was two hundred and sixty castors, paid to a skilful and hard-working young brave whose new squaw was delighted with the colourful blanket and beads which he bought with part of his wealth. This unfortunate Indian did not live long to enjoy his prosperity, being shortly afterwards poisoned by his relatives, who were jealous of his superior abilities as a hunter and envied him the favours shown by the white men. Such murders were commonplace and were always left for the Indian leaders to deal with:

'Thin wiry men,' so Ballantyne describes them, 'not generally muscular, but capable of enduring great fatigue. Their average height is about five feet five inches. The Indian women . . . have an awkward slouching gait, and a downcast look, arising probably from the rude treatment they experience from their husbands; for the North American Indians make complete drudges of their women, obliging them to do all the laborious and dirty work, while they reserve the pleasures of the chase for themselves. Their features are sometimes good, but I never saw a really pretty woman among the Crees. Their colour, as well as that of the men, is a dingy brown, which, together with their extreme filthiness and revolting odour, renders them anything but attractive.'

Each of the Indian tribes kept a large number of slaves, who were the hapless individuals captured in ambushes and battles with neighbouring bands. The Governor, in a report laid before the British Parliament, pictured in harrowing terms the conditions under which these abject creatures had to exist:

These thralls are just as much the property of their masters as so many dogs, with this difference against them, that a man of cruelty and ferocity enjoys a more exquisite pleasure in tasking, or starving, or torturing or killing, a fellow creature, than in treating any one of the lower animals in a similar way. Even in the most inclement weather, a mat or a piece of deer-skin is the slave's only clothing, whether by day or night, whether under cover or in the open air. To eat without permission, in the very midst of an abundance which his toil has procured, is as much as his miserable life is worth; and the only permission which is ever vouchsafed to him is, to pick up the offal thrown out by his unfeeling and imperious lord. Whether in open war or in secret assassination, this cold and hungry wretch invariably occupies the post of danger.

But all this is nothing when compared with the purely wanton atrocities to which these most helpless and pitiable children of the human race are subjected. They are beaten, lacerated and maimed—the mutilating of fingers or toes, the splitting of noses, the scooping out of eyes, being ordinary occurrences. They are butchered, without the excuse or the excitement of a gladiatorial combat, to make holidays. What a proof of the degrading influence of oppression, that men should submit in life to treatment from which the black bondmen of Cuba or Brazil would be glad to escape by suicide![1]

When Ballantyne and his companions arrived at Red River Settlement it proved to be a small township dominated by the stone-built walls of Fort Garry, the local headquarters of the Hudson's Bay Company where Bob was soon taken to be shown his new quarters. The town itself was surrounded by a straggling collection of small farms and homesteads that stretched for sixty miles along the banks of the Red and Assinaboine Rivers. A census taken in 1843 of the town and district revealed a population of over five thousand, and Ballantyne was pleasantly surprised when he stepped ashore at the amenities the settlement had to offer. There were several shops, a church or two, a well-run little school, and a lecture hall used for evening concerts and other social occasions. In the summer the central streets were often full of carriages, and, during the weekends, the river banks were the scene of well-provisioned family picnics to which new clerks soon managed to get themselves invited.

Except for the banks of the two rivers, the country around was treeless; a rolling waste of land upon which scarcely a shrub was to be seen. In summer it was thickly carpeted with a lush green grass on which fed the herds of buffalo, deer and other game, as well as the domesticated animals of the farming community. The strip of woodland which followed the course of the rivers was

[1] From *The Hudson's Bay Territories and Vancouvers Island*, R. M. Martin. London, 1849.

used both for building materials and for fuel, and without these trees it would have been impossible for the inhabitants of the settlement to combat the sub-zero temperature the district experienced every winter.

The day after his arrival Ballantyne was perched on a high office stool, penning accounts of the incoming furs, the pemmican and blanket sales, and totalling inventories of beads, bullets, snow-shoes and rifles. He was never happy doing office work; he loved the open air, and the long hours of confinement passed all too slowly. He counted the days to the weekend break, praying, during the summer months, that the weather would stay fine enough for canoeing; or that, in winter, there would be the crisp clearness of diamond-star-lit nights in which one could stand silent at the edge of the woods and hear the sharp report as a tree split, knifed from top to bottom by the shrinking cold. If these nights were followed by days as clear, sledges and snow-shoes would be brought out by the heavily fur-clad clerks, and a hunting party of excited young men would disappear into the wilderness, not to be seen again until supper, when the thoughts of a roaring log fire, brought them back from the powdered woods. But Ballantyne thought the worst monotonies were the long summer weekday afternoons, when he sat tied to a boring ledger, the minutes creeping and the clock hands seeming to stand still:

It is needless to describe the agonies I endured while sitting, hour after hour, on a long-legged stool, my limbs quivering from want of their accustomed exercise, while the twittering of birds, barking of dogs, lowing of cows, and neighing of horses, seemed to invite me to join them in the woods; and anon, as my weary pen scratched the paper, their voices seemed to change to hoarse derisive laughter, as if they thought that the little mis-shapen frogs croaking and whistling in the marshes were freer far than their proud masters, who coop themselves up in smoky houses during the live-long day, and call themselves the free, unshackled 'lords of Creation!'[1]

[1] *Hudson's Bay*, by R. M. Ballantyne, Edinburgh, 1848.

But life at the fort had its compensations and was by no means all work and no play. Ballantyne and the friends he made there, mostly young men of about his own age, seemed to be for ever shouldering their guns and filing into the tree-lined river banks in search of pigeons and game. They seldom returned without a few brace of grey grouse and other delicacies for the table. Coupled with the wonderful fishing the unspoilt rivers provided, the summer horse-riding when they raced across the prairie in hot pursuit of real or imaginary buffalo, and the flirtations and affairs they had with the pretty half-caste local girls, life cannot have been too unpleasant for the young bachelors of Fort Garry. When out of the office Bob had few complaints, and thoroughly enjoyed the hunting and fishing, the mad prairie gallops, and the canoe trips down river to the rapids, where the bottom of more than one of the birch-bark eggshells they hired from the natives was stoved in, as each tried to outdo the rest of the party by being first to arrive at the deep pool at the lower end of the boiling race of water. In his letters to his parents, no mention was made of the young ladies of Red River Settlement. This does not necessarily mean that his hunting was confined solely to fur-bearing animals and birds to grace the table; but in early manhood he always exhibited a shyness when in the company of girls, especially pretty ones, and to some extent this embarrassment remained with him throughout his life. If he had affairs of an amorous nature while abroad he was careful to see that his mother knew nothing about them.

Bob's tolerance of the privations of a bunkhouse existence (for the winter blizzards sometimes kept the entire staff confined indoors for a week at a time) and the good-humour he usually displayed on these occasions of inspissated gloom, when tempers became frayed and quarrels were frequent, helped to make him one of the most popular members of the 'Fraternity of Quill-Drivers.' This was the title which the clerks of Fort Garry had bestowed upon themselves, and a name they toasted in tankards of mulled beer (into which a red-hot poker had been dipped in order to fizz the bubbles) at every available opportunity, festive or otherwise. Ballantyne displayed a surprising facility for linking them all into a brotherhood of song and dance, extremely wild at times but very energy-consuming, by which some of the long winter evenings were shortened considerably. All of them smoked like chimneys, usually both pipes and cigars, and the atmosphere in the close quarters of the bunkhouse, with only the flue of the fire and perhaps an unsuspected crack for ventilation, must have approached the smoke-filled cribs of Alaskan igloos in degree of heat-laden fumes and smell of overcrowded humanity.

Cut off from the tidings of the outside world for months at a time, local gossip and the occasional refreshment of a Red River scandal took the place of news from the old country, until the arrival of a loaded canoe from York Factory with letters and newspapers from the folks back home, once again set the trappers' wives exchanging titbits of information about friends and relations thousands of miles away. Once in a while the settlement supplied its own drama, and one such incident occurred soon after Bob arrived. The previous summer a Mr. Thomas Simpson, an explorer who had once come within an ace of discovering the long-sought North-West Passage, had started from Red River to make his way back across the plains to the United States. The journey was a long one and he was accompanied by a party of half-breed porters and labourers who were to act as carriers for the valuable supplies and equipment he was taking home. Not long after his departure, however, several of the labourers returned to the settlement with a wild tale that shocked the town and gave rise to dark rumours of evil deeds. The half-breed guides swore that Simpson, in a sudden fit of insanity, had rushed screaming from his tent shooting wildly at the sleeping figures of his companions, killing two of them before blowing his own brains out on the spot. Rather than leave his body to the timber wolves they had buried him and had then hurried back to bring the town the melancholy news of his sudden death. Few of the settlers believed this story. It was thought far more likely that, during an attempt on Simpson's life, he had fought back, killing two of his assailants before a bullet in the head finally laid him low. Rumours persisted until the Company despatched their resident doctor to the scene of the drama with instructions to exhume the body and ascertain the cause of death. However, when Dr. Bunn and his assistants reached the spot and opened the grave it was discovered that the remains had reached such a state of decomposition as to render an autopsy of little value. They brought back Simpson's body for Christian burial, and the service in the little wooden church was attended by practically the entire population of the town. The mystery of how the explorer met his death remains unsolved to this day.

The remainder of the winter passed uneventfully, but with the coming of spring a growing sense of expectancy and excitement began to pervade the young clerks of Fort Garry, for they knew that as soon as conditions permitted canoes to travel in safety, a list of exchanges and postings would appear on the office notice board which might well consign one or more of them to the other end of the continent. The heavy duffle-coats and moose-skin jackets began to vanish as the year advanced, the warm fur-caps with their long ear-flaps giving way to the lightweight 'bonnet rouge,' a style they had borrowed from the French-Canadian trappers. As the weather became warmer, the hard-frozen streams and rills began to trickle with a sound that was as sweet to the ears of the settlers and their wives as the well-remembered voice of a long-absent friend. Soon the dark roofs of the houses appeared once more from beneath the heavy eiderdown of snow, so that the little town, viewed from the elevation of the near-by hill, looked like a chequerboard of black and white. After April had given way to May the solid sheath of snow-covered ice over the rivers began to groan and crack until the long-looked-for day when, almost imperceptibly at first, the close-packed mass started to move slowly downstream. Soon it was heaving and breaking into vast slabs which shrank in size with each passing day; the smaller tributaries becoming rushing torrents, while the floes on Red River moved ponderously down to Lake Winnipeg, buffeting and straining at the ice barring their way.

Even before the waterways were clear enough for navigation the bustle of preparing supplies for despatch to the various isolated trading posts had begun in earnest, and with it the notification of the transfer of personnel to fill the gaps caused by those leaving the service due to ill-health, retirement or promotion to other positions. Ballantyne, who had mentally kept his fingers crossed for several weeks in the hope of being lucky in the draw,

45

was at last summoned to the Chief Factor's office early one June morning and told to pack his kit for the journey to Norway House, a Company post at the far end of Lake Winnipeg, a distance of about three hundred and fifty miles. Within a few days, amid the envious good wishes and handshakes of the clerks he was leaving behind, to whom any change of location always seemed to impart a sense of adventures to come, Bob and his fellow travellers boarded one of the large transport canoes and were soon moving swiftly down-river on the strong current, waving as the image of their friends receded and the first bend in the stream hid them from sight.

A week later he and his companions stepped ashore at Playgreen Lake, at the mouth of Jack River, to be greeted by the trader-in-charge and his wife as the first arrivals of the season. Ballantyne spent the next twelve months at Norway House. His duties were much the same as those he had fulfilled at Fort Garry, but with the welcome advantage of having the rest of the day free when the work in hand was finished. Trout and goldeneye abounded in the near-by rivers, and most summer afternoons were passed sitting with rod and line, or canoeing to Indian villages in company with a fellow clerk, Mr. Ross. This thin, dark-haired young man was about Ballantyne's own age and was starting his second year at the post, and with him as a companion to explore the lakes and rivers of the district the summer months were a pleasant interlude before the onset of another winter. Neither of them looked forward with any relish to the chilly prospect before them, with the tedium of months of confinement with few, if any, visitors. The arrival of a trapper or a trader from another outpost was the only event to break the monotony, and when, in late December, a hard-bitten backwoodsman in the shape of Mr. Cummings shook the snow from his furs and entered the wooden portals of Norway House, he was greeted like a long-lost friend. Cummings was a tall, bearded, bald-headed man of about forty-five, and he had tracked his way alone from his remote trading post, a distance of nearly two hundred miles, in order to enjoy some well-earned leave. He had covered most of the way on snow-shoes, a feat Bob at first found hard to credit. Not long after his arrival, with several platefuls of hot buffalo stew inside him, the trapper was seated by the red-hot stove in the clerks' room, intent on making their hair curl with stories of his adventures. One of his tales is repeated here as being typical of many which Ballantyne heard while in the service of the Hudson's Bay Company, and which he copied down at the time in order to regale his family back home. He had no doubt that the story was a true one:

'My adventure with the bear,' said Mr. Cummings, drawing at his pipe as the young men gathered round the stove, 'started when I set off on snow-shoes, accompanied by an Indian, to a small lake to fetch fish caught in the autumn. I always have them laid in a tight little log hut near the water's edge, where they quickly freeze solid. We return to collect them later in the winter when supplies start running low.

'The lake was about ten miles off, and we started before dawn so as to get back to the camp the same day. On this occasion we had proceeded about six or seven miles and the first streaks of day were just beginning to lighten the eastern horizon, when my Indian suddenly paused and bent down to examine some large footprints in the snow. He rose from his knees excitedly and muttered the words "Bear! Big bear!" indicating to me that the animal had passed that way only a short time before and that he would follow the spoor in the hope of catching up with it. No sooner did I give him permission to go than he threw his gun over his shoulder and was off, quickly being lost to my sight in the forest. For about a quarter of an hour I plodded on behind the dogs, urging them along as they flagged and panted in the deep snow, at the same time keeping my ears open for the sound of a shot from my Indian's gun.

'At last he fired, and almost immediately afterwards fired again. Some of the more experienced Indian hunters can reload so fast that two shots from their single-barrelled guns can sound almost as fast as two from a double-barrelled weapon. Shortly after, I heard another shot; and then, as all became silent, I concluded that he must have killed the bear, and that I should soon find him cutting it up. You can imagine my horror when I suddenly heard the fierce growl of a bear and the cry of a man's voice. Seizing my pistol, I rushed forward and, as I came nearer, I heard my Indian's voice again. 'Come Death!' he groaned weakly, 'You have got me at last, but the Indian does not fear you!' Another loud and angry growl came from the huge black bear as he saw me rushing over the top of the mound, at the bottom of which they both lay. The Indian was on his back, while the bear stood over him, holding one of his arms in its mouth. In rushing up the mound I unfortunately stumbled and filled my pistol with snow; so that when the bear left the Indian and rushed towards me it missed fire, and the only chance I had left was to stun the animal with the butt end. As he reared on his hind-legs I saw the Indian's axe, which lay almost at my feet; and seizing it, I brought it down with all my strength on the bear's head, just at the moment that he fell upon me, and we rolled down the hill together. Upon recovering myself, I found that the blow of the axe had killed him instantly, and that I was uninjured. Not so the poor Indian, however. The whole of the calf of his left leg was hanging off, and his body was dreadfully lacerated. He was conscious, although very weak and faint, and managed to speak to me when I stopped to examine his wounds. I tied him up as best I could, and got him back to the Fort on the sledge; and to my surprise he slowly recovered, although, of course, he never regained the full use of his leg. He still hobbles round the fort, cutting firewood, or paddling about the lake in search of ducks and geese in his bark canoe.'

Allowing, as one must, for exaggeration of the more dramatic details in this and similar stories, and knowing that the dangers allegedly encountered probably increased in fearsomeness with each new telling, it is nevertheless true that the Hudson's Bay territory in the 1840's was no place for weaklings. The smaller posts were often hundreds of miles apart, manned by only one or two white men, and mysterious deaths and fatal disappearances were not uncommon. The Indians, although subdued, were certainly not always to be trusted, and there is no doubt that, during some of the more severe winters, groups in territories remote from the trading posts were often driven to cannibalism in order to survive.

A story which Ballantyne often related on his return to Scotland concerned a Cree Indian, by name Wisagun, who, towards the middle of a biting winter, removed his encampment many miles to the south as game had almost completely disappeared from the area in which they had spent the autumn. For nearly the whole of the previous month they had been forced to exist on scraps of discarded offal, berries and bark they had collected from the surrounding woods, together with a few dried fish and the carcase of a dog which had been the children's summer pet.

The group consisted of Wisagun's wife, his son aged about eight or nine, and two or three other children, plus several of his wife's relations; in all he was the leader of twelve half-famished and vicious Crees, who were now driven to scraping the rocks for edible moss and whose every thought was spiked by the craving for food. After a few days they pitched their camp in a clearing, having suffered agonies of slow starvation on the journey, and without discovering the tracks of either buffalo or deer. For a week they remained at this site, feeding only on a few small birds they shot, and were finally reduced by necessity to consuming their moccasins and leather coats, having first singed them over a fire to render them a little more palatable. Exhausted and near despair, their hopes of a kill were suddenly revived by a scout's discovery of the tracks of many buffaloes within a mile of the camp, and minutes after he brought this news, a small herd was seen silhouetted against the trees at the edge of the prairie.

Weak though they were, they scrambled to load their guns and lace on their snow-shoes, and the males of the hungry party, some staggering with weakness, set off after the moving animals, leaving Wisagun's wife and children and a teenage girl in the largest of the wigwams. The buffaloes had already caught the scent of the hunters and lumbered away into the distance and within a few hours the famished Indians were forced to give up the chase. Some of the weakest had already dropped far behind

49

and were collecting bark, while Wisagun and his son Natappe, reluctantly abandoned the hunt and returned leaden-footed to the encampment.

On their arrival the place seemed deserted, but hearing a peculiar noise, Wisagun peeped through the chinks of the laced wigwam and saw his wife busily engaged in cutting up one of her own children, preparatory to cooking it. Furious with rage that his squaw should dare to commit such an act without his sanction, the Indian slashed through the cords of the tent and immediately stabbed both her, and her young woman assistant, to death. He knew that the rest of the Crees, two of whom were brothers of his wife, would not be long in returning, and, fearing the wrath to come, he fled with his son into the woods.

One can imagine the sight that greeted the despondent hunters when they entered the fatal tent, but they were so exhausted by their previous sufferings that they could only gaze on the mutilated bodies in despair and vow everlasting vengeance on the murderer. The drama, however, was by no means over. Under cover of darkness, the chief and his son returned stealthily to the camp, and Wisagun, with his tomahawk, coldbloodedly butchered the whole party as they lay asleep. He wanted no witnesses to survive to tell the tale, and he knew well what his own fate would have been if his wife's brothers had survived to hunt him down. Death would have been a welcome release from the tortures he could have expected had he fallen into their hands.

Some weeks later Natappe and his father were discovered in what seemed good physical condition by another party of Indians, although there was now no game in the area, and famine and desolation had scythed their way through many hundreds of miles of territory. They were questioned about their plumpness and accounted for it by saying they had been lucky enough to shoot a deer, but that the rest of their group were found dead by starvation when they managed to return with the meat. The young boy looked uneasy and the demeanour of the pair began to arouse suspicion. Before long rumours of what might have happened to Wisagun's unfortunate companions reached Norway House and the ears of the Chief Trader there, and on the Indian's next visit to trade furs he was viewed with a morbid interest by Ballantyne and the rest of the clerks. Under the influence of most of the contents of a quart bottle of Hudson Bay firewater, he was subjected to a barrage of questions by the trader and his assistants, finally admitting the truth, but excusing himself by saying that most of his relations had died before he and his son started to eat what they considered the most appetising portions of them. Had white men been involved both he and his son would have been hanged on the spot, but the policy of the Company was to let the natives settle these affairs in their own way and Wisagun was allowed to return to his wigwam as soon as he had become sufficiently sober. But within a few weeks, his body was discovered drifting downstream in a canoe, a bullet hole in the head: an assassin hidden amongst the trees of the thickly wooded bank had at last evened the score.

In July 1843, Ballantyne found himself once again at York Factory, having been transferred to replace a clerk whose term of service had expired. And there, in Bachelors' Hall, he was to remain for the next two years, breakfasting each day at nine, and then sitting, quill pen in hand, on the long-legged stools in the store-room office working at the ledgers, until, with breaks for lunch and tea, their spell of duty was ended at eight in the evening by the tolling of the watch-tower bell signalling an end to their labour for the day. It was then that he and the rest of the clerks would troop over to their quarters for a hot supper, followed by the inevitable mugs of mulled beer and the clay pipes which even the youngest of them smoked in the most manly fashion around the roaring log fire.

A number of them made an attempt at playing musical instruments of one sort and another, and in the winter evenings the smoke-blacked logs of the walls shook with the raucous choruses of songs that would have scandalised their mothers and brought a blush to the cheeks of their girl friends back home. Many of these all-male jamborees ended with wild variations of the Scottish reel and sword dance, furious and hilarious gyrations in which Ballantyne performed as vigorously, and sometimes as drunkenly, as the rest of his rowdy companions. He took part in a four-piece band they formed, but his duties were limited to clashing a battered pair of cymbals at any moment he thought appropriate. He also gave spirited solos in a voice that now fluctuated between tenor and baritone, and which he was seldom loth to use, having a growing faith in its artistic quality; a faith that was increased immeasurably by the prolonged applause his singing of the ballads of old Scotland invariably brought forth from his uncritical young friends.

There were occasions, on fine clear nights, when fur-muffled clerks would don their snow-shoes and set off to pay a visit to their own private traps hidden amongst the pines and spruces along the banks of the Hayes River. Once or twice in a hard winter, a fortunate individual might discover that most valuable of all Canadian fur-bearing animals, a black fox, maimed but defiant in the steel jaws of a snow-covered trap. A blow with the butt end of an axe-head on the tender nose of the helpless creature (for a bullet would damage the pelt), the pressing down with a moccasined foot of the heavy spring which held tight the spiked jaws of the trap, and the prize was his. Then back through the forest to the gates of the stockade, the fox tied by its feet across the shoulders of the jubilant trapper (for thus he could now expect to be mockingly called by his companions), a banging and shouting at the door of Bachelors' Hall, and the envious inmates would be out of bed within minutes to crowd round the limp carcase deposited on the wooden floor.

Great care had to be taken when the cold was intense not to accidentally touch any metallic object such as the barrel of a rifle or the head of an axe, for the bare hand would instantly be frozen tight to the steel and could seldom be removed without the loss of a portion of skin. If guns were brought back into a warm room after a winter hunting expedition the barrels, and every bit of metal upon them, instantly became as white as ground glass, as the room's moisture condensed on the extremely cold steel.

A favourite trick played upon a new apprentice, fresh out from Britain, was to make him wager that it was impossible for liquid quicksilver to knock a hole through a thick plank of wood. With the mid-winter temperature at York Factory sometimes fifty degrees below zero Fahrenheit, the method used was simple. A bullet mould was filled with mercury, put outside to freeze, and, when solid, was rammed down an equally cold gun barrel and fired at the thick plank. It says much for the quality of the guns that there were not more burst barrels due to this kind of experiment, although with the cheap grades supplied to the Indians, fatal accidents were commonplace enough.

After Bob had been back at York Factory for about a year, the Chief Factor wrote to the Governor:

2nd June, 1844

Dear Sir George,

My young friends Ballantyne and [Thomas] Charles are both fine boys and attentive to their duties The former begins to be useful in the Counting House, and both, I have no doubt, will turn out well. . .

Your much obliged and grateful servant,

J[ames] Hargrave.

It was during his stay here that the young man composed a poem, a feat which ranks as his first literary effort. He called it 'Hudson's Bay,' and it was written in the lazy summer hours when he sat fishing for goldeneye, his hook baited with the grasshoppers that swarmed in the thick grass. It is some two hundred lines in length, and the mental contortions of the young author-to-be can be judged by the amount of crossings-out and substitutions in the original manuscript. Ballantyne at no time in his life made any pretensions to being even a minor poet, but, as an example of his earliest literary work, the first verse deserves the honour of appearing in print.

> Upon the shores of Hudson's Bay,
> Where Arctic winters, stern and grey,
> Freeze the salt-waters of the Deep
> In a long, silent icy sleep;
> Where willows and the stunted pine
> Can scarcely live in such a clime,
> Where Arctic fox and polar bear,
> Clad in a coat of snow-white hair,
> Prowl forth to snuff the tainted gale
> And feast on walrus or the whale;

With snow and ice encompassed round,
And built on low and swampy ground,
Through which Haye's River takes its way
And slowly joins the frozen Bay;
There in its cold and icy lands,
Silent and grim, York Factory stands.

Letters from home were eagerly awaited, and it was only twice a year, amid great excitement on the part of the young clerks, and the rest of the staff, that the sealed, important-looking packets arrived. By this time the Ballantyne family had moved to Portobello, just outside Edinburgh, where Sandy had managed to raise a mortgage for the purchase of a small house in the better part of the town. From here, at the end of 1844, Randall wrote to her son:

16 *West Brighton Crescent,*
Nov. 19th, 1844.

My darling! My own beloved Bob,

It is utterly impossible to describe our joy at the receipt of your charming packet! But to amuse you I will tell you the manner of receiving it. First, however, I must give you the comfort to know that we are *all* well, and shall leave *no* stone unturned to get you back amongst us at the end of your term.

Well, my darling, this being settled I may proceed. We had not heard from you since the month of April (when John was in Italy) and you may believe we longed for the arrival of the Ship, and counted every day after October began, and on Sunday the 20th of this month, I went to pass a quiet day with Aunt Hunter. In the evening I said to her, 'Well Jane, my darling packet *must* come tomorrow, for if it does not arrive till Wednesday (Mary Michael's wedding day!!) I cannot go to the wedding, as there will be no time to read my letters, adorn myself for the wedding, and drive up to Edinburgh, before 11 o'clock.' Thus said, I fixed that if the letters should arrive on the Wednesday I would stay at home and enjoy them, but hoped that they would come two days sooner, and then I might enjoy both treats. You must observe that the letters usually given out on the Monday morning may be got on Sunday evening if called for, and Mina,[1] who was passing the Post Office on her way to a Sunday School meeting, saw people getting their letters and thought she might enquire if there were any for us—when to her astonishment and perfect delight, your packet was handed over!

Home she flew! But where was Mamma? At Aunt Hunter's to be sure, where Aunt had just rung for the tea things, telling the servant that two cups would do, little dreaming of the party that was throwing on bonnets and shawls to rush in with the news! Suddenly, Aunt's drawing-room door was flung open to the hinges! Then to our astonishment, there stood Papa, quiet and erect—with Mary, Jane, Madalina, Randall and Mina pushing him forward, while he presented your packet to our bewildered gaze! A momentary calm followed the first burst of joy, and Mary was appointed to read aloud the whole contents, and the only regret was, when she came to the last page, that there was no more— every word was honey! All our complaints were cured and we devoured your Aunt's tea and toast with an appetite unknown to us for months.

Thursday the 21st.

And now for some news! Your brother James has just been married to Violet Roberton! You stare! But it is quite true— we have just returned from the wedding, where all went off delightfully, and 'the happy pair' went off on their marriage trip to Glasgow, from whence they will return to their own house in a few days. It is to be hoped that the next letter we write to you will have a batch of marriages amongst your sisters, but all in good time—neither Papa nor I have any great desire to get quit of them, the dear pets—and I am sure I would rather keep them for ever than let them go to India. I do wish you could see us all dressed in new winter dresses, bought with Bob's money! Maddle and Randall are resplendent in green tartan!

[1] Williamina Ballantyne, their youngest daughter.

(*27th*) I have just heard that Mrs and Miss Greig, those most estimable, most generous of women, have sent James and Violet a present of a fine old family Bible, which James and John used to read out of, and study the pictures, when they were little boys, and accompanying the Bible is a pocket book containing twenty pounds! And this from two ladies of very limited income! How noble of them! Their generous spirits are just like your own, my darling, but we cannot help regretting that we take such advantage of your goodness. (Now Papa wishes to add a line.)

May God forever bless you, my dear Bob.

A.B.

Oh! my darling, how I do hate to stop—I could go on for ever! But the paper can't hold any more. I am determined to live till you come home at the end of your five years. It will go quickly, my darling—for who could imagine you had been so long away from us! Only take good care of your precious health. Once again, farewell my beloved, my own Bob!

Your affect. mother,
R. S. Ballantyne.

During the short but hot northern summer, the climate and environment at York Factory were anything but salubrious, as the swampy nature of the surrounding countryside meant that mosquitoes and flies swarmed in their millions. Many of the young clerks were afflicted at this time of the year with a variety of stomach complaints, and during July Bob was laid low for several weeks with a severe attack of fever. He was back on duty at the end of August, but the illness had left him weak and he had several renewed attacks during the following winter, with the result that the Chief Factor advised the Governor that the lad ought to be moved to a more healthy situation.

And so, the following June, Bob began the long journey back to Red River Settlement, carrying in his pocket a letter from the Chief Factor to Sir George Simpson who, by marriage, was himself a distant relative of the Ballantynes:

Dear Sir George,

Mr. Ballantyne is just about starting for Norway House and I hasten to address to you a few lines in acknowledgment of your much valued favour of the 1st inst. In reply to your enquiry regarding that young gentleman's habits and character, I feel bound to speak of both in favourable terms.

He came very young to the country and was at first stationed where he had comparatively little work to do; and, in consequence, had made little progress in knowledge of business when he was sent to this place. Since he came under my orders I have every reason to speak well of his application, improvement and docility. He is not yet fitted to take charge of any important trust in business or accounts; but under a superintendent, who would set him a good example, I am certain that he would give satisfaction.

The worst feature of his character that I have observed is youthful thoughtlessness—which time & reflection are sure to remedy. At first there was also about him a little of what characterises most town-bred boys—forwardness and flippancy. York discipline, however, I believe, has withered all such; and on the whole, I beg to speak of him as a young man well fitted to become useful in the service, under proper tuition and a Bourgeois who would take pains to render him so. . .

Yours most faithfully,
J[ames] Hargrave[1]

Upon his arrival at Red River he was allocated a junior position in the Company office, but he was destined to work for only a few weeks at headquarters. It soon became obvious to his employers that young Mr. Ballantyne was restless, hated being continually tied to a desk, and was more eager for a job in which he could use his own initiative. The thought of another year perched high and quilling seemed to appal him, and he pestered the Chief Factor to give him the opportunity of proving his worth in a more

[1] Hudson's Bay Company archives D.5/14, fo. 94.

responsible position. What arguments he used to excuse his youth cannot now be ascertained, but after a final interview with the Factor, he 'skipped rather than walked' to the clerks' room, with the treasured transfer slip in his pocket.

The next few days were full of the excitement of packing and repacking for the long journey, followed by final visits and good-byes, until on the 20th August, 1845, the express canoe, manned by a crew of eight and with Mr. and Mrs. McLean and the eager young clerk as passengers, started on the 2,300-mile trip from Red River to the King's Posts, situated along the northern shores of the lower St. Lawrence near Quebec:

> The beautifully shaped canoe floated lightly on the river, notwithstanding her heavy cargo, and the water rippled gently against her sides as it swept slowly past. This frail craft, on which our safety and progression depended, was made of birch bark sewed together, lined on the inside with thin laths of wood, and pitched on the seams with gum. It was about thirty-six feet long and five broad in the middle, from whence it tapered either way to a sharp edge. It could carry twenty to twenty-five hundredweight, with eight or nine men, besides three passengers and provisions for a month. And yet, so light was it, that two men could carry it for a quarter of a mile without resting.[1]

Bob's appearance was now such that his own parents would have had difficulty in recognising him. Wearing his old blue capote,[2] a pair of corduroys, brightly embroidered moccasins and a battered straw hat, his face burned brown by the sun—he looked as tough and wiry as any trapper from the backwoods. He was now an excellent shot, and during the canoe's many overland portages, he would disappear into the woods, his leather belt heavy with powderhorn, knife and shot, to return more often than not with game or wild duck, a very welcome change from the pemmican and dried fish which were the staple diet for long-distance travelling.

Week after week they paddled down the rivers and across the

---

[1] *Hudson's Bay*, by R. M. Ballantyne. Edinburgh, 1848.
[2] Capote—a long shaggy cloak or overcoat, with a hood. (O.E.D.)

lakes of Rupert's Land into Canada, sometimes carrying the canoe for miles to the next stretch of water; at others shooting through the rocks and eddies of the fast-flowing rapids and then paddling madly to reach the quiet waters of the lee shore. For hours at a time they were soaked to the skin by rain and spray, and on other occasions sweltered for days in the close-packed canoes under the towering sun.

They shortened the long miles by singing canoe songs, keeping time to the steady dip, dip, dip of the paddles. The voyageurs would take up a song individually, first one then another joining in until the whole crew were singing. Bob thoroughly enjoyed using what he now considered to be a better than average voice, and the canoe chants he learned on that trip he later sang many times to crowded halls during his lectures back in his native Scotland.

The young and pretty Mrs. McLean helped with the cooking and kept the men's clothes in repair, acting as nurse for several weeks when one of the French-Canadian labourers became critically ill. One can only admire the pluck and endurance of this early Victorian lady of twenty-three, hampered with the long skirts and flounces of the period and surrounded with as rough and tough a crew as the backwoods could provide. She was expected to be as uncomplaining as the Indian guides and halfbreed porters with whom she travelled, and never for a moment show that she felt the slightest fear of being hundreds of miles from any form of civilisation. It was not until the 25th October, after nine gruelling weeks, when, no doubt to her immense relief, they finally reached their journey's end at Lachine. For sixty-six days they had tracked across the waste of rivers and lakes and un-inhabited forest, averaging thirty-five miles or more a day and camping at night on the river bank, plagued by swarms of persistent mosquitoes and the constant fear of attack by bands of thieving Indians to whom the equipment lying about a sleeping camp was a most welcome source of supplies. They suffered no attacks, and arrived safely at their destination, there to find the Chief Factor, Duncan Findlayson, to greet them. Ballantyne was the first ashore, where Findlayson grasped his nail-hard hand with the words: 'Welcome to Lachine. I think you will find that I have just the job for a man like you.' With visions of being asked to command a patrol to track down and annihilate a marauding band of Redskins in full war-paint, Bob swelled with pride and felt inches taller as he walked towards his quarters. But some hours later, to his infinite dismay, he learned that he had been selected for training for the post of shorthand secretary to Sir George Simpson and that he was likely to spend the rest of his service with the Company indoors.

Chapter Four

LACHINE, A FEW MILES FROM MONTREAL, was the head-quarters of the 'King's Posts' area of Canada, as the Company called the lower St. Lawrence district, and it was here that the Governor and his wife resided. After the rough life he had been leading the civilisation and social amenities of the small town, with its wheeled carriages and groomed horses, its comfortable quarters and well-heated rooms, and the joy of once more sleeping in a feather bed, made Bob wish that he could finish his Hudson's Bay Company service in this cosy, well-found spot. Provided, that is, he could find a job to his liking.

After a hearty meal washed down with an unaccustomed bottle of wine, he walked a little unsteadily to his bedroom, there to be greeted by his own reflection in the wall mirror. The sight came as a shock to him, for he realised that the blue capote was now filthy, as were the worn corduroy trousers and tattered shirt, while his deeply sunburned face was half hidden under a straggling mass of long, greasy dark hair. This was the first time he had had a chance to use a mirror since leaving Norway House, and he thought he looked more like an Indian than a white man. 'I had no cause to be proud of my appearance', he told his parents in his next letter home. He had been given the whole of the following day to unpack and make himself respectable, and during the morning he 'had two baths and a hair-cut and donned a complete new outfit of clothes.' He must have felt and smelt like a new man as he took his first walk around the town that afternoon. The next morning he was summoned by Mr. Findlayson to drive with him to Montreal to meet the Governor's wife and Mrs. Findlayson, who was sister to Lady Simpson and her constant companion. The ladies had intimated that they would like to be introduced to the fortunate young man Sir George had chosen as his secretary, and although the Governor was away for a few days, they were both at home, seated in the drawing room, when Bob and the Chief Factor were shown into the house and ushered to the door of the room.

At that fearsome door, young Ballantyne, his 'knees trembling, mouth[1] dry and brain incapable of thought' came to a full stop. To the amusement of the ladies. it took a hard push in the back from Duncan Findlayson to propel him into the room, still wearing, to his horror, the new cap he had been issued with the day before. But both ladies were impressed with the demeanour of the slim, shy and awkward young gentleman, and Lady Simpson wrote later to his mother that she had been most pleased with 'his amiable disposition and perfect good temper, and that he is, without exception, the handsomest young man I have seen in Canada.' Even so, the possessor of these sterling qualities was extremely glad when the front door shut behind him at the end of the interview and he was able to escape once more into the crowded streets of Montreal.

Soon after his arrival at Lachine, winter set in, and, with the first snow, the wheeled carriages quickly disappeared to be replaced by carioles and sledges of all descriptions. These often beautifully carved and decorated vehicles were usually drawn by one horse, the harness and trappings of which were profusely covered with small round bells. So silent were the sledges as they slid swiftly along on the soft snow that the merry jingling was a necessary warning to other travellers of their speedy approach. This cheerful tinkling music heard on the Canadian snow-covered roads entranced Bob, and there was little he liked better than a fast, fur-covered ride on a swiftly moving sledge, with the flanks of the trotting horse steaming and the steel runners hissing and sliding beneath him.

Until his move to the Montreal area he had been able to receive mail from home only twice a year and box or parcel post once every twelve months when the Company ship called at York Factory. His family in Edinburgh, although living in reduced circumstances, never failed to send him a box, packed tight with comforts and presents and containing an accumulation of letters from relatives and friends, and he savoured the pleasure of its arrival for weeks before it actually appeared. The books and newspapers he rationed by discipline to last for as many weeks as possible after the opening, and the long closely written letters he

[1] Letter to his mother, November 1845.

spun out carefully, enjoying the nostalgia for home they invariably seemed to bring. A list of contents was always put on the top of the packed box, a typical example being that of the 8th May, 1845.

Contents of the Box

6 shirts—four of them coloured.

2 Lamb's wool, tartan cravats for the neck (The blue one 'The Prince Albert,' the green one 'Mackenzie Tartan.')

A fine flute.

Book of instructions for ditto.

A flageolet (a present from James Michael).

6 boxes of percussion caps.

6 pencils.

Cake of China ink.

2 large vols. of Chambers 'Information for the People.'

Various small vols.

2 set of buttons for shooting jacket.

1 set for fishing jacket.

4 pairs of 'Muffatoes' worked by Aunt Madalina for 'Darling Bob.'

Newspapers.

Pinned to this list was a short note from his mother. 'Be sure to tell me what you need most next box. My delight is to pack up the things, my own darling. Papa bids me tell you that as your cousin James Michael is so kind as to send you a flageolet you are bound to receive it and thank him for it—but you are *not bound* to play on it, as it is quite false and will spoil your ear, and also ruin your mouth for the flute. What a lovely flute it is!' (Here his father interjected a line.) 'It is false on D! A.B.' 'Write by next opportunity to kind Mrs. and Miss Grieg,' his mother went on, 'thanking them for the flute, and as they are very clever, intelligent ladies, it would please them if you were to give them some interesting account of any of the wonders of the frozen regions—they are great admirers of your letters. We were very much amused by the expression Miss G. made use of when she sent the money (under the wing of a turkey she sent to James)

'Pray get a recreative article for Master Bob.' I suppose she was afraid we would lay it out in waistcoats.

Your own,
R.S.B.

Miss Greig was to play a very important part in Bob's life when he returned to Scotland. She and her mother had been close friends of the Ballantynes since the family's early days in Kelso, and had offered their assistance on several occasions when times had been particularly hard. They were aware that Sandy was finding it increasingly difficult to make ends meet and that he had not prospered since his youngest son had boarded the ship for Canada. About 1843 he had agreed to accept his late brother James's share in the *Edinburgh Weekly Journal* in exchange for giving his undertaking to withdraw from the printing business, which the remaining partners promptly renamed 'Ballantyne & Hughes.' Sandy soon discovered that John Hughes and John Alexander Ballantyne (his late brother James's eldest son) had sold him a business that was going rapidly downhill, and by 1844 he was thankful to be able to dispose of the newspaper at a price which did at least allow him to retain a small balance in cash. With five unmarried daughters still at home, he was finding it much harder to pay his way and he was now forced to live almost entirely on capital. What he had in the bank consisted of the balance remaining from the sale of the *Weekly Journal* after the settlement of his various outstanding debts. This amounted to only a few hundred pounds, and his income, such as it was, now came from some Water Company shares, plus the interest paid him by a Mr. George Watt who owed him the sum of four hundred pounds. Watt had once acted as manager of the Ballantyne store in Kelso and had set up on his own account some years before as a candle-maker and provision merchant. Under his proprietorship his shop in Kelso prospered, the interest on Sandy's loan was always paid on the dot, and Ballantyne was content to leave the money invested for as long as he possibly could. 'Once this capital is withdrawn,' he wrote to his son James, 'I fear it will melt like butter on the hob.'

Both James and John were now making their own way in the

world and helping their parents whenever they could. But by the spring of 1845, with his bank balance dwindling every week, Sandy would have been thankful to receive help from any quarter. Randall's sharp sense of family dignity and pride in being independent prevented their acceptance of anything which hinted at charity, or of a loan they might not be able to repay, whether it came from Miss Greig or anyone else. This feeling of hers for what she considered right and proper for a middle-class family, albeit an impoverished one, put a stop, at least for the time being, to the ideas her daughters had of taking posts as teachers in Edinburgh, despite the benefit this would have brought to the family's financial affairs.

Just as things were at their blackest they received news which helped for a time to dispel the depression about their future which had enveloped Sandy and his wife for many months. In February a letter arrived appointing Bob's eldest brother, James, as principal of the East India Company's Sanscrit College at Benares in India, at a starting salary of seven hundred pounds per annum. Soon afterwards, to the intense pride of his parents, the degree of Doctor of Laws was conferred upon him by Edinburgh University. Randall's joy knew no bounds and she gladly devoted her energies to helping her daughter-in-law with the numerous tasks of shopping and packing for the long journey to Benares. The new Dr. Ballantyne and his wife, after an exhausting round of visits and farewells, sailed in July on the *Glorian*, en route for Cape Town and India, amid the tearful farewells of a host of relatives. On 8th September, during the voyage out, Violet Ballantyne presented her husband with a baby son, to James's great delight and satisfaction, and they promptly named the boy Alexander. Sandy heard this news with pride in the first message the family received from the happy pair, and tales of little Ally's activities soon began to fill the pages of James's letters.

His younger brother, John, after many false starts, was at last commanding a regular income as a portrait painter, and with a brand-new bank balance and what appeared to be a future full of promise, was now making serious overtures to his second cousin, a somewhat precocious young lady named Christina Hogarth, who both permitted and encouraged his endearments. John viewed with assurance his professional career as an artist and the young couple were soon busy planning their new home, including in their dreams a well-lit studio, servants' quarters and other expensive amenities, the whole to be furnished in the most modern taste.

Randall had now passed her sixtieth birthday, but was still upright, slim and active, and her well-cut face with large, dark eyes and impeccably straight nose bore traces yet of the beauty which had captivated her husband some forty years before. Her grey hair she wore parted in the middle and gathered at the back in a bun, and her head was invariably surmounted by a spotlessly white lace cap. The children all thought the world of her, and their dear, unlucky Papa was content to be mothered like the rest of the family. In her letters to her youngest son, Randall revealed practically nothing of their financial plight, and was as cheerful and as gossipy as her loving heart could make her.

Her boy was not with the Governor's entourage for long, whether from his inability to learn shorthand or a disinclination to be Sir George's secretary is not known, but on a bright winter's day in January 1846 he was interviewed and told to hold himself in readiness to start early the following morning with Mr. George Barnston for Tadousac—being given the added information that he would probably be required to spend the approaching summer at Seven Islands.

As Tadousac was a situation about three hundred miles below Montreal at the mouth of the River Saguenay, and Seven Islands was nearly two hundred miles below Tadousac, the journey was not a short one. On a crisply cold morning, well before dawn, the two men entered a waiting sleigh and slid noiselessly over the silent streets of Lachine, Ballantyne 'feeling as excited as any schoolboy released for the holidays.'

The stars shone brightly as we glided over the crunching snow, and the sleigh-bells tinkled merrily as our horse sped along the deserted road. Groups of white cottages, and solitary giant trees, flew past us, looking in the uncertain light, like large snow drifts; save where the twinkling of a candle, or the first blue flames of the morning fire, indicated that the industrious inhabitant had risen to his daily toil. In silence we glided on our way, till the distant lights of Montreal awakened us from our reveries, and we met at intervals a solitary pedestrian, or a sleigh load of laughing, fur-encompassed faces, returning from an evening party. . .

About seven o'clock we arrived at the hotel from which the stage was to start for Quebec. The stage, however, was full, but the driver informed us that an 'extra' (or separate sleigh of smaller dimensions than the stage) had been provided for us; so that we enjoyed the enviable advantage of having it all to ourselves.

There is something very agreeable in the motion of a sleigh along a good road. The soft muffled sound of the runners gliding over the snow harmonises well with the tinkling bells; and the rapid motion through the frosty air, together with the occasional jolt of going into a hollow, or over a hillock, is very exhilarating—and we enjoyed the drive very much for the first hour or so. But alas! human happiness is seldom of long duration, as we soon discovered; for, just as I was falling into a comfortable doze, bang! went the sleigh into a deep 'cahoe', which most effectually wakened me. Now these same 'cahoes' are among the disadvantages attending sleigh travelling in Canada. They are nothing more or less than deep hollows or undulations in the road, into which the sleighs unexpectedly plunge, thereby pitching the traveller roughly forward; and upon the horses jerking the vehicles out of them, throwing him backward in a way that is pretty sure to bring his head into closer acquaintance with the back of the sleigh. Those we now encountered were certainly the worst I ever travelled over, rising in succession like the waves of the sea, and making our conveyance plunge sometimes so roughly that I expected it to go to pieces. Indeed I cannot understand how wood and iron could stand the crashes to which we were exposed. . .

During the day our sleighs were upset several times; but Mr. Barnston and I, in the 'extra', suffered more in this way than those in the regular stage, as it was much narrower, and consequently, more liable to tip over. Upon upsetting, it unaccountably happened that poor Mr. Barnston was always undermost. But he submitted to his fate most stoically. . .[1]

The two men passed three days in Quebec, rising late and breakfasting at leisure; wandering round the town in the afternoons sightseeing and buying small presents to send back home. There was no regular transport which proceeded even in the general direction of Tadousac, and it was necessary to solicit a lift from a private sledge travelling that way. On the fourth day they bargained two places on a farmer's sleigh and shortly afterwards found themselves sitting behind the jingling bells of a fast-trotting horse, the snow-covered pine woods sliding quickly past on either side. As they advanced, the signs of civilisation began gradually to disappear—villages became scarcer and roads worse, until they saw only an occasional woodcutter's shanty or remote farmhouse:

> Our driver happened to be a very agreeable man, and more intelligent than most Canadians of his class; moreover, he had a good voice, and when we came to a level part of the road I requested him to sing me a song—which he did at once, singing with a clear, strong, manly voice the most beautiful French air I ever heard. He then asked me to sing —which I did without further ceremony, treating him to one of the ancient melodies of Scotland; and thus, with solos and duets, we beguiled the tedium of the road and filled the woods with melody.

They said goodbye to their driver as he turned off to his farm, and Bob and his companion, their packs strapped high on their backs with their snow-shoes laid crossways on the top, started the long walk to the post. After a few more miles the rough track they were following gradually petered out, the snow became thicker, and they were forced to don their snow-shoes and tramp deep into the forest in order to reach the banks of the River

[1] *Hudson's Bay*, by R. M. Ballantyne, Edinburgh, 1848, chapter XI. In the book he used the name 'Stone' to disguise George Barnston's real identity.

Saguenay. Barnston had travelled the route several times and knew the landmarks well, amazing Ballantyne by his ability to find his way through what appeared to be trackless miles of forest, eventually striking the river bank within a few yards of where a small boat was moored in readiness for their crossing. Even in the depths of winter this river did not freeze, its immense depth at the mouth holding sufficient warmth to prevent ice forming into a continuous sheet, and they had little difficulty in rowing to the entrance of a small creek on the other side.

On the evening of the 7th February, the two tired travellers finally arrived at Tadousac, at that time little more than a group of log houses loosely scattered in a hollow of the mountains close to the river. The Hudson's Bay Company used it more as a store and staging post than as a site for trading furs, and Bob found life very quiet indeed:

Nothing worth mentioning took place at Tadousac during my residence there. The winter became severe and stormy, confining us much to the house, and obliging us to lead very humdrum sort of lives. Indeed, the only thing that I can recollect as being at all interesting or amusing—except, of course, the society of my scientific and agreeable friend Mr. Barnston and his amiable family—was a huge barrel-organ, which, like the one I found at Oxford House, played a rich variety of psalm tunes, and a choice selection of Scotch reels —the grinding out of which formed the chief solace of my life. . .

Within a month of his arrival, fresh orders were received for him to proceed at once to Isle Jeremie, a post situated sixty miles down the Gulf of St. Lawrence and an even more solitary spot than his present location. For what must have seemed the hundredth time Bob dutifully packed his kit, and accompanied this time by a silent and rough-looking French-Canadian named Bezeau, who had been detailed to act as his porter, he boarded a small boat which was to take them the first twenty miles of their journey. The two men were put ashore at the mouth of the Esquimain River, close to the hut of an impoverished seal-fisher and his wife, whose family, plus five or six labourers from a near-by saw-mill, were the only inhabitants of this lonely spot. That night they were all crowded into the only hut, and here, in an atmosphere reeking of rancid blubber and wood-smoke, and the smell of the unwashed bodies of his companions, Ballantyne was reluctantly compelled to spend the night. The snores and stenches of his uncouth room-mates and the nauseating smell of the blubber drove the unfortunate lad out of doors on more than one occasion, only to find himself quickly forced inside again by the intense cold. He awoke next morning, stiff, clammy and un-refreshed, but with the immense relief of knowing that he would be spared the ordeal of passing another night in that vile and air-less chamber. In his haste to depart he forgot to pay the sealer his pittance for the worst night's lodging he had ever spent in his life.

He noted in his journal that his porter Bezeau 'was dressed in a blue striped cotton shirt of very coarse quality, and a pair of corduroys, strapped round his waist with a scarlet belt. Over these he wore a pair of blue cloth leggins, neatly bound with orange-coloured ribbon. A Glengarry bonnet covered his head; and two pairs of flannel socks, under a pair of raw seal-shoes, protected his feet from the cold. His burden consisted of my carpet-bag, two days' provisions, and a blue cloth capote which later he carried on his shoulder, the weather becoming warm. My own dress consisted of a scarlet flannel shirt, and a pair of *etteffe du pays* trousers, which were fastened round my waist by a leathern belt, from which was suspended a small hunting knife; a foraging cap and deer-skin moccasins completed my costume. My burden was a large green blanket, a greatcoat, and a tin tea-kettle. Our only arms were the little hunting-knife and a small axe for felling trees, should we wish to make a fire.'

In this garb the oddly assorted pair started their journey from the hut at Esquimain River. Neither had ever travelled that route before and they had only the roughest of directions to guide them on the next stages of their trip to Isle Jeremie. Within an hour of their starting, the track they were following petered out at what seemed to be a vast stretch of snow-covered marshland, tussocked with hummocks of frozen grass and the whitened vegetation of the previous summer. The ice, over which they were forced to make their way, had been overlaid with about six inches of watery snow, and on top of this the sharp frost of the previous night had laid a thin cake of fresh ice. Through this brittle sheet their snow-shoes broke every few steps, sinking them over their ankles in watery slush, '. . . to extricate our feet from which, almost pulled our legs out of their sockets.'

When darkness at last began to fall the two had plodded painfully along for nearly eighteen miles, by which time even the tough, hard-bitten French-Canadian was streaked with sweat and showing signs of exhaustion. A considerable distance behind him staggered Ballantyne, his slim figure bent nearly double, soaked to the skin by his falls and drenched in perspiration. As he mechanically lifted one squelching, aching snow-shoe after the other, the sardonic backward glances of his companion had not been lost on the younger man and had only strengthened his determination not to give in before the backwoodsman called a halt for the night. Under a clump of pines on a slight hillock Bezeau finally threw down his pack as a signal to pitch camp, and, by the time Ballantyne had completed the last agonising half-mile, he had succeeded in lighting a fire and was busily engaged in digging a shelter in the snow to protect their sleeping-bags. Exhausted, Bob slumped wearily against the trunk of a tree while his companion heaped logs on the quickening fire, waiting until he had recovered sufficient strength to unlace his snow-shoes and drag himself beneath the blankets of his sleeping-bag. Before long the taciturn individual who accompanied him had handed over a supper of steaming hot tea, plus thick slices of bread and salt butter, and with these inside him, as the sparks spiralled upwards to be lost amidst the snow-covered branches of the spruces, a grateful Bob Ballantyne closed his eyes and fell into an exhausted sleep.

Soon after dawn next morning he found himself positively groaning with pain as he carefully eased his body out of the ice-covered sleeping-bag, his feet a mass of blisters and his whole frame 'stiffer than the rustiest hinge.' Bezeau had already prepared breakfast and before long they started their journey of a few miles to the log farmhouse of a settler and his wife at Port Neuf, Ballantyne limping painfully behind. At Port Neuf they were given shelter for the next three days as the state of Bob's feet made it impossible for them to continue and the weather was far too warm to make progress easy. During a thaw, as Ballantyne had discovered to his cost, it was impossible to go far on snow-shoes; the soft and sticky snow and watery slush quickly drenched the feet and shoe-strings, making them painfully heavy by the weight clinging to them. But in keen frosty weather, the snow being dry, crisp and fine, it fell through the network of strings without leaving a feather's weight behind, and even a novice could cover many miles without undue fatigue.

On the third night of their stay there was a sudden sharp frost, the thermometer plunging well below zero. Next morning the two men bade goodbye to the farmer and his wife and set out early for the site of a small saw-mill about nine miles away where they had been told they might find a boat. After a search, they discovered a small, flat-bottomed punt, which was just capable of carrying two men, and this they hopefully launched on the near-by Gulf of St. Lawrence, expecting to be able to row the rest of the way. But, after a few miles, a pack of ice stretching far out to sea, forced them to beach their boat and once more lace on their snow-shoes to their already swollen feet:

> The last ten miles of our journey now lay before us; and we sat down before starting, to have a bite of bread and a pull at the rum bottle; after which we trudged along in silence. The peculiar compression of my guide's lips, and the length of step he now adopted, showed me that he had made up his mind to get through the last part of the journey without stopping; so, tightening my belt and bending my head forward, I plodded grimly on.[1]

It was about five in the afternoon, after gaining the summit of a small eminence that, to the immense relief of at least one member of the pair, they finally beheld the trading post of Isle Jeremie. Like the vast majority of the establishments of the Hudson's Bay Company, it turned out to be nothing more than a collection of scattered wooden buildings, most of which were storehouses and stabling, the most imposing edifice being a small

[1] *Hudson's Bay*, by R. M. Ballantyne, Edinburgh, 1848.

Roman Catholic church. The two men made their way slowly down the slope surrounded by a barking chorus of sleigh dogs, the sound of which brought the trader and his wife to the door of their log-built house before Ballantyne and his companion had reached the cluster of outbuildings at the edge of the settlement. Within minutes their packs had been discarded, their snow-shoes kicked off, and they were both sitting before a cheerful fire devouring platefuls of steaming buffalo stew, washed down with tankards of mulled beer, while the trader's wife plied them with questions regarding the happenings in the outside world. The whole of the next day the still sore and aching young man was forced to stay in his bunk, and for more than a week his newly blistered feet would barely allow him to limp painfully around the camp.

For most of the six weeks he was there, Ballantyne was in sole charge of the post, with little to do except read or wander off on hunting expeditions. The trader-in-charge had left to visit other posts in the vicinity, taking his wife with him, and the Indians who were expected to arrive to trade furs did not put in an appearance. With the leisure his enforced idleness gave him, Bob began in a desultory way to make notes of his experiences since he landed at York Factory, jotting down his memories of the more exciting events of the past months and bringing up to date the journal he had started. Since his arrival at Hudson Bay, he had never failed to send his family, by every available post, long and well-written letters, full of humorous anecdotes and containing minute descriptions of his life and adventures in the Canadian wilderness. All these letters were carefully preserved by his mother, who secreted them in a silk-embroidered wallet in her bedroom,[1] bringing them out for inspection only when a friend or relative called who had not enjoyed them before. It was at Isle Jeremie, and later at Seven Islands, that Ballantyne started systematically to record in his journal every interesting event, jotting down all he could remember of what had gone before. These notes, with the contents of the letters which Randall so carefully cherished, were later to form the main

[1] This silk wallet, marked in his mother's hand—'Bob's letters'—by a lucky chance has survived.

source of information for the writing of *Hudson's Bay*, the first of his many books.

In the middle of April orders came through that he was to relieve Alexander Robertson, the young man who acted as trader-in-charge at Seven Islands, a post one hundred and twenty miles east of his present situation. The journey was made by canoe and, due to contrary winds and a storm which blew up suddenly from the sea, the trip took nearly ten days. But on Bob's twenty-first birthday, the 24th April, 1846, both he and his recently acquired Newfoundland dog 'Humbug' stepped safely ashore, to be instantly and exuberantly greeted by a handshaking, back-thumping young gentleman who made no effort to conceal his jubilation at the long-awaited arrival of his relief. Alexander Robertson had passed nearly six long years at this isolated cluster of rough-hewn wooden buildings, and for the last twelve months, or so he informed Ballantyne, had been counting the days to his departure for Scotland and the many comforts provided by the fair sex, which he had been so long denied. The enthusiastic welcome he gave to Bob was followed by a most appetising meal of fresh salmon, garnished with all the delicacies the post could muster, the feast being finished off with a cherished bottle of wine and a gill of brandy to settle the food in place. Despite the fatigue of his long journey, Bob kept his new companion company until dawn, smoking and yarning before the leaping flames of the log fire. From this first acquaintanceship the two became firm friends.

During his four months in charge of the trading post, Ballantyne found Seven Islands a lonely and desolate spot, the only place he could visit being a salmon fishery at the mouth of a river some twenty miles distant. When the day at last dawned for Robertson to return to Tadousac on the first stage of his long journey home, Ballantyne found himself left with only a French-Canadian labourer to keep him company in the months ahead. In front of the station lazed the mighty Gulf of St. Lawrence, stretching out to the far horizon, while behind rustled the vast pine forest, with hardly a break in its primeval wildness until it swept down to the rocky shores of the far-distant Pacific Ocean.

When the last goodbyes had been said and the small boat bearing his new-found friend had been lost to sight as it rounded the distant point, the remoteness of his situation, the tiny dot he represented in that immense wilderness, flooded across Bob's mind as he turned back to the cluster of wooden buildings that were to be his home for many months.

I walked up to the house, and wandered like a ghost through its empty rooms, feeling inexpressible melancholy, and began to have extremely unpleasant anticipations of spending the winter at this lonely spot. But the sight of my dog Humbug caused me to take a more philosophical view of affairs. I began to gaze round upon my domain, and whisper to myself that I was 'monarch of all I surveyed.' All the mighty trees in the woods were mine—if I chose to cut them down; all the fish in the sea were mine—if I could only catch them; and the palace of Seven Islands was also mine. The regal feeling inspired by these considerations induced me to call in a kingly tone for my man, who politely answered, 'Oui, Monsieur.' 'Dinner!' said I, falling back on my throne, and contemplating, through the palace window, my vast dominions.[1]

Within a few days Ballantyne had settled down in his new home and soon found himself enjoying the experience of being in sole charge of his own trading post. He passed many hours in solitary hunting and shooting expeditions or out fishing in the bay; the days when bad weather kept him indoors being spent in writing further pages of his journal of experiences in North America.

But as the end of his five-year engagement with the Company drew near, his loneliness and nostalgia for home and his family back in Edinburgh became more pronounced, and no sooner did his term expire in June, than he wrote immediately to his employers asking to be relieved of further duties. To his dismay the reply he received from the Chief Factor pointed out that, as he had not given a year's notice of his intention to terminate his engagement, he would have to stay in the Company's employment for another twelve months. But apparently sensing the

[1] *Hudson's Bay*, by R. M. Ballantyne, Edinburgh, 1848.

disappointment this news would cause the young man he added a promise to write to the head office in London for a final decision.

Hudson's Bay House.
Lachine. 27th July, 1846.

[1]Archibald Barclay Esquire.
(Secretary, H.B.C., London).
Sir,

. . . The engagement of Robert Ballantyne, Apprentice Clerk, now stationed at the Kings Posts, expired on the 1st of June last, and his friends at home, being desirous of his returning to Scotland immediately, have requested him to do so, but as he has omitted to give a year's notice of his intention to retire from the service, according to a clause in his agreement, he feels himself bound to remain for one year longer. May I therefore request the favor of being informed per return of mail, whether he will be permitted to retire immediately or not. . .

Your obedient servant,
Dun[can] Finlayson C[hief] F[actor]

By return of mail came the reply.

London. August 18th, 1846.

[2]Dunn. Finlayson Esq.
Lachine.

I have to acknowledge the receipt of your letter of the 27th ulto. . .

There is no wish on the part of the Governor and Committee to enforce the rule of the service against Robert Ballantyne. They will send out an apprentice Clerk to take his place and as soon as he shall arrive, or sooner if his services can be dispensed with, Mr. Ballantyne may be allowed to retire. . .

Your obedt. Servt.
A[rchibald] B[arclay] Secy.

[1] Hudson's Bay Company archives A.11/28, fo. 264d.
[2] Hudson's Bay Company archives A.6/27, pp. 85 and 86.

In August the Chief Factor sent a replacement clerk to Seven Islands, and Ballantyne was instructed to return to Tadousac and remain there until relieved by the apprentice who was expected to arrive from Scotland. With the winter rapidly closing in, Ballantyne anxiously wrote again to Lachine.

Tadousac.

28th September, 1846

[1] Dear Sir,

I received your favour of the 17th inst, and have to thank you for obtaining for me permission to quit the Service this season.

I shall hold myself in readiness to leave Tadousac as soon as a person shall arrive to replace me (which I hope will be soon, as the season is now pretty far advanced), and proceed pr. the first opportunity to Lachine.

I am

Dear Sir

Your obedt. Servant,

Robt. M. Ballantyne.

The eagerly expected replacement did not, however, arrive as promised, and Bob found himself marooned at Tadousac throughout another long and dreary winter. Time seemed to crawl as the dark and icy months dragged by, but he loyally carried out his duties for the Company in spite of a bitter feeling that advantage had been taken of his ignorance of the rules of service. Having signed on for only five years, he had assumed that at the end of this period he would automatically be entitled to return home, providing that he did not contract to serve a further term. He wrote his mother that in future he would be careful to read the small print in any agreement he might have to sign, but for the present he would stick it out until the new young man from Scotland came to take his place.

It was not until May that the clerk appeared, and Bob was packed and ready within twenty-four hours. A note in the Tadousac post journal records his long-delayed departure.

[1] Hudson's Bay Company archives B.134/c/62, fo. 341.

1847, 9 *May, Sunday.*

. . . The *Otter*[1] left for Quebec at 9 o'clock. The passengers were Mr. Barnston and Mr. Ballantyne.

Travelling lazily through the beautiful lakes of Canada and the United States, Bob arrived at last in New York, spending a gay three days in the city and indulging in a few of the extravagances he had been forced to deny himself for so long. The gift he selected for his mother was a 'Daguerrotype' of his own likeness, dressed in the tight new clothes he had just bought, and for which he was made to sit rigidly still, his head supported by a concealed iron bracket, until the photographer called an end to the long exposure.[2]

On the 25th May, 1847, I bade adieu to the Western hemisphere and sailed for England in the good ship *New York*. The air was light and warm and the sun unclouded as we floated slowly out to sea, and ere long the vessel bathed her swelling bows in the broad Atlantic. I turned my eyes for the last time upon the distant shore; the blue hills quivered for a while on the horizon, as if to bid us all a long farewell, and then sank slowly into the liquid bosom of the ocean.[3]

The last letter he had received from his family at home mentioned that his father had not been so well of late, and he noticed that Sandy's usual line of greeting was missing from the bottom of the folded sheet. But not until he reached London and found only his brother John to meet him did Bob learn that Alexander Ballantyne had died in Edinburgh on the 28th May.

[1] The *Otter*, a 35-ton schooner belonging to the Company, had been laid up at Tadousac during the winter.
[2] See plate 2.
[3] *Hudson's Bay*, by R. M. Ballantyne, Edinburgh, 1848.

Chapter Five

His FATHER HAD KNOWN for some months that the heart trouble[1] from which he had been suffering was likely to prove fatal, but had managed to conceal the true seriousness of his condition even from his all-knowing wife. But in March a particularly bad attack rendered further pretence useless, and after his doctor had warned him that his condition was now precarious, Sandy dictated and signed his Will. Two days later he added a codicil making plain his wishes regarding the house.

> In addition to any settlement of the seventh current, I hereby dispose, convey and make over, my house No. 16, West Brighton Crescent, Portobello, with the grounds and pertinents and all my other habitable property, with the writings and titles thereof, to my wife Randall Scott Ballantyne, whom failing, to my daughters, Mary Howard, Jane Barclay, Madalina, Randall Hunter, and Williamina, equally, share and share alike. In witness thereof I have subscribed these presents at Portobello this 9th day of March, one thousand eight hundred and forty seven years, before these witnesses.
>
> (*Signed*) Alex. Ballantyne.

Wm. Hill witness
            (Surgeon of Portobello)
Henry Calder witness
            (Grocer of same)

Instead of the bell-ringing welcome and gay, all-night party he had been promised, Bob returned glumly to a black-suited family and the heavily curtained windows of a house in deep mourning. His widowed mother hardly recognised the handsome young stalwart, bronzed and fit, who presented himself as her youngest son, and the comfort his homecoming brought to her and his sisters

---

[1] Canongate Register of Deaths, Edinburgh, June 1847—'Alexander Ballantyne—cause of death, disease of the heart.'

helped them to forget their grief as nothing else could. The flowers on the grave in Canongate churchyard had faded when Bob stood bareheaded at the side of the fresh-turned earth—as his father's hopes had slowly faded since those faraway summers at Walton Hall a quarter of a century ago, when the future had seemed bright and the prosperity of the family assured for many years to come.

A few days later John presided over a sum totalling of the remaining wealth of the Ballantynes, the family sitting in the black-draped parlour in West Brighton Crescent as he read the contents of his father's Will. The list of assets he detailed was short, comprising the sum of £118 in the bank, the house in which they now lived, a debt of £400 owing by George Watt of Kelso, and some shares in the Edinburgh Water Company.[1]

With this amount of worldly goods Mrs. Ballantyne had to keep herself and five unmarried daughters and also provide for her son until he could find employment. John helped her as much as he could, but he had his own wife to support, and James sent twenty pounds from India. Except for a few pounds annual dividend paid by the Water Company, the family had no income whatsoever, and within weeks the balance in the bank started to melt away, with little chance, as far as Randall could see, of the drain being arrested. George Watt acknowledged owing the four hundred pounds and promised to repay as soon as he could raise the money, but this did not immediately help the Ballantynes and, frugal and careful as they tried to be, they appeared to eat into their capital at what seemed a gluttonous rate. It was to Bob that the women now appealed for help and advice. As the new master of the house, his mother and the girls looked to him for decisions in much the same way that they had awaited Alexander's nod of approval in the past. But their father had merely set his seal on previously cut-and-dried feminine schemes which Randall was careful to present to him in so disingenuous

---

[1] In 1854 these shares were valued as follows. 'Four and one fifth shares in the original stock of the Edinburgh Water Company at £32 per share = £134 8s. 0d. Fifteen shares in the New Stock of the Edinburgh Water Company at £15 10s. 0d. per share, now valued at £180 0s. 0d.' (These details are taken from Randall's Will, but at the time of the death of her husband the shares were worth slightly less.)

and artless a manner that her husband was usually made to believe that the original plan had emanated from himself. However, Mrs. Ballantyne's good-looking son was not nearly so malleable as had been the old man; he propounded and the females of the family acquiesced, and within a few months of his return were pleased to be disciplined into grateful obedience by what they considered his logic. They fussed and fluttered round him, darning his clothes, vying one with another to present his food, and thrusting bed-warmers between the sheets before they would allow him to retire for the night. Only the youngest of the family, Williamina, took no part in the lavish displays of affection showered on her brother, feeling herself swamped by the effusions of her elder sisters, but, as she wrote to Bob later, 'loving you just as much, but not in the sickly, spoiling way of the rest of the family.' In after years it was always to their youngest brother that the sisters turned when in trouble—he was as soft-hearted with them as they had previously been with him; his sympathetic understanding and generosity made him a comforting shoulder to cry on—and they seldom cried in vain.

Within two months of his return from the wilds, Ballantyne had secured employment as a clerk with the North British Railway Company, and was also busily engaged in putting the family's financial affairs into some sort of order. His sisters presented the biggest problem. Mary, Jane, Madalina, Randall and Williamina —five healthy young women and not earning a penny piece between them! Mary and Randall were currently engaged on writing stories for children, but even if they could find a publisher they were unlikely to benefit by more than a few pounds. Dare he suggest to their mother that they should find some kind of job, even of the most genteel and ladylike nature? He enlisted the help of the girls in an approach to Mrs. Ballantyne, with the suggestion that she might consider allowing them to become children's governesses. But to this idea Mamma refused to give her consent—her daughters would be scattered and she would be left alone in West Brighton Crescent, deprived of the comfort of her family and with Bob visiting her only at weekends from his job in Edinburgh. If their employment allowed them to live at home, then she might reconsider the matter, but for the present it was quite unthinkable that she should approve of her un-married daughters leaving her parental care.

And that appeared to be that—until the problem was un-expectedly solved by four of the girls secretly applying at a newly opened private school in Portobello for posts as teachers, and to their delight and the immense relief of their brother, being accepted at salaries that would enable them to support them-selves without recourse to the family exchequer. A secret con-ference took place that evening, and next day the four eldest girls nervously presented their mother with the *fait accompli*, expecting a monumental row. But they were agreeably surprised when, after some perfunctory grumbles and head-shaking, Ran-dall accepted the situation and gave her blessing to the action her daughters had taken. Williamina, who was only eighteen, was to stay at home to help her mother, to that spirited young lady's extreme annoyance.

From that time events started to move rapidly. Within a few months of taking the job at the school, Madalina was bubbling with the news that her hand had been sought by the Reverend Macadam Grigor, a Free Church minister with whom she had been keeping company: he had asked her to marry him soon after being appointed to the living of Kettle and Coults. At the age of thirty, Madalina had almost resigned herself to being left on the shelf, and the whole family was overjoyed at her good fortune. Christina, John's wife (who was known to all her relations and friends as 'Teenie'), offered her house at 8 Wemyss Place, Edin-burgh, for the wedding. On the 4th January, 1848, amid the splendour reserved for such occasions, the ceremony was per-formed by the Rev. Horatius Bonor of Kelso, a minister well known for the thunder of his sermons and famous for the rousing hymns and tracts he composed on the Free Kirk's behalf.

Among those who attended the marriage and the reception which followed was Miss Mary Greig,[1] their neighbour and friend when they had lived in Kelso, and whom Randall had

[1] Mrs. Elizabeth Greig died on 18th January, 1847, aged ninety-three. Her daughter, Miss Mary Turner Greig, died on 11th January, 1864, aged eighty-two, at Belmount Place, Kelso. Miss Greig left an estate of approximately £3,000.

invited to be her guest for a few days. Bob still had the flute she had sent him at Lachine and on which he had taught himself to play many of the old Scottish airs she so liked to hear, and on the way back home in the coach, after the bride and groom had departed, he regaled both her and the rest of the family, who were packed around him, with a series of spirited tunes, no doubt rendered more fluent by champagne.

The elderly spinster, Miss Greig, had been impatiently awaiting her visit to Portobello for some weeks. No sooner did she succeed in finding Bob alone than she confided to the incredulous young Mr. Ballantyne the startling news that she was prepared to pay for the private publication of the letters he had sent his mother while abroad and that she would be pleased if he could arrange for an estimate to be obtained for their being printed in the form of a book. When the thunderstruck young gentleman realised that she was serious he stuttered his thanks and rushed to tell the goods news to the rest of the family. Amid great excitement, the embroidered silk wallet was hurriedly brought down from his mother's bedroom and long extracts from the carefully preserved letters read aloud to the kind-hearted old lady, who was thoroughly enjoying the sensation her announcement had caused. Miss Greig had looked forward to the arrival of each packet from Hudson's Bay Territory with almost as much eager expectation as had Randall herself, and she and her mother had pledged themselves months ago to this scheme of publication. Only the death of Alexander Ballantyne had prevented them from revealing the closely kept secret as soon as Bob returned home.

The author-to-be was, of course, delighted with the offer, but on his mother's insistence he told Miss Greig that he must treat it as a loan repayable by the subscription sales, and to this the old lady had finally to agree. The next day the family met in council to plan a campaign to launch the book, the girls vying with each other as to the number of letters they would write to possible subscribers, while Ballantyne hurriedly searched for the drawings he had made abroad, and collected together all the notes and correspondence he had sent home, ready for his return to his lodgings. From that time onwards he devoted every spare moment to the work of rewriting and editing. He consulted his cousin James, who was now in charge of his late father's old printing firm of Ballantyne & Hughes, and with his help and advice the book began gradually to take shape. By the late summer his cousin had read and approved the final draft of the manuscript, and had also persuaded Messrs. William Blackwood and Sons to handle the local sales for Edinburgh and district and to give the title-page the honour of their imprint. An edition of one thousand copies was decided upon at an agreed price, and the completed volumes were ready for distribution in good time for Christmas.

Thus it was, that in mid-December, 1847, Robert M. Ballantyne's name appeared for the first time on the title-page of a book, and one can well imagine his pride at seeing in print the magic words, and in handling the grey, cloth-bound volumes with their gold-lettered spines and exciting smell of printer's ink. '*Hudson's Bay*,' they shouted. 'Every-Day Life in the Wilds of North America—with Illustrations by Robert M. Ballantyne—for Private Circulation, and Copies to be had of William Blackwood & Sons, 45 George Street, M.DCCC.XLVIII.'

Copies were immediately despatched to the hundreds of subscibers in both Britain and Canada whom he, and his sisters, relations and friends had induced to order the book before publication. Uncles had been cajoled into taking six or more copies for presentation to nephews at Christmas, while Sir George Simpson authorised the purchase of a large quantity for sale to the trappers and settlers through the Hudson's Bay Company stores. Ballantyne's story of his adventures in the Far North was well received and gained high praise from the many readers who wrote and thanked him for the pleasure it had given them. By late January, 1848, the last copies remaining with the publishing house had been sold, the sum owing to Miss Greig was gratefully repaid, in spite of the old lady's protests, and the author found himself in pocket by over twenty pounds 'to his most entire satisfaction.'

One of the subscribers who read and enjoyed the book was Mr. John Blackwood, the editor of *Blackwood's Magazine* and a partner in the publishing company of the same name; he so liked the tale that he offered to print one thousand copies for public sale, any profit (or loss) to be divided equally between Robert Ballantyne Esquire and Messrs. William Blackwood & Sons, who were to be the publishers. The twenty-three-year-old author accepted the offer by return of post with the most extreme politeness, and then, hardly able to contain himself with pride at his new-found professional status, caught the next available coach home to break the news to his family.

The original edition had been printed at cut-price terms by Ballantyne and Hughes, but in a slovenly, careless manner and criticism had been levelled at the volume on account of its many typographical inaccuracies. It was full of spelling mistakes, incorrect pagination and errata of all kinds, and Blackwoods therefore ordered the new edition to have the text reset and the proof sheets carefully checked by both their own reader and the author.

On the 7th March, 1848, this second edition of one thousand and forty copies appeared for sale in the bookshops at nine shillings each, bound in a similar style to the previous issue, but this time with the publisher's imprint in gold, on the spine. Bob awaited news of the first month's sales with expectant heart—but, alas, he had yet to learn that there is a world of difference in disposing by subscription of a newly issued book amongst one's own friends and relations and their own friends and relations, and in having the second thousand volumes of the same work of a new young author appear for sale on the counters of London and the provinces where he was completely unknown. Financially this edition was a failure and it was not until the end of 1853 that the publishers were finally able to clear their shelves of the remaining stock of *Hudson's Bay*. Ballantyne had hopefully purchased one hundred volumes of the book, not realising that almost everyone he knew had already bought the first edition, with the result that he now found himself stuck with about eighty unsaleable copies. Fifty of these, due to the help of his old friend Duncan Finlayson of Lachine, he sold to Mr. Benjamin Dawson, a bookseller of Montreal, and a further twenty-five were taken back into stock by the publishers. John Blackwood treated him very well over the affair as these two letters reveal:

31 *St. Andrew Square,*
Edinburgh.
25th Oct. 1853.

Mr. Simpson.

Dear Sir,

The last statement of *Hudson's Bay* shows a balance
against the book of £7 5s. 10d. I have just received a settlement from Mr. Dawson of Montreal, to whom I sold the
remnant, and I shall be happy to pay you this balance on
learning from you that it is correct.

I am,
Yours truly,
R. M. Ballantyne.[1]

31 *St. Andrew Square,*
Edinburgh
29th Oct. 1853.

John Blackwood Esquire.

Dear Sir,

I beg to acknowledge receipt of your note of yesterday
and to express to yourself and your brother my sense of the
very handsome manner in which you declined to take payment of the balance of my *Hudson's Bay* account.

Pray accept of my sincere thanks for your kindness.

Yours very truly,
R. M. Ballantyne.

Blackwoods were at fault in not preparing the volume for a
juvenile readership, having issued it in a style similar to that
chosen for the first edition by the inexperienced Mr. Ballantyne.
The austere, plain grey cloth cover, unrelieved by any spirited
embellishments in the form of gold-blocked pictures, was far too
dignified a format. The exterior of the book appeared so uninteresting that it is most unlikely that it induced boys to take it
down from the bookseller's shelf or entreat parents to purchase it

---

[1] These two letters are printed by permission of the National Library
of Scotland, in whose collection they are housed.

on their behalf. In the adult market it was swamped by a glut of travel books, written, it seemed, by practically every titled lady and gentleman who had completed the Grand Tour, and also by the chattering rows of three-decker novels with which the shops were filled. *Hudson's Bay* stayed glumly on the shelves, and, far from this time sharing in the division of any profits, the author finished by owing the publishers money. The episode had a depressing effect on a young man who had in any case become an author almost by accident, for there does not appear to have been any compelling literary urge to create, or any deep-seated desire to embrace a career as a writer. Hopes Ballantyne may possibly have had in this direction were dashed for the time being, and it was many years before he wrote again for publication.

In the autumn a tragedy occurred which far overshadowed his own troubles. His sister, Madalina, was expecting her first baby and had moved into Mrs. Ballantyne's house in Portobello to be near her mother for the last few weeks of pregnancy. A nursery had been prepared for the infant, complete with new cot and a layette of pressed and tissued baby clothes which her sisters had knitted for the new little nephew- or niece-to-be. As Madalina's time drew near, Randall hovered anxiously around her daughter, waiting for the first signs that the baby was due to arrive and, with the onset of the pains, she sent instantly for the midwife, taking command herself of the background operations necessary in preparing for the birth, relaying instructions to her daughters for hot water, warm towels and smelling salts, and reassuring the Reverend Macadam Grigor as he paced the drawing-room floor.

For a time all appeared to be well—but when, after several hours, there was no sign of the baby being delivered, the old lady went scurrying round for the doctor. His grave demeanour after first examining the expectant mother sent a chill through the waiting family gathered at the foot of the stairs, and his sombre advice to the white-faced husband to pray for his wife's recovery did nothing to allay their deep anxiety, Randall's sobs only confirming their worst fears. Throughout the whole of that night the poor, weak and exhausted girl was in labour, and it was the afternoon of the following day before a massive haemorrhage mercifully put an end to her sufferings. Her mother was not to be comforted and desolation filled the house for many weeks. 'The only consolation,' said Madalina's grief-stricken husband after the funeral, 'was that she died praising God.'

Coming so soon after that of his father, his sister's tragic death affected Bob very deeply. Theirs was a close-knit, affectionate relationship which bound the whole family freely to one another, and the loss of his sister caused a wound that took many years to heal. From the time of the funeral, he started to attend church regularly, and it was seldom that a Sunday went by when he did not go to both morning and evening services. He formed a Bible-reading class for working men and was most assiduous in his duties, giving almost all his spare time to religious work of one sort or another. His new-found fervour so impressed the local clergy that, at the end of the following year, on his minister's recommendation, and at the age of only twenty-four, Bob was elected an elder of the Free Church of Scotland.

From this point in his life his letters become far more heavily tinged with religious quotations and exhortations to Godliness, and one can sometimes detect an underlying feeling of guilt, as though he imagined that some act or omission had caused him to receive the heavy punishment of the loss of his kinsfolk. The emotional stress under which he suffered left a lasting mark on his character; he abandoned a light-hearted book on which for his own amusement he had been engaged, and started to take an interest in the tortuous theological discussions and arguments in which the elders of the Free Kirk seemed to be constantly enmeshed. He disputed abstruse points of doctrine with an earnestness that totally belied his youth, and for a time, the stalwart young backswoodsman from Hudson's Bay seemed to shrink, becoming a Bible-black silhouette of the husky individual who strode so briskly down the gangplank of the good ship *New York* only eighteen months before.

Troubles seldom come singly. The private school where his sisters had been teaching ran into financial difficulties and suddenly failed, while owing them two months' salary. Mrs. Ballantyne then flatly refused to live any longer in the house where her daughter had died and became every week more melancholy and depressed, until finally the girls begged Bob to find a place with less harrowing memories in which they could all reside, and perhaps where another school could offer them fresh employment.

It was on a visit to Kelso to discuss with George Watt the repayment of the debt that he owed his late father that a solution of their immediate financial problems was presented to Bob. He was making a courtesy call on Miss Greig, when she mentioned that a large house she owned in The Terrace, Kelso, had become vacant. Would the Ballantyne family be interested in occupying it if she could offer the building at a small enough rental? It was perhaps a little too large for just themselves, but they might consider taking a few paying guests of the correct type, or the girls might establish a small school and thus augment their income.

The family correspondence reveals that the matter was discussed and mulled over for several weeks, with Bob doing his best to induce his mother to accept the idea. George Watt had made clear that he could repay only two hundred pounds immediately; the balance would have to be settled at a later date. Ballantyne now approached him again with an offer to accept two hundred and fifty pounds down and the rest of the debt to be cleared by his accepting goods and victuals from Watt's shop over a period of months in order to furnish and supply the proposed new school. In addition, he suggested that Mr. Watt's daughter, Jane, who was at present working as a teacher at another establishment, could take a place in the school and further help to reduce the balance of the debt by working for a smaller salary than would normally be paid.

In a few days all was agreed between the two men and Ballantyne jubilantly broke the good news to his family whose last remaining doubts regarding the soundness of the scheme seem to have been overcome. Mrs. Ballantyne herself was quickly won over; she liked Kelso immensely and knew that most of her old friends still lived there, besides the fact that most of the happiest years of her married life had been spent in the town. Within a few weeks the family had moved into temporary accommodation provided by Miss Greig, and the girls held an excited council with Miss Watt to decide the plan of campaign. Before long preparations were in full swing to furnish the classrooms and provide the essentials for the start of the new venture on which the future well-being of the family so greatly depended. There was much preparation to be done, but they had great hopes of opening in time for the start of the summer term, and the following advertisement appeared in *The Kelso Mail* on the 30th November, 1848:

> The Misses Ballantyne will open a boarding school, for young ladies, in Kelso, in the beginning of May 1849, in which the following branches will be taught:
> *English, in all its branches,*
> *French—Italian—German*
> *Drawing—Music (Piano-forte and guitar.)*
> For further information apply to Mr. Geo. Watt, The Square, Kelso, and Mrs. Ballantyne, 8 Wemyss Place, Edinburgh.[1]

The school could not have been quite ready in time, for another advertisement appeared in the same paper on the 7th June, 1849:

> The Misses Ballantyne announce that they commence their classes for the instruction of young ladies on Monday, the 11th inst.
> *The Terrace, Kelso, June 6th,* 1849.

The sisters, no doubt with the help of their many friends in Kelso, were soon teaching a number of young females the rudiments of what passed for a refined education and a well-bred knowledge of the world. Moreover, to their intense delight, within a few months they were earning enough to ensure both their mother and themselves a sufficient income for their immediate needs. They were also thoroughly enjoying the experience and Randall wrote ecstatically:

> . . . cannot understand why we did not think of it before! Dear, dear Bob, we all love you so very much and much

[1] This was the address of John Ballantyne and his wife.

more since you have made us undertake this wonderful plan. Do you believe it, but Mamma teaches painting with much success!

Having let the Portobello house at a good rent, the Rev. Gigor retaining one room, Ballantyne took new lodgings in James Square, Edinburgh, in a residence conducted in a most impeccable fashion by an elderly Miss Rutherford, who had been strictly commissioned by his mother to 'keep a guid eye on the lad.'

Not that his mother needed to worry unduly about her son's moral welfare, for he seems to have spent most of his spare time immersed in the social and religious work of the Free Church of Scotland. As well as conducting an evening Bible meeting for young men, he now taught a class of children at Sunday School, was an active member of the church choir, and had the distinction of being the youngest Elder of the Free Kirk. In several of his letters he reveals that his self-imposed religious tasks were a gladly accepted penance that would one day cleanse his soul of unspecified sins of the flesh committed in the dark days of his past. The unbidden erotic thoughts of a virile young bachelor would have been fiercely condemned by the outwardly austere Presbyterians with whom Bob associated, and condemned in terms which would have conjured up visions of eternal damnation to an impressionable mind. At this period of his life, any family tragedy he viewed as a direct intervention on the part of the Almighty to punish the erring Mr. R. M. Ballantyne, with the result that he developed a guilt complex which remained with him, in greater or lesser degree, for the remainder of his life.

In the late spring, the depression which had gripped him so strongly after his sister's death had been somewhat dissipated, and his mother at Kelso was cheered by the return of her favourite son's good humour.

James Square,
29th May, 1849.

My own darling mother,
   I find that I have half an hour to spare before going to the office so I shall devote it to writing you a screed. We

have been flitting the office during the last weeks so that I have had several holidays! ! ! One of which, Saturday, I devoted to excursions and went all the way to Perth!

Yesterday I went to John's new house, No. 70 Northumberland Street, where I spent the whole day in helping to put it in order. It is, without exception, the very best house that John has ever been in. The rooms are large, elegant and *light* and, being near the corner of the street, we can look into Howe Street. The painting room is not so good, certainly, as the one in No. 8,[1] but it's good enough. My room is a capital one. There are two views to be obtained from the window by sitting in different parts of the room. If I feel in a lightsome mood I shall sit in a corner from which I have a view of blue sky and several trees with chimney pots in the background. If, on the contrary, I desire to indulge in gloomy ideas, by changing my position I have an admirable view of the side of a house, without a speck, not even a window to break its monotony. The room moreover is large and on the upper flat, so in fact I'm quite pleased with it. I expect to get into it tomorrow; at present I still live with Miss Rutherford. . .

We are all well comparatively. I am *very very* glad, my own sweet mother, to hear of your improved health. Let us thank God for it. Change of air and scene etc., may be the direct causes of this improvement, but it is God's blessing which makes these effications and without this not all the most felicitous combinations of circumstances could restore you to health. Once more adieu, my dearest mother,

Your affectionate Son,
R. M. Ballantyne.

Ballantyne's script was always clear and legible and there is little variation in the quality of his fine flowing hand until the final months of his last illness. The habit he had of signing even correspondence to his family with his full name continued throughout his life; intimate letters to his wife, written later, invariably had the same formal signature.

[1] They previously lived at 8, Wemyss Place, Edinburgh.

By now he was looking around for fresh employment. His family had never viewed his situation with the railway company as anything more than a temporary expedient, and that summer he secured a post in the office of Alexander Cowan & Company, the Edinburgh firm of paper-makers. Within a few months he had become a firm friend of the owner's son, James Cowan, who was about his own age, with the result that he received an invitation to spend his summer holiday aboard the Cowan family yacht. While on the trip he was supposed to act as his boss's personal secretary, but the post carried only the lightest of duties and the two young men quickly became inseparable companions. Both were keen fishermen, vying with each other in the size of the catch each was able to land, a contest in which Ballantyne's Hudson Bay experience stood him in good stead. For the rest of Bob's life, James Cowan remained one of his closest friends.

During this same year, Bob was fortunate enough to be advanced a small capital sum as an interest-free loan by the wealthy Alexander Cowan. This enabled him to purchase a junior partnership in the reconstituted printing and publishing firm of Thomas Constable & Company. The company had by this time recovered completely from the financial disaster which had ruined Sir Walter Scott and the previous owners, and had been appointed Her Majesty's Printer and Publisher in Edinburgh. Bob's salary under his new agreement amounted to only one hundred pounds per annum, and the ledger shows his share in the profits of the business at the end of 1852 as being a mere £16 18s. 11d., so it would not at first appear that he had contracted a particularly good bargain by joining the company.

But the fact that he was now a partner and enjoyed the privileges that this position carried with it probably appealed to his family's sense of pride and his own self-respect, and his new salary may have compared quite favourably with what he earned as a clerk with Cowan & Company. When one remembers that this was the year that saw the publication of Charles Dickens's *Bleak House* and Harriet Beecher Stowe's *Uncle Tom's Cabin*, one hundred golden sovereigns a year was no doubt quite a tidy sum to support a young bachelor of abstemious habits and Free

Church connections. He had given up smoking completely on his return from Hudson Bay, seldom drank what he termed 'ardent spirits' and generally seems to have lived a modest existence. Since the death of his sister Madalina, the occasional excesses he permitted himself, the nights out with the boys and the rip-roaring parties with his weekend bachelor friends, had been replaced by an almost Calvinistic attitude towards life, with his leisure punctuated by frequent church-going and the shunning of even the mildest of the sins of the flesh.

His interest in the Arctic Regions had prompted him to buy a copy of Patrick Fraser Tytler's travel book, *A View of the Progress and Discovery of the Northern Coasts of America*, which had been first issued in 1832. Despite his unfortunate experience with the second edition of *Hudson's Bay*, Ballantyne had now become convinced that he had the ability to write another work of a similar nature which could enjoy a successful sale in competition with travel books by other authors. Urged on by his sister-in-law, Teenie, who by this time was taking an almost more than sisterly interest in her handsome young lodger, Bob set to work to rewrite Tytler's text in an endeavour to make it more suitable for juvenile readers, adding three new chapters at the end to bring the book up to date. The finished manuscript was offered to Thomas Nelson & Sons, the Edinburgh and London publishing house, who were sufficiently impressed to offer Ballantyne twenty-five pounds for its purchase. Illustrations were supplied by Birket Foster after sketches by Ballantyne, and the work of producing the volume was immediately put in hand.

Notwithstanding the fact that he had rewritten the entire work and considerably extended its length, when Nelson's first issued the book in 1853 they omitted Ballantyne's name from the title-page, although they did accord him a mention on the spine of the volume under that of the name of P. Fraser Tytler. When fiery little Teenie saw the sheets of the finished book which Bob brought home just before its publication, she nearly exploded with wrath, realising immediately that her brother-in-law was being denied his proper share of the credit of authorship. And when Mrs. John Ballantyne was on the warpath it behoved any offending male in the vicinity to make himself scarce! She was a domineering young woman who expected unswerving loyalty and devotion from all her male subjects, and woe betide her husband if he did not write to her every day when he was away painting a portrait. Bob, willingly or unwillingly, found himself subject to the same rules.

Dark haired, with a well-cut oval face and slim figure, and with that spoilt little-girl look which many men found irresistible, Teenie demanded, and apparently found, obedience from both her men. With Bob her ambitions centred on what she thought were his neglected abilities as a writer, and she bullied and nagged the young man in a way which convinced him that it was all for his own good. She was furious that he had been so naïve as not to insist that his name should appear on the title-page, and tight-lipped and fuming, she threatened that if he did not demand that the injustice be instantly righted, she would herself go to see the Nelson partner responsible and force him to correct the omission immediately. The threat was enough; Ballantyne was at the publisher's office next morning and did not leave until he had a firm promise that the 'mistake,' as he preferred to call it, would be rectified without delay. The printers were instructed to prepare a substitute title-page with, in heavy type, the words 'With Continuation by R. M. Ballantyne, Author of *Hudson's Bay; or Every-Day Life in the Wilds of North America*.' The original title-page was cut out and the newly printed sheet tipped in in its place, but too late to prevent a few copies inadvertently escaping before the offending leaf had been removed.[1]

Bob took the whole affair in good part and the Nelson family soon became friends. This friendship did not, however, cause the partners to soften the terms on which they conducted business with the budding young author, and William Nelson subsequently earned the unenvied distinction of being referred to as 'a mean old codger' in some of the later letters of the Ballantyne family. To persuade an author to part with the copyright of a manuscript for the smallest possible lump sum was the policy

[1] The first issue of *The Northern Coasts of America, and The Hudson's Bay Territories*, dated 1853, without Ballantyne's name on the title-page, is very rare. The only copy I have located is that in the Bodleian Library. The substitute title-page of the second issue is dated 1854.

which seemed invariably to guide his dealings with those unfortunates not strong enough to resist the temptation of an immediate cash payment. Bob's previous disappointing experience in retaining the copyright of a book and sharing the profits on a royalty basis, as he did with *Hudson's Bay*, had rendered him peculiarly liable to Nelson's blandishments, acceptance of whose terms was to cost him dear in future years.

Under its new title, *The Northern Coasts of America, and the Hudson's Bay Territories—A Narrative of Discovery and Adventure*, the book proved a great success, and before the end of 1854 two new issues had already been sold and a further edition was being prepared. Its red-cloth covers, heavily blocked in gold, with a large picture of a hunter with gun and snow-shoes, apparently induced many a boy to take it down from the bookseller's shelves, and the spirited illustrations showing Red Indians chasing buffalo or escaping death by inches as their canoe was swept by the current ever nearer the edge of precipitous falls, must surely often have completed the sale without the shopkeeper saying a word.

William Nelson was attracted by the treatment the hopeful new writer had given the original text and borrowed a copy of his first book in order to gain a clearer knowledge of his style. Reading Ballantyne's autobiographical account of his adventures in Rupert's Land impressed upon the publisher that here was an author who could write a quick-moving adventure story sufficiently exciting to retain his youthful readers' interest until the very last page, and then keep them on the look-out for the next work from his pen. He must have believed that he had found himself a potential money-spinner, for he immediately approached Bob with a suggestion that he should submit a fictional story of adventure for boys, possibly based once more on his own experiences in the Arctic wastes of the Far North.

With his thirtieth birthday already behind him, Ballantyne's restless spirit had already driven him to ask himself where exactly his life was drifting; but about one thing he was quite determined—he would not allow himself to be cooped forever in a printer's office. Nelson's offer presented a heaven-sent opportunity to escape, for although he had never attempted a fictional work, he now felt absolutely sure[1] that he could weave a tale of deeds of daring and danger with sufficient power to grip the imagination of any red-blooded boy alive. He set about the task with enthusiasm and was soon absorbed with the fictional exploits of the fur traders and trappers of the Arctic, laying for the unsuspecting hunters a series of ruthless Red Indian ambushes from which his youthful heroes extricated themselves by hair's-breadth escapes. By the end of the summer the manuscript was half completed, had been read and ardently approved by his sister Randall, and Bob had hopes of seeing it finished in time to appear in the bookshops before Christmas. But quite suddenly, after enjoying the best of health for many years, his mother was taken seriously ill. On receipt of an urgent summons, Bob rushed round to the house at 2 Windsor Street, Edinburgh, where she had been staying, insisted on calling in another doctor to aid her own physician, and saw to it that she was given the very best treatment available. But in spite of every effort the doctors made, she died on the 10th September within only a few days of first complaining of pain.

A bachelor son is often closer to his mother and more affectionate than a married man of the same age, and Mrs. Ballantyne's sudden death shocked and grieved him far more than the loss of his father. After the funeral in Canongate churchyard his life seemed empty of purpose and he lost all interest in the book he was writing, finding what relief he could by immersing himself even deeper in church activities and walking miles through the darkened streets of the town every evening, sometimes not returning to his brother John's house until long after midnight. For many months both he and his sisters never ventured abroad unless swathed in the deepest black, their clothes carrying all the trappings of sombre ribbons and veils, while Bob's tall silk hat fluttered with visible signs of his loss. Every Sabbath the members of the family who were in Edinburgh walked in procession to the graveside, making their way back home in a

---

[1] Ballantyne later told his wife, that 'having prayed for guidance before commencing to write the work,' as his daughter confirms he did over all his books, he then felt convinced that he could write a tale that any boy would relish and one that would hold his interest to the end.

slow-moving crocodile of arm-linked couples, each as bible-black as their companions and all intent that the ritual conventions of mourning should be strictly observed.

Ballantyne's guilty depression and ridiculous assumption, as revealed by his letters, that he was somehow partly responsible for his mother's sudden death, seem gradually to have given way to a more commonsense attitude towards the natural course of events. It was impossible for the sombre charade and woeful deportment to continue indefinitely, and, as the months slowly passed, the wound healed and he regained much of his old buoyancy of spirits. By the following summer his letters reveal him to be back on his old form, and in one he wrote to Teenie he lightheartedly describes himself stumbling full length in the river while attempting to land a fine salmon he had hooked. 'I've had a truly wonderful day's sport,' he wrote, 'and feel more fit than I've done for months. Indeed my appetite is the talk of the household here, and I feel quite ashamed of it! Thank God that I can enjoy life again.'

His sister-in-law's two young daughters were growing rapidly, and she now also had a little son, Randal[1], in whose company Bob delighted, keeping the lad supplied with a constant succession of 'monkeys-on-the-stick' which he contrived to carve out of bits of wood and which twitched and contorted on the pulling of a string. Uncle Bob was in constant demand to draw funny faces and invent comic strips for the amusement of the two girls, and they seldom went to bed without persuading him to tell them one of his stories, making him continue for several nights the serial he had started days before. Their favourite uncle could be relied upon to produce the most wonderful oddities from the huge inside pockets of the cape he wore, and they would greet his return from the office with noses pressed hard against the parlour window, shouting and waving as the slim, bearded figure in the striped trousers and tall silk hat strode up the front garden path at the end of his day's work.

While he was still working at Constable's, he drew for the

---

[1] John named his son after his mother, dropping the final letter of her name; so that, as Mrs. Randall Ballantyne leaves the story, Randal, the boy, joins it.

children a comic series of pictures on a lithographic stone, and had the foreman on the printing workshop pull a few copies for their amusement. He called the sheet 'The Life and Adventures of Simon Gupple,' and the similarity between the antics of young Master Gupple and those of their own young brother Randal, sent Dot and Edith into peals of laughter. This was the first occasion when he made use of the pseudonym 'Ralph Rover,' which he was to employ in several of his subsequent books —making one of his *Coral Island* heroes answer to the same name. There is no evidence that 'The Life and Adventures of Simon Gupple' proceeded beyond the original sheet, but as this is lettered with the figure '1', it is likely that Ballantyne had hopes of extending the infant's adventures at some future date.[1]

During this same year, his sister Jane, who had a fluent knowledge of the French language, translated Champfleury's[2] *Les Souffrances du Professeur Delteil* into English. Bob acted as editor of the finished text and drew a full set of illustrations to accompany the story, now titled *Naughty Boys, or the Sufferings of Mr. Delteil*. He showed the manuscript to Mr. Constable and managed to persuade him to print and publish it. Exactly how many volumes were produced is not known, but the books of the firm show an entry dated 31st December, 1855, with the words 'Cost of the *Naughty Boys* publication—£26 13s. 4d.' so it can be presumed the issue amounted to only a few hundred copies. Neither of the Ballantynes' names appear on the title page[3] and, as far as is known, no second edition was ever published.

Some months later a chance meeting in the street with William Nelson prompted the publisher to enquire what had happened to the manuscript of the adventure story on which Ballantyne had been engaged, and Bob was forced to admit that he had not touched it since his mother's death. He promised to submit the portion he had written to enable Nelson to advise him if he

---

[1] The only copy of this ephemeral publication which has been discovered was the sheet preserved by the author.

[2] 'Champfleury' was the pseudonym of Jules François Felix Husson (1821–89), a French writer of the *réaliste* school.

[3] R. M. Ballantyne's initials appear under at least one of the illustrations.

thought it worth while his continuing with the tale, and was amazed and elated when, a week later, a letter arrived from the publishing house offering him fifty pounds for the completed manuscript. Amid a chorus of 'I told you so's' from Teenie, he was soon hard at work again on the story, writing by candle-light well into the small hours of the morning with a new-found enthusiasm for an author's life.

Within a fortnight of the Nelson offer, a letter arrived from his friend James Cowan, inviting him to a three-months holiday in Norway with all expenses paid. The party was to live aboard the Cowan family yacht, and Ballantyne was to be accorded a small single cabin where he could work in privacy on his manuscript if he so desired. 'My luck must at last have changed,' Bob wrote to his brother James, 'for I have never known two such strokes of fortune.'

Teenie was not slow to seize this golden opportunity of once again advocating a course of action she had been pressing him to adopt for the previous two years—namely, that he should give up his office job and accept writing as a profession. Ballantyne had listened patiently to her arguments before, but had not dared to renounce a regular income for the gamble of trying to earn a living by his pen. But the fifty pounds which Nelson now dangled before him put a new complexion on the matter; it represented nearly half his present yearly earnings, and, by writing two books every twelve months, lecturing in the evenings and selling a few of the watercolours he like to paint, it seemed quite possible that he could earn a comfortable living. And, as his sister-in-law stressed, who could tell what a benevolent fate might have in store regarding the ultimate profits from the sale of his future books? His share of the yearly profits of Constable & Company brought him in very little, and after Nelson's glowing praise of his style, the thought of making literature his profession, with the rise in social status this conferred and the freedom from routine which it promised, had a very strong appeal indeed. The decision was a big one to take alone and of such moment to the whole family that he decided to extend to them the courtesy of asking their collective advice.

The conference that took place that May weekend lasted some

hours and was by no means peaceable. Years later, Ballantyne wrote to his wife—'Mr. Constable was the first to tell me that, whatever I did, I should not take to literature! John long ago told me for any sake to avoid painting! ! Teenie told me that I should not attempt lecturing! ! !'

He could have added that his sisters were horrified at the idea of his leaving regular employment, and advanced every possible argument to persuade him not to renounce his junior partnership with the printers. It was after tea at his brother's house that the argument began in earnest, and when Bob finally rose to signal an end to the discussion, no decision had been arrived at and the whole family were still hard at it—Teenie urging him not to waste his talents cooped up in an office, and his sisters, one after another, tearfully reminding him of his spendthrift Uncle John, and of his father's impoverished old age.

'I shall ask guidance,' said Ballantyne dramatically, as the meeting finally broke up, 'I shall ask guidance from God.'

What advice the Almighty gave him has not been revealed, but it is sufficient for us to know that within three weeks he was happily engaged in attempting to hook his first salmon, standing up to his knees in water and 'bursting ever and again into song' as he flashed the spinner through the cool Norwegian air.

Chapter Six

HE HAD A WONDERFUL START to his holiday with three weeks of fine sunny weather, living on board the yacht when it was anchored in remote and peaceful Norwegian fjords, or tramping inland with his companions to stay at some isolated village whose local river boasted fish of a size unheard of in Scotland. Once more Bob's Hudson Bay experience stood him in good stead in the daily competition for the heaviest catch and the other five males in the party soon came to seek his advice on matters of technique. This was especially evident when they took part in an eagle-hunting expedition, which involved climbing some of the less precipitous mountains in what turned out to be a successful attempt to bag a specimen of the king of the birds. The members of the party enjoyed themselves like a crowd of schoolboys released for the summer holidays, scrambling over rocks, soaking themselves in streams, cooking the midday meal over a fire of sticks, and spending the evenings drinking the local beer round the fire of some rustic inn.

All went well until they arrived at the small town of Torning, where they had intended to stay for three days, but soon after they had settled at the local hotel Ballantyne complained of feeling unwell and succumbed next day to a bad attack of influenza. He was in bed for over a week, listening miserably to the tales of the wonderful salmon hooked by his companions and to the sounds of the evening feasting and revelry which came from the rooms below. During his illness he had not made any effort to shave, and for the remainder of his Scandinavian holiday he let his beard grow unchecked, arriving back in Edinburgh sunburned and weather-beaten and with a now luxuriant growth of deep brown hair masking the lower half of his face.

Striding down the gangplank of the Cowan's yacht he looked a very handsome figure,[1] and for once both Teenie and his sisters, who seldom saw eye to eye, all agreed in telling him that his

[1] See frontispiece. This photograph was taken soon after his return from Norway.

appearance was much improved. For the rest of his life he remained bearded, and when later he came to address the audiences which attended his lectures, clothed in his Rupert's Land leather jacket and trousers, moccasins on his feet and with a long-barrelled gun under his arm, he looked the sort of colourful personality from the backwoods which the public delighted to see. The beard strongly appealed to his juvenile readers, who pictured the author of *Hudson's Bay* as the sort of romantic, adventurous-looking individual which his photographs now showed him to be.

When he relinquished his partnership with Messrs. Constable & Company, he had been able to withdraw his capital from the firm, so that he could now take things very easily, spending his days in painting a few pictures, passing long weekends fishing in the Highlands. In the evenings he worked on the manuscript of his book, which he had now provisionally entitled *Snowflakes and Sunbeams—A Tale of the Far North*. In addition, he wrote a number of letters to various societies in and around Edinburgh, offering his services as a lecturer on the subject of Hudson Bay and other far-northern territories, advising them that his fee would be five pounds plus expenses. On two occasions, before leaving for Norway, he had delivered a talk before a public audience, both in aid of Free Church charities, and had been gratified by the congratulations he had received and the genuine interest the lectures had aroused. He therefore resolved to augment his income by advertising his services professionally. Over the years his voice had deepened into a fine baritone and he worked out a scheme for interspersing his talks with some of the canoeing songs he had learned on his long Canadian trips. After a hesitant start, he soon became a popular figure in church halls and lecture rooms, striding on to the stage dressed in the trapper's clothing he had brought back with him and with the stage table strewn with bows and arrows, snow-shoes, head-dresses, animal skins and other Canadian souvenirs. The bearded figure of 'the brave Mr. Ballantyne,' as the young ladies had joyfully dubbed him, kept his listeners fascinated as he told them lurid stories of Indian raids, or sang the French-Canadian songs of the hunters, dramatically terminating his talk by firing his blank-loaded long-barrelled gun at the (now stuffed) Norwegian eagle set high over the stage, which a jerk of a hidden string sent crashing down on to the platform amid the horrified screams of the ladies and the enthusiastic applause of the men. These affairs inflated his ego to an extent that made him only half-heartedly deny some of the more lurid fictional tales of his prowess that the eager young ladies delightedly repeated about their new-found hero.

His sisters were dismayed at this new mode of life and prophesied a dissolute existence leading to early ruin, at the same time doing their best to restore him to a regular job. They secretly explored all sorts of avenues and in October he was surprised to receive a letter from, of all places, Bucharest.

> *British Residency, Bucharest.*
> *28th Sept.* 1855.

My dear Sir,

In July last my friend and Secretary Mr. Cobbold received an appointment in the Diplomatic Service. I mentioned the circumstances to my sister Mrs. Voucher at Lucca & she wrote me that your sister was very desirous of seeing you employed, & suggested that you might like to replace Mr. Cobbold as my Secretary. [Here follow four pages of detailed instructions as to routes, clothing required, etc., etc.]

As I have many applications for the office of Secretary, I will beg you immediately on receipt of this, to *telegraph* to me your decision. Bring plenty of warm clothing for our winters here are severe.

> Very Truly yours,
> R. G. Colquhoun.

His sister Randall was the culprit this time and Bob was by no means pleased at having to find the cost of the telegraphed message of refusal. 'I like the freedom I have obtained,' he wrote her smugly, 'and am quite confident of being able to make my own way in the world.'

1855 had witnessed the dissolution of the Kelso school for young ladies, at least as far as the Ballantyne girls were concerned. With other private schools competing and charging very low fees, the concern began to run into debt and the girls found themselves unable to draw sufficient salary for their needs. A note amongst Ballantyne's papers states:

> When Mrs. Ballantyne died, she left all her property to her four daughters by holograph Will, i.e. to Mary, Jane, Randall and Williamina. The property thus left consisted of the shares in the Water Company, the furniture at Windsor Street, and her personal clothing. . .[1]

The amount they received, although by no means large, enabled the girls to take advantage of their fluency in languages and seek teaching posts abroad. Williamina, as pretty and as independent as ever, was soon happily teaching English at a German school. Jane took a job in Paris, and Randall found a situation in an English school at Pisa, Italy. The eldest daughter, Mary, had married a Mr. Hector McKenzie in 1849, and was now at Fort William on the Ottawa River, Canada, where her husband held the lucrative post of Chief Factor of the trading post. It was here, in 1852, that their only child, Isobel, was born.

Ballantyne was by this time working on the manuscript of his new book every evening, and by September 1856 it was complete. He sent the text and a full set of illustrations to Nelson, who declared himself delighted with both story and pictures. The proofs were promptly corrected and returned, and, amid a flourish of advertising in the trade press, the volume appeared in the shops in November, clothed in the familiar red cloth, with the same gold-blocked figure of a hunter on the spine that had proved so attractive on the binding of *The Northern Coasts of America, and the Hudson's Bay Territories*. As a five-shilling adventure book for boys it sold excellently that Christmas and within a few weeks repeat orders started to flow into the publisher's office as the recommendations of the critics and those who had already read the book began to have their effect.

Bob (or perhaps Teenie, whose advice he always sought) had originally favoured 'Snowflakes and Sunbeams' as the title, but

---

[1] John and Robert Ballantyne were named as executors of their mother's Will, which revealed total assets of £337 18s. 2d., plus the house in Portobello which Mrs. Ballantyne had held on trust for her daughters.

the more commercially minded William Nelson had been against this and had blocked only the words 'The Young Fur Traders' on the spine, believing this title to have a more powerful impact on juvenile minds. A compromise had been reached by having both versions on the title page, giving *Snowflakes and Sunbeams; or, the Young Fur Traders*, but the publisher saw to it that the first part of the title was quietly dropped after the first few editions.

Most of the newspapers that noticed the volume gave the book a warm welcome, a typical review being that of *The Athenaeum*.

> This is a charming book, and will be the delight of high-spirited boys. It is full of fun and adventure. The description of hunter-life in the backwoods, and the society and manners at the trading-stations of the Hudson's Bay Company, are excellent, and have unmistakeable signs of having been drawn from life. The adventures and escapes are very exciting, and are told with great freedom and spirit. It is one of the most fascinating books of the kind; and fortunate will those youngsters be who find it hanging on their branch of the Christmas-tree.

The whole story has a strong autobiographical flavour to one who knows the history of the author's life while an employee in the service of the Hudson's Bay Company: one is not long in gaining the impression that the tale of young Charley Kennedy's adventures displays, in a highly coloured and romanticised form, the sort of life Ballantyne himself had hoped to be able to lead while he was in the snow-covered wilderness of Rupert's Land. In the first chapter we are told that fifteen-year-old Charles, who lives with his parents and surviving sister near to Red River Settlement (the rest of the Kennedys' numerous offspring having died during a smallpox epidemic), has made up his mind to run away rather than be apprenticed as a clerk to the Hudson's Bay Company at Fort Garry, a place his parents are determined he shall stay at for several years. He refuses to allow himself to be tied to an office desk, with the result that Mr. Grant, the Chief Factor in charge of the depot, is delegated by Frank Kennedy, the boy's irascible and stubborn old father, who has himself spent a lifetime in the Company's service, to give the unruly young lad some sound advice as to the merits of a safe, sedentary occupation.

'Charley, my boy,' began Mr. Grant, standing with his back to fire, his feet pretty wide apart, and his coat-tails under his arms—'Charley, my boy, your father has just been speaking of you. He is very anxious that you should enter the service of the Hudson's Bay Company; and as you are a clever boy and a good penman, we think that you would be likely to get on if placed for a year or so in our office here. I need scarcely point out to you, my boy, that in such a position you would be sure to obtain more rapid promotion than if you were placed in one of the distant outposts, where you would have very little to do, and perhaps little to eat, and no one to converse with you except one or two men. Of course, we would merely place you here on trial to see how you suited us; and if you prove steady and diligent, there is no saying how fast you might get on. Why, you might even come to fill *my* place in course of time! Come now, Charley, what do you think of it?'

Charley's eyes had been cast on the ground while Mr. Grant was speaking. He now raised them, looked at his father, then at his interrogator, and said-

'It is very kind of you both to be so anxious about my prospects.

'I thank you, indeed, very much; but I— I—'

'Don't like the desk?' said his father, in an angry tone. 'Is that it, eh?'

In order to convince his son of the advantages of an indoor life, his father waxes eloquent on the dangers lurking in the backwoods, but only ends up by removing the last remaining doubts in the lad's mind that the freedom of the wilds is the only life for him.

'In fact,' broke in the impatient father. . . 'You'll have to rough it, as I did, when I went up the Mackenzie River district, where I was sent to establish a new post, and had to travel for weeks and weeks through a wild country, where none of us had ever been before—where we shot our own meat, caught our own fish, and built our own house,—and were very near being murdered by the Indians—though, to be sure, afterwards they became the most civil fellows in the country, and brought us plenty of skins. Ay, lad, you'll repent your obstinacy when you come to have to hunt your own dinner, as I've done many a day up the Saskatchewan, where I've had to fight with redskins and grizzly bears, and to chase the buffaloes over miles and miles of prairie on rough-going nags till my bones ached and I scarce knew whether I sat on—'

'Oh! exclaimed Charley—starting to his feet, while his eyes flashed and his chest heaved with emotion—'that's the place for me, father! Do please, Mr. Grant, send me there, and I'll work for you with all my might!'

As might be expected, the author permits his young hero to escape from parental care and the boring routine of an office job in much the same way he must have often longed to escape himself. For the rest of the story Charles Kennedy leads an adventurous and daredevil life such as any boy might envy, packed full of exciting and often bloodthirsty incidents, until he wins his way to the inevitable happy ending in the final chapter. The narration of the various adventures that befall young Kennedy and his friends derive an unusual force and vividness from the author's personal experience of the scenes he describes, and his hero being of much the same age as the young stalwarts who read the book, made it easy for them to identify themselves with the brave deeds and daring escapes with which the pages are filled. One must admit that the chain of events strung together by the passage of time are hardly stiffened by anything approaching what one could call a plot, and this was a fault that marred a great number of the tales which Ballantyne wrote. But the strength of his writing lay in the meticulous accuracy of the backgrounds in which he set his tales, and one has only to read any of his stories that are located in a situation of which he had direct personal knowledge to perceive the trouble he went to in order that his readers should not be misled.

His publishers were very satisfied with the bargain they had made and wrote to Bob to inform him that they would be interested in marketing any further books he might write. This letter brought an immediate reply from the author, saying that he already had something prepared for their approval, and in a few days Ballantyne brought them the text and drawings of the bedtime stories he had recited for his young nieces and which he had spent a considerable amount of time converting into nursery picture books. The stories were quite unlike anything that Nelson's had published previously, but, after inspecting the manuscripts and the gaily coloured pictures that accompanied them, they agreed on a trial issue of the story entitled *The Three Little Kittens*. If this was a success, they informed the author, the rest of the series would follow in due course. But when it came to a discussion of the terms he might be expected to receive, the only offer that Ballantyne could elicit from them was a nebulous promise that they would pay him in proportion to what the books earned in profit.

When he had first drawn the pictures for the children and composed the original text, he had never imagined that they would ever earn him a fee, and although he had since spent some time in revision of the wording and alteration of the illustrations, he was happy to think that the stories could earn him anything at all. He therefore accepted the publisher's verbal offer, trusting them to treat him fairly if the tales proved successful. He was already working on his next full-length story for boys and informed Nelson that he would prefer not to have his name appear on the title-page of any of the nursery books, believing that this would injure his reputation with the tough young adventurers who composed his regular readership. To this the publishers agreed and when the nursery series of children's books appeared, the author's true identity was hidden under the pseudonym of 'Comus.'

Whether because of a last-minute decision regarding this, or for some other reason, the book appears to have been first issued in quarto size in December 1856, without a title-page. It is possible that the rush to be in time for the Christmas trade prevented a reprinting of the preliminary pages after some error had been discovered, but for whatever reason, the copies in the national libraries all lack this page, as do several others which have survived in private collections. Nelson's reissued the book in the following year, dated 1857, and this time the title-page is duly present, reading 'Three Little Kittens by Comus.' The volume contains the first appearance in Britain of the now famous nursery rhyme:[1]

> Three little kittens they lost their mittens,
>   And they began to cry.
> Oh, mother dear, we sadly fear
>   That we have lost our mittens.
> What! Lost your mittens, you naughty kittens!
>   Then you shall have no pie.
> Mee-ow, mee-ow, mee-ow.
>   No, you shall have no pie.

The book was an immediate success with young children and Nelson's quickly published others in the series, *Mister Fox, My Mother, The Butterfly's Ball*, and *The Life of a Ship*, all appearing in time for Christmas 1857.

With his success as an author made obvious by the reprinting of his works, Bob was becoming far from happy about the payment he was receiving from his publishers. He wrote to Teenie, telling her of an interview he had with the Nelson brothers.

> Well, I've had two hours of it with T. Nelson—the result is not so satisfactory as I could have wished but more so than I expected. They are a contradictory pair.
>
> They *admit* that I was paid too little for the 3 Little Kittens, also for the Young Fur Traders, and they offer me the munificent sum of £50.—I said that that was simply offering me £20 for my copyrights, because the other £30 simply met the short payment of the Young Fur Traders.

[1] This nursery rhyme is usually ascribed to Eliza Follen (1787–1860), a New England writer of children's books. They appear at the end of *New Nursery Songs for All Good Children*, which appeared about 1843, but even here the verses are described as 'traditional.'

Of course they can 'see' nothing. After admitting these two points and granting that some sort of conversation was had on the subject of giving me an interest in my books, they deny everything *generally* and make out that they have had small profits on my books and are due me nothing whatever except as a matter of free grace!

I declined the offer and begged them to go into the matter again and drop me a note. So we shall see what we shall see.

I must post this now. I write it in Cowan's office.

Ever your afft. brother,

R.M.B.

According to Ballantyne, Thomas and William Nelson had promised him ten pounds in royalties for every extra five hundred copies sold of *The Young Fur Traders*, after the disposal of the initial printing of fifteeen hundred volumes. This was a verbal offer, originally made when Bob handed over the manuscript, and had helped to induce him to part with the copyright of the book to the publishers. Not having been subject to a written agreement, it had no legal standing, and Thomas Nelson argued that if they did make the author any further payment in recognition of the high sales of the work, it would be merely to show their appreciation of his talents and would certainly not bind them to further payments for future editions. In the case of *The Three Little Kittens*, and the other books in this series, they agreed to pay Ballantyne one-quarter of the net profits of the first editions, the copyright to remain with the publishers and any subsequent editions to be their own concern. With the naïvety of one unversed with an author's privileges under the Copyright Act, Bob finally accepted their second offer of seventy-five pounds as a conclusive payment for both books, but later, when his eyes were opened by both the works going through dozens of editions for which he did not receive an extra penny, he more than once told his wife that he was bitterly disappointed by the way he had been treated. He considered that a sharp commercial trick had been perpetrated by a wealthy firm on a writer new to the publishing business.

In the last few months of his life the firm wrote to him, asking for details about the 'Kitten' books, which were still going through edition after edition and proving a most profitable speculation for the company. The members of the firm who had known Bob in the past had all long since died or retired, and the records of the company had been lost in a disastrous fire in Edinburgh, so that queries from readers could not be answered. The draft of the letter in reply, in the author's hand, has been preserved, and the final sentence reveals that Ballantyne still felt resentment at his treatment:

> C/o F. A. Searle Esq.
> San Antonio,
> Tivoli,
> Italy.
> 9th November, 1893.

Messrs. T. Nelson & Sons,
Edinburgh.
Dear Sirs,

Yours of the 2nd inst; has been forwarded to me.

I am not the author of the poem in *The Three Little Kittens*—only the letter press story founded on it & of the illustrations. Neither am I the author of the poem of *Mister Fox*—only the story and cuts. In regard to the other volumes of the series (*The Robber Kitten*, *My Mother*, etc.) I composed the poems and prose, besides drawing the illustrations on the wood.

It might perhaps interest you to know that for the copyright of each of these books I received nine pounds!

I am,

> Yours faithfully,
> R. M. BALLANTYNE.

The year 1857[1] saw the publication of what proved to be two of the most popular stories Ballantyne ever wrote. The success of *The Young Fur Traders* made Nelson's press him for another

[1] Although published late in 1857, both volumes are dated 1858. Dating a book forward was a common practice in Victorian days, especially if the volume appeared during the Christmas period.

tale of the Far North and Bob started work on a new adventure story, this time set amongst the Esquimaux of Ungava Bay.

> When casting about in my mind for a suitable subject, I happened to meet with an old retired 'Nor'wester' who had spent an adventurous life in Rupert's Land. Among other duties he had been sent to establish an outpost of the Hudson's Bay Company at Ungava Bay, one of the most dreary parts of a desolate region. On hearing what I wanted he sat down and wrote a long narrative of his proceedings there, which he placed at my disposal, and thus furnished me with the foundation of 'Ungava.'[1]

By early summer the manuscript was completed and within a few days of submitting it to his publishers he received an offer of sixty pounds cash, plus a promise that he could have a small share of any profits accruing from the first edition, providing he assigned to them the copyright of the book and relinquished any claim to a financial interest in subsequent editions should these be called for. To these terms the author gave his consent, and in June, on the strength of the thirty golden sovereigns he had received in part payment, he bade goodbye to John, Teenie and the children, and, with brushes and paints, notebooks and pencils, set off on a month's holiday by the seaside.

He took lodgings in a house on the seafront at Burntisland, just across the Firth of Forth opposite Edinburgh, passing part of every day on the beach and spending hours walking alone along the coast and cliffs of Fife. He had promised Teenie that he would try and return with at least three chapters of a new story completed, but at first both the subject and the setting of the tale eluded him:

> By now I had reached the end of my tether, and when a third story was wanted I was compelled to seek new fields of adventure in the books of travellers.[1]

From his bedroom window in the lodging-house he was able to look across the Forth to the island of Inchkeith about four miles

[1] Both these quotations come from an interview Ballantyne gave to *The Idler Magazine* (vol. III, p. 531).

away, and it was while sitting at his table before the window, idly gazing out to sea, that the sight of the little island shimmering in the distant sunlight brought suddenly to his mind the idea of making the characters of his next tale castaways on just such a place. He decided to make it a tropical island, uninhabited and wild, but crowded with a multitude of dangers through which his youthful heroes would have to fight their way to a happy ending. Next day (or so he told his wife in later years) he caught the morning ferry back to Edinburgh, and borrowed from amongst Nelson's file-copies several works of reference dealing with the Pacific Ocean and the islands and people there. Amongst their recent publications he must have noticed a book which had appeared in 1852, entitled *The Island Home; or, The Young Cast-Aways*, written by an American author, James F. Bowman, who used the pseudonym of Christopher Romaunt. There seems little doubt that he took this volume along with the rest.[1] With the parcel of books under his arm he arrived back in Burntisland the same afternoon and immediately began the task of absorbing sufficient facts about desert islands in the South Seas to enable him to give an authentic ring to an adventure story set in a part of the world about which he had no first-hand knowledge.

He entitled the new work *The Coral Island* and within a few days had completed the first chapter of what was to become his most famous book, the one that probably did more to endear him to generation after generation of young men than anything else he wrote. But if one reads James Bowman's *The Island Home; or, The Young Cast-Aways*, one can feel little doubt that many of the incidents which appear in Ballantyne's best-seller were culled by the author from this obscure fictional work by the American writer, a work which had been published in Boston and Edinburgh some five years before. There is no question of plagiarism in its worst form—the lifting of whole paragraphs from Bowman's work for insertion into his own—this certainly does not occur

[1] *The Island Home* was first published by D. Lothrop & Company, Boston, in 1851. The only copy located of the first edition is in the Bancroft Library of the University of California, at Berkeley, U.S.A. I have a copy of the first English edition, published by Thomas Nelson and Sons in 1852, which was the text Ballantyne used.

and is something Ballantyne would not even have contemplated; but a number of dramatic situations which appear in *The Island Home* seem to have been rewritten by Bob to change their form somewhat, and then woven into the story of the adventures of Ralph Rover, Jack Martin and Peterkin Gay, as he named his three young heroes.

There is little plot in either book, and what there is varies in many particulars one from the other, but there are enough similarities between the two stories to make it difficult to ascribe all of them to mere coincidence. Bowman has five young Americans and a Scot marooned on a coral island in the Pacific by mutineers, while Ballantyne chooses a similar setting but has his three young men shipwrecked. In the course of their adventures the boys in both stories scramble up palm trees to drink the 'lemonade' from coconuts, rub sticks together to make fire,[1] find the deserted hut and carved intials of a former white inhabitant and avail themselves of the abandoned utensils discovered there; both groups become frightened by a mysterious noise which they later believe is made by a species of penguin, and both witness a ferocious club fight between rival parties of cannibals in which they themselves become involved. Even the celebrated attack by a shark is duplicated although in dissimilar terms. Here is Bowman's version:

> [2]A somewhat startling incident put an end to these interesting reminiscences. Charlie was leaning over the gunwale, and with his face almost touching the surface, and his hands playing in the water, was peering down into the lagoon, probably on the look-out for another turtle, when a large shark, coming, as it seemed, from beneath the boat, rose suddenly but quietly, and made a snatch at him. Charlie saw the monster barely in time; for just as he sprung up with a cry of affright, and fell backwards into the boat, the shark's shovel-nose shot four feet above water at our stern, his jaws snapping together as he disappeared again, with a

[1] Although the boys in both stories hold the wood against their chest, they use different methods to cause enough friction to ignite a flame.
[2] Pages 230 *et seq.*

sound like the springing of a powerful steel-trap. Though baffled in his first attack, the voracious fish continued to follow us, watching closely an opportunity for a more successful attempt. . .

His flattened head, and long leather-like snout, together with a pair of projecting eyes, so situated as to command a view both in front and rear, and which he kept turning restlessly on every side, contributed greatly to enhance his forbidding aspect. Every moment he seemed to grow fiercer and bolder, and at length he actually laid hold of our keel next the rudder, and fairly shook the boat from stem to stern. To our great relief he soon desisted from this, for such was his bulk and strength, that we hardly knew what he might not effect in his furious efforts. His next move was to make a sudden dash at Max's oar, which had probably given him offence by coming too near his nose, and which he jerked from his hands.

Max seemed to regard this last exploit as a personal affront, and loudly declared that 'this was going altogether too far, and that he would stand it no longer.' He accordingly proceeded with great energy to lash his cutlass to the handle of one of the remaining oars with some twine which he found in the locker, threatening all sorts of terrible things against the unsuspecting object of his wrath. Meanwhile Morton succeeded in fishing up the lost oar, which the vigilance and activity of our attentive escort rendered a somewhat dangerous undertaking; when recovered, the marks of six rows of formidable teeth were found deeply indented upon its blade.

Max having completed his novel weapon, Browne, who had been engaged in an unprofitable attempt to strike the shark across the eyes with his cutlass, inquired 'what he was going to do with that clumsy contrivance?'

'That clumsy contrivance, as you rashly term it,' replied Max with dignity, 'is designed as a shark exterminator, with which I intend forthwith to pay my respects to this audacious sea-bully. We have stood on the defensive quite long enough, and I am now about to carry the war into Africa.'

He accordingly jumped upon the middle seat of the yawl,

where, in spite of all attempts at dissuasion, he stood watching a favourable opportunity for a thrust. This was soon presented. All unconscious of the unfriendly designs cherished against him, the shark came propelling himself carelessly alongside, and directly under Max's nose, with his back fin quite above water. The temptation was not to be resisted. Max braced himself as firmly as possible in his position. Arthur expostulated, and begged him at least to get down and stand in the boat. Morton exhorted him a caution. But he only answered by a wave of the hand and a grim smile; then requesting Browne to lay fast hold of his waistband, to assist him in preserving the centre of the gravity, he raised his weapon in both hands, and giving it a preliminary flourish, brought it down with his full force, aiming at the broadest part of the fish's back, just forward of the dorsal fin. But the weapon was too dull, or the blow too feeble, to pierce the tough hide of the 'sea-attorney,' for it glanced smoothly off, and Max, losing his balance, went headlong into the sea. Browne, in a hasty effort to save him, came near going over also, while the boat careened until the water poured in over the gunwale, and for a moment there was imminent danger of capsizing. Max came to the surface almost paralysed with fright, and clutched convulsively at the side of the boat; when we drew him on board unharmed, but pale and shivering, as he well might be, after so extraordinary an escape.

Ballantyne's heroes faced a similar danger but had neither boat nor cutlasses and were fishing from a log when they were attacked:

[1]Now, while we were thus intent upon our sport, our attention was suddenly attracted by a ripple on the sea, just a few yards away from us. Peterkin shouted to us to paddle in that direction, as he thought it was a big fish, and we might have a chance of catching it. But Jack, instead of complying, said, in a deep, earnest tone of voice, which I never before heard him use—

[1] Pages 74 *et seq.*

'Haul up your line, Peterkin; seize your paddle; quick—its a shark!'

The horror with which we heard this may well be imagined, for it must be remember that our legs were hanging down in the water, and we could not venture to pull them up without upsetting the log. Peterkin instantly hauled up the line; and, grasping his paddle, exerted himself to the utmost, while we also did our best to make for the shore. But we were a good way off, and the log being, as I have before said, very heavy, moved but slowly through the water. We now saw the shark quite distinctly swimming round and round us, its sharp fin every now and then protruding above the water. From its active and unsteady motions, Jack knew it was making up its mind to attack us, so he urged us vehemently to paddle for our lives, while he himself set us the example. Suddenly he shouted 'Look out!—there he comes!' and in a second we saw the monstrous fish dive close under us, and turn half over on his side. But we all made a great commotion with our paddles, which no doubt frightened it away for that time, as we saw it immediately after circling round us as before.

'Throw the fish to him,' cried Jack, in a quick, suppressed voice; 'we'll make the shore in time yet if we can keep him off for a few minutes.'

Peterkin stopped one instant to obey the command, and then plied his paddle again with all his might. No sooner had the fish fallen on the water than we observed the shark to sink. In another second we saw its white breast rising; for sharks always turn over on their sides when about to seize their prey, and their mouths being not at the point of their heads like those of other fish, but, as it were, under their chins. In another moment his snout rose above the water,—his wide jaws, armed with a terrific double row of teeth, appeared. The dead fish was engulfed, and the shark sank out of sight. But Jack was mistaken in supposing that it would be satisfied. In a very few minutes it returned to us, and its quick motions led us to fear that it would attack us at once.

'Stop paddling,' cried Jack suddenly. 'I see it coming up behind us. Now, obey my orders quickly. Our lives may depend on it. Ralph, Peterkin, do your best to balance the log. Don't look out for the shark. Don't glance behind you. Do nothing but balance the log.'

Peterkin and I instantly did as we were ordered, being only too glad to do anything that afforded us a chance or a hope of escape, for we had implicit confidence in Jack's courage and wisdom. For a few seconds, that seemed long minutes to my mind, we sat thus silently; but I could not resist glancing backwards, despite the orders to the contrary. On doing so, I saw Jack sitting rigid like a statue, with his paddle raised, his lips compressed, and his eyebrows bent over his eyes, which glared savagely from beneath them down into the water. I saw also the shark, to my horror, quite close under the log, in the act of darting towards Jack's foot. I could scarce suppress a cry on beholding this. In another moment the shark rose. Jack drew his leg suddenly from the water, and threw it over the log. The monster's snout rubbed against the log as it passed, and revealed its huge jaws, into which Jack instantly plunged the paddle, and thrust it down its throat. So violent was this act that Jack rose to his feet in performing it; the log was thereby rolled completely over, and we were once more plunged into the water. We all rose, spluttering and gasping, in a moment.

'Now, then, strike out for the shore,' cried Jack. 'Here, Peterkin, catch hold of my collar, and kick out with a will.'

Peterkin did as he was desired, and Jack struck out with such force that he cut through the water like a boat; while I being free from all encumbrance, succeeded in keeping up with them. As we had by this time drawn pretty near to the shore, a few minutes more sufficed to carry us into shallow water; and, finally, we landed in safety, though very much exhausted, and not a little frightened by our terrible adventure.

The Island Home may now be accorded a greater measure of recognition by students of literature than it has so far received,[1]

[1] As far as I am aware, the connection between Bowman's *The Island Home* and Ballantyne's book *The Coral Island* has not before been remarked upon. Little is known about this Californian author and no other

for as the source from which came many of the incidents portrayed in *The Coral Island* (itself a book which exercised a considerable influence over the boyhood imagination of Robert Louis Stevenson), it helped youth develop a taste for the romance of the Southern Seas and for the mystery and excitement of those far-off coral strands. The author of *Treasure Island*, that classical example of an adventure story for boys, had himself read and thoroughly enjoyed *The Coral Island*, and, as is shown later, his love of the romantic islands of the Pacific was almost certainly first awakened by reading Ballantyne's book. The neglected Mr. James Bowman is to be thanked for unwittingly contriving a train of narrative which culminated in Stevenson's unsurpassed romance, in which we have, for the first time in English juvenile literature, an adventure story that is both unmoralised and unashamed, and in which priggishness and didacticism find no place. No doubt Bowman would himself have been the first to acknowledge his own debt to Daniel Defoe, Johann Wyss, and Captain Marryatt.[1]

Ungava and *The Coral Island* both appeared in the bookshops early in December 1857, the first selling at five shillings a copy,

separate publication by him has been discovered, although he contributed articles about Anglo-Saxon writers to *The Hesperian*, and sentimental lyrics entitled "Homesick" and "At the Ball" to the *Californian*. He was for many years the editor of the *San Francisco Chronicle*. There are references to Bowman in John P. Young's *Journalism in California*, published by the Chronicle Publishing Company in San Francisco (1915); also in Franklin Walker's *San Francisco's Literary Frontier*, published by Knopf in New York, 1939, from which the following description is taken.

'In San Francisco the favourite poets-of-the-day were Bret Harte, Frank Soule, James F. Bowman, and William H. Rhodes. Among these . . . Bowman had the greatest stock of classical allusions and was sure to lend dignity, erudition, and fire to any patriotic gathering.

'. . . finally, James F. Bowman's death from cancer of the stomach (on the 30th April, 1883) marked the end of the terrible decade. "Little Johnny Bowman," with his wizened face, his sparkling black eyes, his Absalom-like ebon locks, and his legs which reminded one of Quilp would no longer lecture on Anglo-Saxon poetry, write interminable serials on a wager, or worry his friends with his drinking. During his life he produced every kind of literature that the frontier knew and had experienced all the vicissitudes of its writers except success.'

[1] The authors respectively of *Robinson Crusoe*, *The Swiss Family Robinson* and *Mr. Midshipman Easy*.

and the second, by virtue of its coloured plates, at a shilling extra.[1] Both works had an instant and enduring success, generations of young readers taking them to their hearts and consuming edition after edition. *The Coral Island*, especially, proved tremendously popular, and has been continually reprinted ever since it first appeared, being translated into practically every European language before the end of the nineteenth century. For the copyright of each of these two books, the author received only sixty pounds, plus *ex gratia* payments amounting to a further thirty. As far as is known, and this is confirmed by letters Ballantyne wrote to the firm in the last years of his life, he was paid nothing for the many subsequent issues of these two titles, and derived no extra benefit whatsoever from the many thousands of volumes which were printed after the first editions were exhausted.

The original manuscript of *The Coral Island* was retrieved by the author from the publishers, and later presented, enclosed in a cloth case, to Teenie's young son, Randal, as a Christmas present. Could the author have realised its eventual fate, and seen what the money obtained by its sale was to be spent upon, he would, one can be sure, have kept it secure in his roll-top desk.[2]

[1] Ballantyne supplied the illustrations for both books.
[2] In later life, Randal Ballantyne became an alcoholic. According to family legend, he sold the manuscript of *The Coral Island* to a London secondhand bookshop for the sum of five pounds, in order to obtain funds for drink.

Chapter Seven

THE NEW YEAR found Ballantyne tasting the sweet fruits of literary success and the fame which his attainments brought with them. The Press had been unanimous in showering praise on his last two books and the speed with which the first edition of both volumes was disposed of exceeded his publisher's most sanguine expectations.

His friends now delighted to introduce him as—'My friend, Robert Ballantyne, the author,' or, 'Mr. Ballantyne, the well-known author,' and before long no Free Church social occasion seemed quite complete unless the young and handsome Mr. Ballantyne was present. Teenie fussed and clucked around him, accepting and declining invitations, and generally chaperoning him like an overgrown schoolboy, in spite of his thirty-three years. She accompanied him to all mixed functions, no doubt to the annoyance of the matrons who had unmarried daughters on their hands and for whom the eligible young author would have made an excellent catch. But Teenie's task was not a difficult one —her brother-in-law was shy with the ladies, hating dancing, and confessed to feeling most awkward if left alone with 'one of the creatures.' He was content with the company of his sister-in-law, and she, it seems, with his.

Amongst the notes John Ballantyne made for a short family history was the following description of his brother:

In the late 'fifties I remember Bob as being a brisk & energetic figure, slim of build like the rest of us Ballantynes, active in his movements, and with a fine baritone voice which he used with great effect at our musical evenings. He had the lowland accent of an Edinburgh Scot like myself. Before his marriage he wore his hair long, much in the style of the hunters of the forests of the Frozen North that he knew so well; his face gave one the impression of being bronzed, no matter what the season, and was considered extremely handsome by the ladies. His eyes were keen, & much of his face was hidden by his full-flowing moustache & thick, brown beard. His entrance into a drawing-room would cause every female head to turn & the conversation to give pause; which fact embarrassed him immensely as he professed to be not in the least vain about his appearance.

A brother artist asked me to persuade him to sit for a head of Christ upon which he was then engaged,[1] & to this Bob reluctantly gave his consent. But the identity of the model becoming known, he very much regretted giving his permission & confessed himself ashamed of having impersonated his Saviour.

Bob seems to have been quite happy to leave the management of all his social affairs in the hands of his petulant little sister-in-law, and while he was lodging in her house it appears she had only to command and he invariably obeyed. Many of the letters he wrote her seem to be missing, and pages have been cut from others which have survived, so there is no means of knowing whether in fact the pair were more than good friends. In the light of the available evidence we can only presume that they were spiritually in harmony and on affectionate terms of friendship, and that some of his letters show Bob was positively frightened of incurring her wrath. She was a pretty woman, but also an irascible and domineering one, and he took extremely good care not to offend her on any pretext.

During 1858, Nelson's put a number of easy hackwork tasks in Ballantyne's hands, and his name was soon appearing on the title-pages of such diverse subjects as *Handbook to the New Gold Fields of the Fraser and Thompson Rivers*; *Environs and Vicinity of Edinburgh*; *Ships—The Great Eastern and Lesser Craft*; *The Lakes of Killarney*; etc., all of which brought him a few extra pounds, even if they did little to enhance his literary reputation.

That summer he and his brother John joined the Edinburgh Volunteers, the Victorian equivalent of our present-day Territorial Army. They quickly became keen supporters of the movement,

[1] I have been unable to trace the present whereabouts of this painting. Mrs. Ballantyne informed her daughters that it was eventually given to one of the Scottish art galleries.

standing stiff and important as the drill sergeant roared his instructions, or walking miles on route marches, much to Teenie's amusement. In a letter to her husband she mockingly accused them both at playing at soldiers, but admitted that they looked rather dashing and fierce in their new uniforms and little pill-box caps.

These spare-time occupations took second place to the writing upon which Bob's livelihood now solely depended and he concentrated his energies on completing his next full-length book for boys. By September the neatly written sheets of *Martin Rattler* were in his publisher's hands, terms being agreed between them at seventy-five pounds for the outright sale of the copyright. It was due to his acceptance of those dangling baits of round lump sums that Ballantyne once again lost control of a story that was destined to pass through numerous editions and become an undoubted best-seller in the juvenile market. It is only just to admit, however, that Nelson's, by purchasing the copyright and allowing Ballantyne no further benefit from subsequent editions, were following a practice which was commonplace in the middle of the nineteenth century, but which, as in Bob's case, often denied to the author his proper financial reward.

The Press gave a warm welcome to the author's latest literary creation when the book appeared in late November, the issue of *The Scotsman* for 24th December, 1858, being typical of many:

> Mr. Ballantyne ought to be a decided favourite with young readers, for not content with introducing them to far distant lands—ranging from the cold and cheerless regions of North America to the beautiful islands of the Pacific—he makes young boys the heroes of all his stories, endowing them with wonderful fortitude and perseverence. This book has all the advantages of Mr. Ballantyne's former works; it is both instructive and amusing.

This reviewer had perceived the quality, unique in those days, which above all others was making Ballantyne's books so popular with young people. For the first time in the annals of English juvenile literature, youngsters were able personally to identify themselves with the heroes of the tale they were reading. It was they who rescued helpless natives from a cruel death at the hands of cannibals, or dashed through smoke and flames to the side of the swooning heroine, or plunged without a moment's hesitation into shark-infested waters for the sake of an injured friend; modestly refusing to accept any thanks from the erstwhile victim other than perhaps a firm shake of the gratefully outstretched hand of one whom they had just snatched from the jaws of a fearful death. It was during 1859 that Ballantyne first experienced the agreeable but embarrassing sensation of being followed through the streets of Edinburgh by admiring youngsters, and his autograph became the prized possession of many a young Scots lad.

In *Martin Rattler; or, A Boy's Adventures in the Forests of Brazil*, Ballantyne had woven the threads of his narrative into much the same design as those of his previous adventure tales, but this time choosing as his setting the steaming forests of South America. He prefaced the work by stating 'that all the important points and anecdotes are true; only the minor and unimportant ones being mingled with fiction.' This was the foundation on which he was to base the vast majority of his adventure stories, setting his fictional characters against a background of factual descriptions of the lands and people amongst which the tale was made to unfold. This manner of construction, the fictional tale built on a solid sub-stratum of fact, was a new departure in juvenile literature in mid-Victorian days, and helped to impart to everything he wrote an authentic ring which masked the improbabilities of his plots. It also meant, of course, that his boy readers sometimes had to wade through pages of instructional dialogue, in which the fauna and flora were often minutely described, together with a history of whatever country they happened to be in. But he was always careful enough to sandwich these instructive passages between joints of red-blooded action and suspense, and there was certainly nothing pastel-shaded about his violence. The ferocity of the natives towards the white men and boys they find trespassing on their preserves is only equalled by the ferocity of the white men and boys towards any native or wild animal they can creep near enough to kill.

The story *Martin Rattler* is typical of many that Ballantyne wrote. The young hero after whom the book is named, having been brought up by his old Aunt Dorothy Grumbit, is forced to fight the school bully in order to save his aunt's white kitten from being slowly drowned. After a desperate battle, Martin manages to knock the heavier boy unconscious, and is congratulated by an Irish sailor, Barney O'Flannagan by name, who has happened to witness the fight. The tales Barney tells the boy about his adventures at sea inflame the lad's imagination with a desire for a sailor's life, but his aunt refuses to let him go. At the age of fourteen, Martin Rattler is accidentally swept out to sea in a small punt, only to be saved from drowning by the providential appearance of a ship on her way out to Brazil. One of the tars on deck leaps overboard to the rescue, and this turns out to be none other than Martin's old friend Barney O'Flannagan! The youth becomes one of the crew, and slips overboard with Barney when their ship is attacked and overrun by pirates near the coast of South America. They swim ashore and find themselves on the sandy coast of Brazil, in whose dense tropical forests they quickly become lost—luckily stumbling on the hut of a hermit just when things seemed blackest. After passing the night in the hut, Martin awakens pale and weak, having been attacked by a vampire bat, but under the hermit's care is soon nursed back to health. Having regaled the two shipmates with a long history of Brazil, the hermit finishes his tale with the words—'No truth is taught to the people,—no Bible is read in their ears; religion is not taught,—even morality is not taught; men follow the devices and desires of their own hearts, and there is no voice raised to say, "You are doing wrong." My country is sunk very low; and she cannot hope to rise, for the word of her Maker is not in her hand . . . she has no vital stream. Yes, Brazil, my country, wants the Bible!' To which Martin and his companion echo a loud Amen.

They leave on a hunting expedition, and, in the course of a few hours have succeeded in dashing the brains out of a large iguana by swinging it around by its tail and causing its head to come into violent contact with a tree; have speared a magnificent jaguar to death; and built a fire over a hole into which the hermit had observed an armadillo scuttle, thus driving the unfortunate creature into the open where it is quickly despatched.

After a series of adventures, Martin and Barney reach the Amazon River, and are befriended by a plantation owner who invites them to take part in an alligator hunt.

At sunrise an expressive shout in Portuguese set the black slaves on their feet; and, after a hasty breakfast of alligator-tail and farina, they commenced operations. Alligator-tail is by no means bad food, and after the first mouthful,—taken with hesitation and swallowed with difficulty,—Martin and Barney both pronounced it 'capital'. Sambo (one of the slaves), who had cooked the delicate morsel, and stood watching them, smacked his lips and added, 'Fuss rate.'

All being ready for the hunt, a number of Negroes entered the water, which was nowhere very deep, with long poles in their hands. This appeared to Martin and Barney a very reckless and dangerous thing to do, as no doubt it was. Nevertheless accidents, they were told, very rarely happened.

Sambo, who was the overseer of the party, was the first to dash up to the middle in the water. 'Hi,' exclaimed that dingy individual, making a torrent of remarks in Portuguese while he darted his long pole hither and thither; then, observing that Martin and Barney were gazing at him open mouthed, he shouted, 'Look out, boys! here 'im comes! Take care, ole feller, or he jump right down you' throat!'

As he spoke, a large alligator, having been rudely stirred up from his muddy bed, floundered on the surface of the lake, and Sambo instantly gave it a thump over the back and a blow under the ribs; which had the effect of driving it in the direction of the shore. Here a number of Negroes were ready for him; and the moment he came within reach, a coil of rope with a noose on the end of it, called a lasso, was adroitly thrown over the reptile's head: ten or twelve men then hauled the lasso and dragged it ashore amid shouts of triumph. This alligator was twenty feet long, with an enormous misshapen head and fearful rows of teeth that were terrible to behold. The monster did not submit to be captured, however, without a struggle; and the Negroes grew wild with the excitement as they yelled and leaped madly about seeking to avoid its dangerous jaws and the blows of its powerful tail. After some trouble a second lasso was thrown over the tail, which was thus somewhat restrained in its movements; and Sambo, approaching cautiously with an axe, cut a deep gash at the root of that formidable append-age, which rendered it harmless "Hi!" shouted Sambo in triumph, as he sprang towards the animal's head, and in-flicted a similar gash in its neck; 'dare, you quite finish, ole feller.'

Shortly afterwards, the two friends are taken prisoner by a party of Indians armed with blow-pipes and poisoned arrows, and are separated and taken to different native villages. Martin is made a slave by the Indian tribe, learns a smattering of their language and quickly becomes an expert with the blow-pipe. On being forced to witness a scene of native festivity, in which some of the participants become the worse for drink, Martin leaves the revels 'with a feeling of pity for the poor savages,' and recalls to mind the soulful cry of his erstwhile friend the hermit—'They want the Bible in Brazil.' Sundry other thoughts of an evangelical nature are made to pass through the hero's mind by the author, who seldom missed an opportunity of drawing his young readers' attention to the spiritual shortcomings of those to whom the Word of the Lord had not been vouchsafed.

After several months of slavery, Martin escapes from his captors by plunging over a steep precipice into the swirling waters of a rock-bound pool some hundred feet below. He spends weeks wandering in the dense jungle before luckily meeting with a party of Brazilians who allow him to accompany them to the diamond mines. But here he is at first accorded a cold wel-come by Baron Fagoni, the overseer, being confined for several hours to a dark and cheerless room, wondering what fate has in store. Suddenly a dozen slaves enter with flaming candelabra and trays loaded with steaming dishes of mouth-watering food; followed by the smiling Baron Fagoni, who turns out to be none other than his old friend Barney O'Flannagan in disguise. The two leave the mine together, and, after further adventures, return safe and sound to England, each with four hundred pounds in his pocket, the proceeds of the sale of gold dust and diamonds. Arriving once more at his boyhood home, Martin discovers that his old aunt has disappeared from the rustic surroundings of her native village, but he traces her to a cold and dreary garret in Liverpool where she lies dying. The sight of her long-lost nephew has a miraculous effect and quickly restores the old woman to health, and she proudly returns with him to her ivy-covered cottage. The story ends by telling how Martin Rattler prospers and eventually becomes a wealthy man, spending his leisure hours in visiting the poor and reading the Bible to the sick and bedridden, while himself leading a God-fearing and upright life.

It is difficult to imagine modern youth accepting as genuine traits of character the evangelical fervour displayed by so many of Ballantyne's heroes, and it is more than likely the boys of today would now condemn Martin Rattler out of hand as being both an insufferable prig and a smug, self-righteous show-off. But in the age when his tales appeared, Ballantyne expressed the public mood. The readers for whom he wrote were largely composed of the sons of the rising class of merchants and tradesmen who had been bred out of the Industrial Revolution; little men of first-generation wealth who eagerly embraced the pomposities of Victorian middle-class society, and who believed that their new-found comparative prosperity could be preserved only by the maintenance of the *status quo* in a society that was viciously capitalistic. The façade of respectability behind which so many of these self-made men and their families crouched needed the occasional bolstering of the hard-headed public do-goodism of the soup-kitchen, church-hall-building variety; this was the type of charitable endeavour that would in no way weaken the rigid class-structure of the community in which they lived, or give the lower orders any toe-hold that might enable them to rise above what was known to be their proper station.

A favourite target of genteel benevolence were the indolent and immoral coloured savages of the lands conquered by British grit and determination, and on whom the blessings of the Church had not yet been visited. The raising of funds by bazaars, flag-days and sales of work, so as to despatch yet another black-coated missionary to the far-flung outposts of the Empire in order to bring the Bible to the pagan, were favourite and much used devices which enabled the public-spirited organisers to stand higher in their own esteem and that of their fellow men. Drop-ping a copper or two in the rattling can no doubt helped still the twinges of uneasy conscience that must occasionally have been aroused in the public mind by the methods used to subdue the native peoples of Her Majesty's ever growing dominions—but the mystique of British imperialism was accepted unquestion-ingly. Much of the growing enthusiasm for the works of R. M. Ballantyne can be attributed to his belief, held equally by W. H. G. Kingston, Thomas Mayne Reid, G. A. Henty and other boys' writers, that goodness and power were symbolised by the British Empire. Both he and his contemporaries bowed down before the majesty of the British Raj. He also paid constant lip-service to the noble aims of the newly literate class of merchant adventurers, both at home and abroad, who, once having cushioned themselves against the slings of fortune by the comforting padding which wealth affords, then turned their benevolent minds to charitable works of a religious nature. Most of his heroes ended their days in this manner.

The popularity of his tales amongst the parents who bought them every Christmas for their sons depended in some measure on their desire to instil in their offspring a wish to emulate the Empire builders and captains of industry who had earned them-selves the plaudits of the crowd by being ruthlessly successful in their pursuit of wealth and power. Once having attained these pinnacles, their boys could in their turn buttress the Establish-ment and, if they wished, help butter the loaves of the more deserving of the nation's poor. As to his young readers, there can be no doubt that they thoroughly enjoyed his stories, with all their manifest incongruities and implausible situations, identify-ing themselves with the bloodthirsty teenagers who roamed forest, prairie and coral island, trusting in God and light-heartedly slaughtering man and beast with zestful enthusiasm. Ballantyne gave them all the action they desired, making the blood stream down the pages of his books, but not forgetting to slip in a sermon or two, and having his heroes on their knees at least once during the course of the plot. Before the final pages of his books are turned, it is most unusual if the chief character of the tale does not return home with pockets loaded with gold, which by industry and hard work he quickly converts to a sizeable fortune, in much the manner advocated by the illustrious Samuel Smiles in *Self-Help*. This is virtue rewarded, and the materialistic heart of the young male satisfied, for Ballantyne knew it was no use offering him metaphysical argument—you must leave him with a dream of earthly rewards.

Seemingly, they also accepted without question the author's reiterated *argumentum ad hominem*: provided a lad was clean-living, upright and God-fearing, then the British straight left was more than a match for any half-dozen skulking foreigners, though the blackguards were armed to the teeth with the most fearsome of weapons. But in all his iconic portrayals of sound, healthy, juvenile behaviour and white-manly exhibitionism, Ballantyne was always careful to avoid even the slightest hint of any action on the part of his characters which could be construed as meaning that they were displaying other than a platonic interest in the female sex. The villains and bad men in his stories, although they were allowed to smoke and drink and occasionally swear in unspecified terms, never permitted themselves to be anything but perfect gentlemen in their encounters with the heroine. In those days it was quite unthinkable that they should have acted otherwise. Even if one forgets for the moment the stifling taboos of the author's nineteenth-century environment, the sickly influence of his holier-than-thou predecessors in the same field would have been enough to bridle any desire he might have had to liberalise his boys' emotions. The mincing authors of the past, the long procession of pious aunties and hellfire uncles stretching back in time to mid-Georgian days, the pews of flat-chested spinsters who churned out titles for the Religious Tract Society, and the black-browed Divines sheltering under such genial pseudonymns as 'Mr. Lovechild,' who whiffed brimstone through the nursery and condemned to eternal damnation all who so much as thought of fleshly sins; this legacy of prudery millstoned Victorian juvenile fiction and castrated the teenage heroes of boys' adventure tales. G. A. Henty trespassed only once, and in an interview later[1] he ruefully admitted 'I never touch on love interest. Once I ventured to make a boy of twelve kiss a little girl of eleven, and I received a very indignant letter from a dissenting minister.'

An author who influenced Ballantyne's work was Captain Frederick Marryat, R.N., who in the twenty years following 1829 had written a series of instructional adventure stories for boys, and in whose pages didacticism and priggishness are evident in far greater degree than Bob ever permitted himself. Even so, neither of these once laudable characteristics are ever totally absent from Ballantyne's yarns and he consistently displayed an uncompromisingly hostile and condemnatory attitude to any phrase or action that even so much as hinted at a desire on the part of his characters to experience the milder joys found in the company of the fair sex. The most stirring and realistic of his adventure tales are leavened with a eunuch-like approach to any female that he apologetically allowed to intrude amongst the red-blooded boys who are busily massacring the natives or bagging their fifth rhinoceros.

It is hardly surprising, therefore, that a writer whose youthful heroes were never permitted to whistle after a pretty girl, and whose only desire on rescuing a beautiful coloured princess was to convert her instantly to Christianity, should have discovered, when he attempted to varnish and sophisticate his characters to make them believable to the prosaic and increasingly progressive adult world of the nineteenth century, that his descriptive powers were quite unequal to the task. For despite the fact that he was fast becoming the favourite author of the youth of Britain, Ballantyne on more than one occasion revealed that he resented being driven by the whips of financial necessity into writing solely for boys. His assessment of his own literary abilities persuaded him that he could break into the wider and more rewarding pastures occupied by the novelists and writers of adult popular fiction. He made several fruitless attempts to convince his publishers that he was capable of holding the interest of other age-

[1] Quoted in G. Manville Fenn's biography of George Alfred Henty.

groups than those with whom he was now so firmly established, but, except for a few guide books and pamphlets, they
firmly discouraged him from writing anything for the adult
market.

Much of his difficulty of expression stemmed from the fact that
he was hidebound by his strict Presbyterianism, with the result
that he conveyed the impression that he was acutely embarrassed
by having to mention sex in any form. He finally came to accept,
after several disappointing rejections, that his talents fitted him
only for the role of an author of books for boys, and that therefore he would remain forever outside the boudoir world of the
three-volume novelists so beloved by the countless members of
the Victorian circulating libraries.

In a letter to his sister-in-law in January 1859, Bob at last
acknowledged this situation, but shrouded his acceptance of the
permanent role of writer for juveniles under the guise of his
having received an evangelical 'call.'

> . . . Do you know I have had some serious thoughts this
> forenoon, while travelling, that *young people* are my
> 'mission'! They not only like what I write, but there is no
> doubt now (I think) that I can keep their earnest attention
> for a long time while speaking. May God direct me in this
> thought if it is a correct one. You know I have all along
> kicked at writing for boys. Yet God has given me great suc-
> cess in this very thing. Then I began by lecturing to grown
> up people, yet I found that boys & girls come & they *attend*;
> wh. fact speaks volumes. Last night, at supper, several
> persons remarked about my hold over the young.

However, Ballantyne did have at least one success in the adult
sphere. In the autumn of that year both he and his brother were
commissioned as ensigns in the City of Edinburgh Rifle Volunteer Corps,[1] a rank which they had long coveted, and, for the
benefit of his fellow officers, he dashed off an amusing handbook
on *How Not to Do It—a Manual for the Awkward Squad*, and

[1] In July 1860 R. M. Ballantyne was made a Captain and placed in
command of No. 9 Company of the Edinburgh Rifle Volunteers. He
resigned from the force in February 1863.

this was followed by two others in a similar vein.[1] The work was a skit on the drill movements of the force and he persuaded Messrs. Constable's to give it the honour of their imprint. This little publication, and the others which followed, eventually passed through several editions and must have returned him quite a handsome profit.

Teenie now decided that they should move to a larger house at 6 Abercromby Place, Edinburgh, in order to give better accommodation to her growing children and allow her more scope for entertaining. Considering that her husband John's income was, if anything, diminishing, and that he was finding it harder and harder to find sitters, this was by no means a wise move and both men demurred, Bob going so far as to produce a set of figures to prove that they would have great difficulty in making ends meet, and this despite the fact that he was now able and willing to pay a higher rent. But, as usual, his sister-in-law had her way, and within a few weeks the move was completed and they had settled into their new home.

John had enjoyed some years of popularity as a portrait painter; he was a competent artist without being brilliant and had long been an Associate of the Royal Scottish Academy. In 1855 he had accepted an appointment as teacher to the life class at the Edinburgh School of Design, for although the position carried a salary of only two hundred pounds a year, it ensured a regular income for a member of a somewhat precarious profession. During the early years of his marriage, when he was considered a fashionable painter, he earned respectable fees, sometimes commanding as much as fifty guineas for a single portrait; but the circle of his friends and acquaintances who were willing to sit for him, and then pay for the finished picture, was rapidly diminishing and commissions were increasingly difficult to obtain. The teaching appointment, although consuming most of his working hours, helped keep the wolf from the door, and the occasional outside

---

[1] The other booklets in this series were *The Volunteer Levee*, published in 1860; and *Ensign Sopht's Volunteer Almanack for 1861*. In November 1881 there appeared *The Collected Works of Ensign Sopht— Late of the Volunteers*. This latter work incorporated the above three titles, plus extra material.

work he was able to execute paid for some of the little luxuries in which his wife liked to indulge. For the present, therefore, the family could still live in modest style and enjoy the pleasures of Edinburgh middle-class society. Bob Ballantyne invariably accompanied Teenie and her husband on their occasional visits to the theatre or the concert hall and took a leading part in the frequent musical evenings they arranged at home. Neighbours and friends would be invited to a cold supper, followed by a night made merry with choruses around the piano in the candle-lit drawing room, nights that were recalled and discussed long after the final chords of 'Auld Lang Syne' had died away and the guests had departed to their homes.

The new house became a focal point for members of the Ballantyne family who had left Edinburgh to seek careers elsewhere, and hardly a month passed by without some relative visiting Abercromby Place. James, the eldest Ballantyne brother, had suffered the loss of his wife Violet soon after their marriage, the unfortunate woman succumbing to an attack of cholera within two years of their arrival in India. She left her widowed husband with two small children to care for, and, in the spring of 1859, he returned to Scotland on leave for a two-month stay in Edinburgh. While he was there the Nelsons commissioned Bob to write a new book in which his eldest brother's knowledge of Eastern affairs would prove most valuable, and he wrote his sister-in-law, who was away visiting her parents' home at Scremerston, Berwick-on-Tweed, to acquaint her with the glad news:

Monday evening.
[*April*, 1859]

My dearest Teenie,

I've got two minutes to write & then go to dress to dine at Constable's with Jane.

I went out to Nelson's today & he has decided that the *Overland Route to India* is to be re-written by me—to be 350 pages bigger than *Martin Rattler*—to be illustrated like the old one, *in colours*, and to have my name on the title page. In fact it is an order for a new book by the talented young author R.M.B.!

I came home quite full of it—but alas! who was there to tell it to? It's work that I'll like far before Canada. James will be able to correct me too! and also to suggest.

I'll leave this open and add a line tomorrow. Adieu for tonight, my own pet.

Thine ever,
R.M.B.

With James's expert help with matters oriental, Bob completed the manuscript of *The Overland Route to India* in less than four months, drawing extensively on textbooks which had already been written on the subject. But, after inspecting the manuscript,[1] the Nelson brothers decided against publication, giving as their reason the sudden proliferation of books which had appeared on India due to the outbreak of the mutiny which was then raging with unabated fury. Ballantyne's disappointment was somewhat assuaged by their agreeing to pay him an agreed sum for his labours.

That year also brought the lamentable and prostrating news that his youngest sister, Williamina, had given birth in Germany to a son out of wedlock. This horrifying disclosure sent a shudder through the entire family, whose Free Church of Scotland respectability was utterly scandalised by the unbelievable tidings. The unfortunate young lady was seldom mentioned in polite conversation for many years to come. Even after her marriage to a Mr. Wight and their establishing a home at Stettin, in Germany, her sisters refused to receive any communication from her and it was only through Bob that a desultory correspondence with this gay, attractive, but impetuous and headstrong, member of the Ballantyne family was eventually resumed.

But for her brother there were no amorous entanglements or indeed any thought of any. He must have appeared a most eligible bachelor and a fine catch for any Edinburgh young lady —but he remained quite unassailable, content with the company of John, Teenie and the three children. One can only wonder if the last of these light-hearted verses which Ballantyne carefully

[1] This unpublished manuscript is still amongst R. M. Ballantyne's papers.

copied into a notebook some years later give us any clue as to why at that time he preferred to stay single. Continuing an inviolate bachelor until he was over forty seems to call for some explanation other than a lost childhood sweetheart or a perfectionist attitude towards women.

My Brother John[1]

In form and feature, face and limb,
I grew so like my brother,
That folks got taking me for him,
And each for one another.
It puzzled all our Kith and Kin,
It reached a fearful pitch;
For one of us was born a twin—
And not a soul knew which!

One day to make the matter worse,
Before our names were fixed,
While we were being washed by nurse,
We got completely mixed.
And thus you see, by fate's decree,
Or, rather, nurse's whim,
My brother John was christened me,
And I was christened him!

This fatal likeness even dogged
My footsteps when at school,
And I was always being flogged
For John turned out a fool.
I put this question fruitlessly
To every one I knew;
What would you do if you were me
To prove that I was you?

Our strong resemblance turned the tide
Of my domestic life,
For, somehow, my intended bride
Became my brother's wife!

[1] These verses first appeared in *Carols of Cockayne* by H. S. Leigh, published in 1869.

And thus, from year to year, the same
Absurd mistakes went on;
And when I died, the neighbours came,
An' buried brother John!

In the autumn of 1859, a disaster occurred which shocked all Britain, details of the tragedy filling the pages of the newspapers for several weeks. Seven years before, Teenie's brother and his wife, Peter and Georgina Hogarth, had sailed with their small daughter, Agatha, aboard the *Lord Delaval* for Australia, hoping to strike it rich and make their fortunes at the famed McIvor diggings, where gold had been discovered in considerable quantities. By the time they arrived at their destination, the McIvor strike had been exhausted, and although Peter continued prospecting at various localities for nearly two years, his luck was out, both he and his wife being forced to secure what employment they could in Melbourne. Within a few months of their arrival, young Agatha contracted dysentery and died, but a son, Robert, was born soon afterwards, and tales of his activities filled pages of their letters home.

Only lack of capital made Peter reluctantly give up the search for the elusive gold, and his tales of the fortunes being made by some of his lucky companions finally persuaded his brother, Robert, to join him in Australia. But the two hundred pounds he brought with him soon went the same way as his brother's savings, and, in the summer of 1859, the whole family were forced to make a dispirited return to their native Scotland. They could scrape together only enough money to travel steerage class, but they managed to book passages in the *Royal Charter* steam clipper, a fast boat which was expected to reach Liverpool in about two months.

But on the 25th October, when almost within sight of their destination, a storm of unprecedented violence burst on the heavily laden vessel as she battled her way through the Irish Sea. Tremendous waves battered the leaking ship and, amid scenes of panic and hysteria, she was smashed to pieces on the rocks of the Anglesey coast.

John and Bob Ballantyne had travelled to Liverpool to greet the return of the members of Teenie's family, and were waiting, unsuspecting of the tragedy, with a large group of relatives of the passengers, in a hotel near the landing stage. The violence of the gale had blown down most of the telegraph wires in the area, and it was not until the following morning that news reached the town of the catastrophe. The message contained the words 'Some survivors have been landed at Moelfra,' and a rush was made by the grief-stricken relations and friends of those on the ship to secure transport to the scene of the wreck. It was over twenty-four hours before Bob and his brother were able to reach the village, and there they were greeted by the appalling news that out of a total of over five hundred passengers and crew, only twenty-seven of those on board had survived.

Every tide cast the battered remains of a few of the drowned on the shore at the foot of the cliffs, but most were unrecognisable and had to be identified, when this was possible, by the contents of their pockets and the papers they carried. The Ballantynes stayed for two days in the hope of obtaining the bodies of the Hogarths for burial in Scotland, but were finally forced to return alone to a broken-hearted Teenie and the months of mourning which convention demanded. The bodies of Robert, Peter and Georgina Hogarth were eventually recovered from the beach and buried in Llanallgo churchyard, where the majority of those who perished found a resting place. Little Bobby Hogarth was never found, and neither was a large proportion of the other passengers and crew.[1]

The harrowing scenes he witnessed at Moelfra as the bereaved searched for their dead left an indelible picture in Bob's mind of the human suffering a storm at sea can cause, and the utter helplessness of those on shore, although, as in this case, the stricken vessel may be only a few hundred yards from land. Here was a worthwhile cause that he could espouse, and he told Teenie that he would henceforth devote a portion of his energy to awakening the public conscience to the appalling lack of lifesaving equipment around the coasts of Britain. He made her a promise that

[1] The story of the disaster can be read in *An Authentic Account of the Wreck of the Royal Charter Steam Clipper*, by A. & J. K[ennedy], Dublin, M'Glashan & Gill, 1860; and also *The Golden Wreck*, McVee (Souvenir Press), 1860.

he would do all he could to make those in authority realise that lifeboats and rocket-firing apparatus should be available at every locality that could be considered dangerous to shipping; and, as things turned out, this proved to be no idle resolution to be forgotten at the first opportunity. In fact, as will be seen, it exercised a considerable influence over his future career.

During the early part of the same year he had become smitten with the idea of starting his own magazine for boys, and with this in mind he had spent weeks working on the layout of the proposed paper, preparing material for what he hoped would be the first issue. He put together a prototype for the publisher's inspection and approval, and posted it off with hopeful expectancy. But, to his disappointment, one by one the Edinburgh publishing houses turned down the idea, Nelson's, Blackwood's and Constable's all giving good reasons why they thought they were not the right people to market such a periodical, or in fact have anything to do with it. Disheartened by the refusals, Bob tried the smaller firm of Edmonston and Douglas, of Fores Street, Edinburgh, enclosing the following letter.

30th November, 1859.

My dear Sirs,

According to promise I now send you the first number of the magazine, about which I spoke to you today, and my jottings in reference to it for your own consideration.

It would be named *Ballantyne's Magazine for Young People*, and it will come out in monthly parts consisting of 48 pages, a little larger than crown octavo. It will be printed in double columns and will have four or five illustrations—woodcuts.

The sale of 3000 copies per month at 6*d*. would just about cover the cost of production and pay all expenses *including* publisher's commission at 10 per cent. The sale of 5000 copies at 6*d*. would leave a profit at the end of the year of about £265.

The terms would be that I am to be the sole and independent Editor. I shall furnish most of the material myself, which shall consist of original and selected matter, but the bulk of each number to be original. It shall not be what is termed a 'religious periodical,' but religion shall have a place in it. The first article in each number shall be a portion of a story by the Editor.

This is a rough sketch of what I propose, but the Editor will pledge himself to no rigid plan. He will modify all his arrangements should time and experience render modification advisable. In conclusion, let me say that I am willing to take all the risk of production etc., on my own shoulders. The material in the specimen number herewith sent is about the amount required to fill a monthly part. In the pocket of this number you will find the design for the cover of the magazine and the sketches for the first part.

I shall call on you in a day or two, meanwhile I remain,

My dear Sir,

Yours very truly,

R. M. BALLANTYNE.

P.S.   I may also say that, if it were deemed advisable, I could procure testimonials in favour of my magazine from all the leading men in Edinburgh, besides others throughout the Kingdom. Pray consider this letter strictly private. R.M.B.

The author had completed the prototype only after a great deal of trouble and effort, even incurring the expense of having an eight-page sheet of a serial story[1] specially printed, in order to show the publisher the size of type and quality of paper he would like used. The folder, in which the original material has been preserved, is full of his ideas for puzzles, games, illustrations, and parts of stories, as well as a suggested layout for the title-page and a drawing for the cover. The project must have taken many long hours in preparation, and the polite but definite refusal with which Messrs. Edmonston and Douglas answered his letter must have come as a deep disappointment. With this final rebuttal, his scheme for starting *Ballantyne's Magazine* appears to have been reluctantly abandoned by the aspiring editor, and there is no further evidence that he ever revived the idea.

[1] This tale was entitled *The Golden Dream* and was later published by Messrs. John F. Shaw & Company.

The preparation of the proposed magazine could not have interfered too greatly with his other literary work, and by writing several hours each day he had now reached the stage of being able to complete several full-length books every twelve months, in addition to which he contributed short articles to newspapers and periodicals. *The World of Ice; or Adventures in the Polar Regions* had appeared in November, 1859[1] while a factual narrative called *Discovery and Adventure in the Polar Seas and Regions* to which Ballantyne added a continuation to the text of Sir John Leslie and Hugh Murray, so as to cover the ill-fated Sir John Franklin expedition, was published by Nelson's in midsummer 1860.

By the time this book appeared he had completed yet another adventure story, a tale of the intrepid Dick Varley and his dramatic escapes from Red Indians and grizzly bears in the Rocky Mountains of North America, accompanied by a faithful Newfoundland dog which he had earlier saved from a squaw's cooking-pot. He called this book *The Dog Crusoe*, and finished it in time to accept the Cowan family's invitation to be once more their guest on a yacht trip to Scandinavia. Within a few weeks of completing the manuscript he was back in Norway, fighting the salmon in the fjords and lakes and sketching and painting watercolour views of the magnificent scenery for the benefit of the folks back home.

Life was again sweet and the only upset, happily a comical one, was the letters he kept receiving, including one from his brother James, all pointing out, often in a gleeful manner, the blunder he had made in his book *The Coral Island* regarding the shape, size and appearance of coconuts when in their natural habitat. He admitted the mistake in his autobiographical work published in 1893:[2]

> . . . despite the utmost care of which I was capable, while studying up for the *Coral Island*, I fell into . . . a blunder through ignorance in regard to a familiar fruit.

[1] Like many other books which Thomas Nelson & Sons published, *The World of Ice* was dated forward. Volumes which appeared in the last few months of a year carried the date of the following year—*The World of Ice* being dated 1860.

[2] *Personal Reminiscences in Book-Making*. London, 1893.

I was under the impression that cocoa-nuts grew on their trees in the same form as that in which they are usually presented to us in grocers' windows—namely, about the size of a large fist with three spots, suggestive of a monkey's face, at one end. I sent one of my heroes up a tree for a nut, through the shell of which he bored a hole with a penknife and drank the 'lemonade'. . . . but in fact the cocoa-nut is nearly as large as a man's head, and its outer husk over an inch thick, so that no ordinary penknife could bore into its interior!

It is interesting to note that the first illustration in Bowman's *The Island Home; or, The Young Cast-Aways*, actually shows a boy up a cocoa-palm in the act of throwing down three nuts, and the artist who drew the picture has inadvertently made them look about the size one generally sees them in greengrocers' shops. However, on page ninety-seven of this work the outer husk is, in fact, mentioned:

> . . . Tearing off the outer husk, and punching a hole through the shell, which in the young nut is so soft that this can be done with the finger, we drank off the refreshing liquor with which it is filled . . .

The error he made in *The Coral Island* and other inaccuracies which had occurred in his books helped to persuade Ballantyne that he should not only read up his subject, but also do his best to gain first-hand experience of the locality in which he proposed to set a tale:

> I formed a resolution always to visit—when possible— the scenes in which my stories were laid, converse with the people who, under modification, were to form the *dramatis personae* of the tales, and generally to obtain information in each case, as far as lay in my power, from the fountain head.[1]

On his return from Norway he told Nelson's frankly that in future he would insist upon retaining the copyright of any work he wrote—he had suffered enough annoyance by seeing his books appearing in edition after edition while not earning him another

[1] *Personal Reminiscences in Book-Making.* London, 1893.

penny, and he would henceforth demand a substantial return commensurate with his popularity as an author. He informed them that he would seek terms not only from themselves but from other publishers, and would accept the best rate available while retaining the copyright. The Nelson family had long been personal friends, and had it not been for Teenie pushing him from behind, it is doubtful whether Bob would have been so forthright, but in the event he managed to part company with his old publishers without enmity and for some years afterwards they continued to put a considerable amount of work his way. Ballantyne never failed to call on the family during his visits to Edinburgh after he had moved elsewhere, and he was generous enough to say that it was only in the business sense that he found them a little too shrewd and sagacious with an author who could not in the least pretend to commercial astuteness.

He sold his book, *The Golden Dream*, on a royalty basis to John F. Shaw & Company, a small London firm who specialised in the publication of works dealing with religious subjects, but who had little idea of the marketing of adventure books for boys. Their current publications included such titles as *Moses Right and Bishop Colenso Wrong*, by the Rev. Dr. Cumming; *The Spiritual Casket of Daily Bible Meditations*, by John Evangelist Gossner; *The Midnight Cry*, by Rev. Samuel Garrett; *Lessons for Maidens*, by the Rev. W. Landels, etc., etc., continuing with similar titles for the whole twenty-four pages of the advertisements which they inserted at the back of the volumes they published. Sandwiched between these fist-shaking clerical gnomes was the advertisement for *The Golden Dream*, by R. M. Ballantyne, a rip-roaring story of adventure in the Far West, laced with a little homespun theology, but full of such dramatic incidents as attacks by grizzly bears, lynchings, gunfights, and the feuds and excitements of the great Californian gold rush. With its misleading title and the knell-tolling imprint of Messrs. Shaw & Company, it is little wonder that the boy readers of the sixties believed it to be yet another theological treatise 'modified for younger minds.' They left it severely alone and the unsold balance of the original two thousand copies had later to be 'remaindered' at a give-away price.

This was hardly a good beginning for an author trying to keep his independence and Bob was disheartened by the fate the book suffered. Yet the story was well written and excitingly told, and, when James Nisbet & Company republished the work in 1870, no less than eight new editions were sold in a space of twenty years, with a total volume of eight thousand copies.[1]

Why Ballantyne was so foolish as to choose Shaw & Company in the first place is not known, unless he took the advice of the elders of the local kirk with which he was connected, and through whose hands many of Shaw's publications would probably have passed. But he showed a little more acumen by next approaching Messrs. Routledge, Warne & Routledge, a company who had an excellent reputation for the quality of their children's books and a wide knowledge of the juvenile market. An understanding was reached whereby the publishers agreed to Bob retaining the copyrights of his stories, and they contracted to pay him a royalty for every thousand copies sold. He signed this agreement with Routledge in the new year and almost at once he received a commission from Nelson's for an instructional book for boys, the rate to be three shillings and sixpence for each printed page, and he was free to submit a title and subject of his own choosing. He could hardly quarrel with terms such as these and he immediately accepted the offer, stating that the book would describe man's struggle to conquer the oceans of the world.

At the same time he was contemplating an attempt at a major work in oils, a painting he intended to call *The Lifeboat*, containing all the drama of a storm-tossed, sinking ship, with help appearing just in time to rescue the despairing passengers and crew. If he was able to depict the scene with sufficient vividness, he hoped the painting could be exhibited, and later sold, to raise funds to help purchase a lifeboat for use around the Scottish coast, and for this project he had already gained the support of a number of local societies.

With two books commissioned and a large oil painting to start, Bob obtained leave of absence from the family and moved into a small country cottage where he could work in peace, perhaps

[1] I am able to give accurate details regarding the sales of his books by using the notes which Ballantyne made in respect of them.

doing a little fishing as a pleasant relaxation between spells of work.

It was here that he wrote *The Red Eric; or The Whaler's Last Cruise*, which appeared for sale at three shillings and sixpence a copy in September 1861. He also expended much effort on *Man on the Ocean*, an instructional and historical tale of ships and the art of navigation which Messrs. Nelson's had commissioned; but he found the task laborious and slow moving, much preferring fictional stories which did not entail the continual checking of facts and figures. Ballantyne's account of *Man on the Ocean* brought him in some seventy-five pounds when it finally appeared as a four-hundred-page book, and, had he been able to complete it quickly, it would have shown a profitable return for his labour. But in fact he was working at it, on and off, for some eighteen months, and it slowed down his fictional output at a time when the family finances were once again running into difficulties.

In the spring of 1861, Paul du Chaillu's book, *Exploration in Equatorial Africa*, was published, containing accounts of the activities of the gorilla, a species of animal about which little was then known. His tales of the 'ferocious wild men of the forest,' as he termed the great anthropoid apes, engrossed the public imagination, especially as the book appeared in the midst of the controversy aroused by the publication of Charles Darwin's *On the Origin of the Species*.[1] The Nelson brothers were not slow in perceiving the possibility of an exciting juvenile fictional story being written on the subject, and Ballantyne was offered eighty pounds providing he could complete a tale about gorillas in time for Christmas publication. He set to work immediately, and, by spending days at the printer's offices, correcting proof sheets as they issued from the press, he just managed to accomplish his part of the task on time—but the book did not arrive in the shops until the last week before Christmas. Nelson's sense of timing and business acumen paid dividends, for the publicity given to du Chaillu's work ensured *The Gorilla Hunters* a wide sale; the title appealed to the juvenile imagination, and the fact that Ralph Rover, Jack Martin and Peterkin Gay, whom they had already met in *The Coral Island*, were three characters of this

[1] Darwin's *On the Origin of Species* was published in October 1859.

146

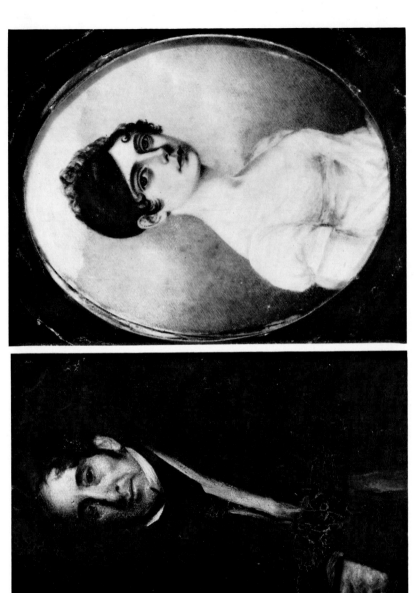

Sandy and Randall Ballantyne

R. M. Ballantyne in New York aged twenty-two

R. M. Ballantyne and his brother, John, in the uniform of the Edinburgh
Volunteer Corps, 1859

Jeanie and Bob. A photograph taken the day before their marriage

Dressed to descend the Botallack tin mine

R. M. Ballantyne after his walk from London to Edinburgh

R. M. Ballantyne in 1893, shortly before he left for Rome

Terrible Encounter with a Shark. Reproduced from the first edition of *Coral Island* published by Thomas Nelson and Sons, 1858

tale also, gave an added stimulus to the popularity of the book.

In his story of *The Gorilla Hunters*, Ballantyne makes his readers suffer several philosophical discourses, revealing to them the *modus vivendi* he thinks they should adopt if they are not to be greeted by their stalwart friends and more manly school-fellows with sardonic sneers and be for ever dubbed as weaklings and 'mimini-pimini muffs.' He sets the tale in the heart of darkest Africa, where the three young heroes are intent on killing the maximum number of gorillas in the minimum possible time, plus any other of the continent's fauna which might inadvertently stray within range of their guns.

The principal characters in this plot to wage relentless war on the animal kingdom consist of the narrator, Ralph Rover, a rather sober-sided individual who acts as the leader of the expedition, Jack Martin, 'a tall, strapping, broad-shouldered youth of eighteen, with a handsome, good-humoured, firm face,' and Peterkin Gay, 'little, quick, funny, decidedly mischievous, and about fourteen years old.' Viewed from the standpoint of an author, this is a very malleable and interesting threesome to work with, the contrasting idiosyncrasies of its members making each easy to identify in the mind of the reader without talented inflexions of emphasis. Ballantyne succeeds in employing quite a modern, sophisticated technique with Ralph Rover, the narrator of the story, by standing back from the character to derive the full benefit of the part he sets him to play, not merely using him as commentator of events.

In his earlier book, *The Coral Island*, the author made full use of the 'Crusoe' tradition, deriving intense reader-identification from the efforts of the three marooned boys to fend for themselves in a strange and hostile environment. The young followers of the tale must often have imagined themselves in a similar situation—cast away on a desert island, with only their own wits and courage holding the balance between survival and a lingering death. And in *The Gorilla Hunters*, Ballantyne once again plays on the deep-seated fears of the young by confronting them with forces which would overwhelm them if not ruthlessly destroyed. Even if one takes the view that most boys are bloodthirsty little savages beneath the veneer which civilised society imparts, one still has to explain why this should be so; and also why a book as cruel and vicious in its treatment of wild animals as *The Gorilla Hunters* turns out to be, should have been so immensely popular with the boys of the latter half of the nineteenth century.

The psychological reasons for this are doubtless many and complex. One can be found in the fact that many children have at some time in their lives experienced a frightening sense of insecurity, perhaps engendered by a parental quarrel or the overhearing of a chance phrase or remark. One result of realising that his world may not after all be inviolate may be that the child has to endure the terrifying dream of being relentlessly pursued by ferocious animals, while his own frantically fleeing feet are slowed to a crawl by quagmire sands stretching away to bottomless cliffs over which he plunges to tearful wakefulness. This type of nightmare is common enough in childhood, and to read about the destruction of their imaginary enemies, be they human or animal, may still sub-conscious fears and rejoice the hearts of boys who would never admit to their fellows that they themselves were not just as brave and courageous as the fictional heroes whose exploits they followed in the lurid and bloodthirsty pages of the books of Ballantyne, Manville Fenn, Kingston or Henty.

The readers of *The Gorilla Hunters* did not have long to wait for action, and before the end of chapter three the trio had already bagged a leopard and killed a fully grown buffalo. Ralph Rover then soliloquises to give a picture of what the author apparently believes to be the type of life a boy should endeavour to lead.

I was deeply impressed with the importance of boys being inured from childhood to trifling risks and slight dangers of every possible description, such as tumbling into ponds and off trees, etc., in order to strengthen their nervous system. . . They ought to practise leaping off heights into deep water. They ought never to hesitate to cross a stream on a narrow unsafe plank for fear of a ducking. They ought never to decline to climb up a tree to pull off fruit, merely because there is a possibility of their falling off and breaking their necks. I firmly believe that boys were intended to encounter all kinds of risks in order to prepare them to meet and grapple with the risks and dangers incident to a man's career with cool, cautious self-possession, a self-possession founded on experimental knowledge of the character and powers of their own spirits and muscles.

The muff is a boy who from natural disposition, or early training, or both, is mild, diffident and gentle. So far he is an estimable character. Were this all, he were not a muff. In order to deserve that title he must be timid and unenthusiastic. He must refuse to venture anything that will subject him to danger, however slight. He must be afraid of a shower of rain; afraid of dogs in general, good and bad alike; disinclined to try bold things; indifferent about learning how to swim. He must object to the game called 'dumps,' because the blows from the ball are sometimes severe, and be a sworn enemy to single-stick, because the whacks are uncommonly painful. So feeling and acting, he will, when he becomes a man, find himself unable to act in the common emergencies of life; to protect a lady from insolence; to guard his home from robbery; or to save his own child should it chance to fall into the water.

Let muffs, therefore, learn to swim, to leap, and to run. Let them wrestle with boys bigger than themselves, regardless of being thrown. Let them practise 'jinking' with their companions, so that if ever they be chased by a mad bull, they will, if unable to get out of his way by running, escape perhaps by jinking. Let them learn to leap off considerable heights into deep water, so that, if ever called on to leap off the end of a pier or the side of a ship to save a fellow creature, they may do so with confidence and promptitude. Let them even put on 'the gloves,' and become regardless of a swelled nose, in order that they may be able to defend themselves or others from sudden assault. So doing they will become sensible fellows, whose character I have thus, to some extent, described. Of course I speak of sensible fellows only with reference to this one subject of training the nerves and muscles. Let it never be forgotten that there are men who, although sensible in this respect, are uncommonly senseless in regard to other things of far higher moment.

The next few chapters are littered with the carcases of the lions, elephants, zebra and other denizens of the jungle which they encountered, until finally they stumble on the spoor of a large gorilla.

Here was the footstep of that creature about which we had heard so many wonderful stories, whose existence the civilised world had, up to within a very short time back, doubted exceedingly, and in regard to which, even now, we knew comparatively very little. . . Shouldering our trusty rifles and buckling tight the belts of our heavy hunting knives, we sallied forth after the manner of American Indians, in single file, keeping, as may well be supposed, a sharp look out as we went along.

Presently we came to a part of the forest where the underwood became so dense that we could scarcely make our way through it at all, and here we began for the first time to have some clearer conception of the immense power of the creature we were in pursuit of, for, in order to clear its way, it had torn down great branches of the trees, and, in one or two places had seized young trees as thick as a man's arm, and snapt them in two as one would snap a walking cane. Following the track with the utmost care for several miles, we at length came to a place where several huge rocks lay among the trees. Here, while we were walking along in silence, Makarooroo made a peculiar noise with his tongue, which we knew meant that he had discovered something worthy of special attention, so we came to an abrupt pause and looked at him.

'What is it, Mak?' inquired Jack.

The guide put his finger on his mouth to impose silence, and stood in a listening attitude with his eyes cast upon the ground, his nostrils distended, and every muscle of his dusky frame rigid as if he were a statue of black marble. We also listened attentively, and presently heard a sound as of the breaking of twigs and branches.

'Dat am be gorilla,' said the guide in a low whisper.

We exchanged looks of eager satisfaction.

Title page from *The Gorilla Hunters*, first published in 1861

Our First Gorilla

'What can he be doing?' said I to the guide, as we stood looking at each other for a few seconds, uncertain how to act.

'Him's breakin' down branches for git at him's food, 'spose.'

'Do you see that?' whispered Peterkin as he pointed to an open space among the bushes. 'Isn't that a bit o' the hairy brute?'

'It looks like it,' replied Jack eagerly.

'Cluck!' ejaculated Makarooroo, making a peculiar noise with his tongue. 'Dat him. Blaze away!'

'But it may not be a mortal part,' objected Peterkin. 'He might escape if only wounded.'

'Nebber fear. Hims come at us if hims be wound. Only we mus' be ready for him.'

'All ready,' said Jack, cocking both barrels of his rifle, 'now, Peterkin, a good aim. If he comes here he shall get a quietus.'

All this was said in the lowest possible whispers. Peterkin took steady aim at the part of the creature that was visible, and fired.

I have gone through many wild adventures since then. I have heard the roar of the lion and tiger in all circumstances, and the laugh of the hyaena, besides many other hideous sounds, but I never in all my life listened to anything that in any degree approached in thundering ferocity the appalling roar that burst upon our ears immediately that shot was fired. . . And it was not uttered once or twice, but again and again until the whole woods trembled with it, and we felt as if our ears could not endure more of it without the tympanums being burst.

For several moments we stood motionless with our guns ready, expecting an immediate attack, and gazing with awe, not unmingled—at least on my part—with fear, at the turmoil of leaves and twigs and broken branches that was going on round the spot where the monster was wounded.

'Come,' cried Jack at length, losing patience and springing forward, 'if he won't attack us we must attack him.'

We followed close at his heels, and the next moment emerged upon a small and comparatively open space, in the midst of which we found the gorilla seated on the ground, tearing up the earth with its hands, grinning horribly and beating its chest, which sent forth a loud hollow sound as if it were a large drum. We saw at once that both its thighs had been broken by Peterkin's shot.

Of all the hideous creatures I had ever seen or heard of, none came up in the least degree to this. Apart altogether from its gigantic size, this monster was calculated to strike terror into the hearts of beholders simply by the expression of its visage, which was quite satanic. I could scarcely persuade myself that I was awake! It seemed as if I were gazing at one of the hideous creatures one beholds when oppressed with night-mare!

But we had little time to indulge in contemplation, for the instant the brute beheld us, it renewed its terrible roar and attempted to spring up, but both its legs at once gave way, and it fell with a passionate growl, biting the earth and twisting and tearing bunches of twigs and leaves in its fury. Suddenly it rushed upon us rapidly by means of its fore legs or arms.

'Look out, Jack!' we cried in alarm.

Jack stood like a rock and deliberately levelled his rifle. Even at this moment of intense excitement I could not help marvelling at the diminutive appearance of my friend when contrasted with the gorilla. In height, indeed, he was of course superior, and would have been so had the gorilla been able to stand erect, but his breadth of shoulder and chest, and his length of arm were strikingly inferior. Just as the monster approached to within three yards of him, Jack sent a ball into its chest, and the king of the African woods fell dead at our feet!

It is impossible to convey in words an idea of the gush of mingled feelings that filled our breasts as we stood beside and gazed at the huge carcase of our victim. Pity at first predominated in my heart; then I felt like an accomplice to a murder; and then an exulting sensation of joy at having obtained a specimen of one of the rarest of animals in the world overwhelmed every other feeling.

This unfortunate beast was only the first victim in a long string of similar killings, until the three boys had almost lost count of their bloody victories:

'It seems to me,' [said Jack], that notwithstanding the short time we stayed in the gorilla country, we have been pretty successful. Haven't we bagged thirty-three altogether?'

'Thirty-six, if you count the babies in arms,' responded Peterkin.

'Of course we are entitled to count those.'

'I think you are both out in your reckoning,' said I, drawing out my note-book; 'the last baby that I shot was our thirty-seventh.'

'What!' cried Peterkin, 'the one with the desperately black face and the horrible squint, that nearly tore all the hair out of Jack's head before he managed to strangle it? That wasn't a baby; it was a big boy, and I have no doubt a big rascal besides.'

'That may be so,' I rejoined; 'but whatever he was, I have him down as number thirty-seven in my list.'

'Pity we didn't make up the forty,' observed Jack.

Whatever a more enlightened age may think of such descriptions of wanton cruelty appearing in the pages of a juvenile adventure book, there can be little doubt that both the author and his publisher were well satisfied with the reception it received in the eighteen-sixties, for the tale passed through numerous editions during the succeeding years. Bob Ballantyne was more than pleased with the lump sum he obtained on its completion, for the various members of his family seemed in constant need of financial help and the windfall was soon dispersed amongst the impoverished brothers and sisters with which he was surrounded.

His brother John was finding it extremely difficult to find clients even at reduced prices, but the biggest drain on Bob's resources was now his sister Randall, who had gone to Pau in France to instruct pupils in English and other languages. A number of Scottish families had taken up residence in the town and she had founded her little school with high hopes of success, believing that later she would be able to enlarge the establishment by employing other teachers. But the persistent dry cough from which she had suffered since her return from Italy never left her, the recurring bouts of debilitating weakness with which it was accompanied becoming more and more frequent, causing constant interruptions to her pupils' studies, until, one by one, they were withdrawn, and poor Randall found herself practically penniless. It was to Bob she turned for help, and in October 1861 she wrote:

> . . . I have alas, now no pupils and no prospect of any, Mrs. Hill and all my old friends having left Pau, and two new German masters having come to settle here. I feel horribly knocked down at present, but am trying hard to cast all my burdens on the Lord, and I think things may yet turn a wee bit brighter. I have already got ready a few things for magazines which I send by Henry Carpenter, who goes to Liverpool on Monday next, and I want you to send them (if you think them fit) to the *Sunday At Home* (the hymn I mean) and the others to any other magazine you like.

She sent her brother a series of stories and poems for inclusion in periodicals of one kind and another, hoping to earn a few pounds by their acceptance and thus lighten the burden which Bob carried by supporting her. The poor man must have suffered the acute embarrassment of breaking the news that they had all been refused, for a careful search of the magazines she named in her letters reveals that not one of them ever appeared.

Only a few months later she died of consumption of the lungs, leaving assets worth less than fifty pounds. Most of this sum went towards paying for the funeral and the erection of a headstone to mark her grave, but the whole of the doctor's bill and the other expenses inevitably incurred in a long illness fell on the shoulders of her uncomplaining youngest brother, who had arrived in Pau a few days before her death in respect to an urgent telegram from her physician. Randall's thin and wasted body was cradled in Bob's arms when she died, and the tears he shed that day were for a sister he loved very dearly. Each of her brothers and sisters sent a wreath, but of all her scattered relatives only Robert Ballantyne followed her coffin to the grave in the Protestant cemetery.

Throughout his life he always seemed to be footing the bill for some impoverished member of his family. He was a singularly unworldly and ungrasping man, who hated arguments about money and usually had to be prodded into action by Teenie (or later, his wife) before he would take any action to recover a debt, or gently remind a borrower of his obligations. With close relatives he insisted on regarding any help given as a gift, perhaps repayable if fortune really smiled, but if not, then he would persuade himself that the pleasure he felt at being able to help was enough recompense. As in the case of George Watt of Kelso, he could demand payment on behalf of others, but seldom for himself.

His brother John was now beginning to feel the pinch of tightened purse-strings, and had at last been forced to accept that he was no longer regarded by the Scottish public as a fashionable and talented portrait painter. In 1860 he had been raised to the rank of Academician in the Royal Scottish Academy, but unfortunately the School of Design, at which he had been a master for the previous seventeen years, was that summer placed under the direction of the London Board of Trustees, who wrote to state that his services as teacher in the Life Class would no longer be required. By way of sweetening the news, they announced that they were prepared to grant him a pension of seventy-eight pounds per annum for the rest of his life. When the shock of learning that his services were being dispensed with had worn off, John professed himself pleased with the opportunity that was now presented to him of starting afresh, for he knew that his teaching had seriously interfered with any prospects he might have had in the field of portrait painting. But all the money they had saved during the fat and prosperous earlier years had gradually dwindled away, and he was compelled by necessity to seek a living elsewhere:

Finding myself thus free from a long & not very profitable servitude, I at once determined to follow out a plan which I had often hoped to have been able to carry out, namely, to pursue my professional career once more in London. But in a manner how different from what I had anticipated did I now find myself returning to the great city! At the age of 47 with a wife & young family & not a halfpenny in my possession except my pension of £78 per annum did I commence an artist's life in London.[1]

It was only after much heart-searching that the decision was finally taken to move south, but the fresh opportunities that could be sought, the chance to augment his income by starting a class of private students, and the fact that most of his contemporaries were now successfully established in the capital and could do much to help him, made the choice an obvious one. In February 1862 he left Edinburgh for London, and at the end of the year Teenie joined him a for a few weeks in order to find a house for the family, leaving the children in the care of their Uncle Bob, aided by Janet the maid.

By this time Bob was much in demand as a lecturer and was fast becoming an old hand at the game, quite enjoying the hold he was able to command over an audience. Instead of waiting to be engaged to speak by a local society, he would sometimes hire a hall himself and advertise the event in the newspapers, often going out a few days before, a satchel of ready pasted posters on his shoulder, surreptitiously sticking them on any vacant spaces he could find. Samples of some of these have been preserved in a scrap book (see page 159).

According to the accounts given in the Press, the lectures were quite a success and they soon became a regular feature of his life. He added further titles to his repertoire, such as 'Norway'; 'The Lifeboat'; and later, 'The Fire Brigade'; 'Cornish Mines', etc. The 'other voices' mentioned on the programme above were usually composed of any local singers whom Ballantyne could train to learn the words in time for the meeting, and some amusing (and awful) moments occurred when carefully rehearsed cues were missed, or the wrong song was suddenly voiced by a dozen eager baritones in the wings. But the result was usually

[1] This is an extract from an autobiographical fragment which John Ballantyne commenced writing in 1843, adding notes at intervals until 1874.

worth all the trouble and anxiety, for if he succeeded in filling the hall, he was able to earn anything up to nine pounds after all expenses were paid, although the average was nearer four or five.

A LECTURE ON HUDSON'S BAY
and
THE FROZEN NORTH
by
R. M. BALLANTYNE
*Embellished with slides from the
Magic Lantern
And the singing of canoe songs by
Mr. Ballantyne
With the assistance of other voices*
Places 2/- each.   Families of three and upwards 1/6*d.* each
Back of the Hall 1/-

Provided he varied the subject matter he was able to appear several times in the same district, and one winter he lectured on five consecutive evenings in the same Edinburgh hall.

One such lecture is described in a letter to Teenie, dated December 1862:

> I spoke pretty well the first lecture, but too fast and did not feel easy because I thought I was not taking. I was mistaken in this so the next night I spoke easily and fluently and more slowly. You know, this is the first time I have ever walked on to a large platform alone (without even a table to go behind) and come forward to the edge of it—visible from head to toe—without paper of any kind, and begun to speak! For you see I did not go to the table and use my notes until the gas was put down. I was a little nervous, but it soon wore off. I'm a hardened villain now—that's a fact!

His eldest brother, James, had returned from India in 1861, but sadly broken in health. Since the loss of his wife he had started to drink more and more heavily and had now reached the stage when he was seldom, if ever, completely sober. Combined with the frequent attacks of malaria from which he suffered, this continual drinking had wreaked havoc with an otherwise sound constitution, and Annabella, his second wife, had tearfully confessed to Bob that on more than one occasion only immediate medical aid had revived him after a heavy and prolonged debauch. On James's premature retirement from Benares, the East India Company had appointed him librarian to the India Office in London, a sinecure post with duties of a nature which permitted leisure for a long convalescence, but unfortunately his health had been so undermined by sixteen years out East, and the ravages of alcohol, that he was rarely well enough to venture far from home. His daughter, Bessie, a first-class amateur pianist, had been cared for and schooled in Edinburgh by John and his wife, while his son, Alexander, had left home to become a midshipman in the Royal Navy.

After Teenie had made temporary arrangements to rent rooms at 24 Russell Place, Fitzroy Square, and the children had joined her and John, it was decided that Bob should remain for the time being in Edinburgh to look after the empty house and furniture until they had found a permanent London home. He worked hard at his writing and in November 1862 Routledge published *The Wild Man of the West*. But Bob was far from satisfied with his new publishers and, in January 1863 he wrote to his sister-in-law:

> . . . moreover, Routledge does *not* pay better than Nelson. For secondary tales in the Magazine[1] he pays the same and I'm not writing anything else for him. I am inclined to think that the *Wild Man* has not sold well; that the *Red Eric*[2] has not gone on selling, and that he has lost conceit of me. Anyhow I'll finish my story for him soon & see how he takes it.

It appears from the above statement and other remarks in Ballantyne's letters that neither party was particularly pleased with the bargain they had made, and it was not long before the author was on the look-out for yet another publishing house.

[1] *Routledge's Magazine for Boys*, which first appeared at Christmas 1861, and continued for many years.
[2] *The Red Eric*, published in September 1861. In fact, Ballantyne did write several more tales for Routledge, in spite of his threat not to do so.

Chapter Eight

JAMES NISBET, one of the founders of the Sunday School Union, had started a book-publishing business under his own name at 21, Berners Street, London, in 1825, specialising in religious books and later in books for children and young people. His manager, James Watson, became proprietor of the firm a few years after Nisbet's death, and it was in 1863, while attending a literary dinner in Edinburgh, that he chanced to sit near to Bob. During their conversation, Ballantyne mentioned his difficulties with his present publishers, and Watson responded by asking that a manuscript should be submitted in order that terms for publication might be agreed.

This was the start of the long relationship between James Nisbet & Company and Robert Ballantyne, which continued without a break until the author's death. *Gascoyne—The Sandal-Wood Trader*, the first book Bob submitted, was published in December 1863 (dated the following year), with the rates agreed at forty pounds for each thousand copies sold, the first edition to be fifteen hundred copies and the copyright to remain with the author. 'I have just received a cheque for £80 from Nisbet's in payment of the first 2000 copies of *Gascoyne*,' he wrote to Teenie late in 1864. 'I never received more from Nelson's for any book.'

An aspect of the new relationship which particularly appealed to Ballantyne was Watson's agreement that the firm should publish, not a magazine, but a series of small books to sell at one shilling each under the general title of *Ballantyne's Miscellany*. The author visualised using these little volumes as a medium for instructing the poorer and less educated members of the community in what he considered to be religious truths, at the same time teaching them something of history, geography and science, but with the whole twisted into the thread of an adventure tale, the knowledge being cunningly imparted without the unsuspecting reader being aware of the educational benefit he was receiving. Thus ran the argument by which Ballantyne persuaded his publisher to give his blessing to the scheme.

The first three volumes, entitled *Fighting the Whales, Away in the Wilderness*, and *Fast in the Ice*, all made their appearance in December 1863, and in April the following year, just after the issue of the fourth volume,[1] no doubt in the hope of boosting sales, the author addressed a stereotype holograph letter to many hundreds of church dignitaries, parish priests and curates, throughout the length and breadth of the British Isles.

> 13 *The Mall—Kensington, W.*
> *April*, 1864.

Revd. Sir,

I enclose a few copies of the prospectus of a Miscellany for the poor which I am at present engaged in publishing.

As the success of this work will, under God, depend entirely on its being known to philanthropists—through whom alone I expect it to reach the class for which it is intended—I adopt this method of making it known to you, in order that you may recommend it if you deem it worthy of recommendation.

The volumes are intended for adults, but I am hopeful that they may be found suitable for the young—for whom I have written books for many years past.

Knowing that your time must be too fully occupied to permit of your giving much attention to the subject of this letter, I venture to ask you to do me the favour of giving the copies of the prospectus to any member of your congregation whom you know to be specially interested in the poor.

Trusting that you will not think I take an unwarrantable liberty in thus addressing you,

> I am,
> Revd. Sir,
> Your most obedient servant,
> R. M. BALLANTYNE.

This appeal so moved one Reverend Sir that he wrote:

The Dean of Carlisle having read several of the little volumes of *Ballantyne's Miscellany* has much pleasure in

[1] The fourth volume was titled *Chasing the Sun.*

162

expressing his opinion that they are written in a very pleasing style, and one well calculated to interest and instruct the classes for which they are intended. The writer appears to have attained the peculiar and rare excellence of so interweaving sound religious instruction with his narratives, as not to burden them with prosy observations, and yet never to lose sight of the manifest object which pervades the whole, to save souls.

The Rev. Dr. Andrew Thomson of Edinburgh went even further:

I have read some of Mr. Ballantyne's little volumes through at one sitting, one chapter carrying me to another. I have read them with the same feeling with which, in boyish days, I have sat and listened to a first-rate story-teller —the dashing and brave spirit of adventure, the fine manly moral tone of the narrative, seem to me to render these little volumes eminently adapted for circulation among working men. It would help to promote the moral health of the community not a little, were thousands to be circulated for every one that is circulated now.

One would think that any desire on the part of the Victorian working man to purchase a volume of the *Miscellany* must have been chilled by reading the advertisements quoted above, or in seeing such statements as—'His books are what Dr. Arnold so anxiously desired to see—books on secular subjects written in a religious spirit.' The series obviously could not have proved to be a commercial success, for the fourth volume, which appeared in March 1864, was the last issued by the publishers for nearly six years.

Yet the stories were lively and exciting, although laced with soul-saving evangelism and death-bed repentances, but the exterior appearance of the early volumes was not nearly attractive enough to make the artisan wish to part with his hard-earned shilling. The plain spines of the little books looked drab and uninteresting against the gaiety of the lavishly gilt backs and bright colours of rival publications, but the failure of the original four volumes, in spite of their coloured plates, may well have been that, at a shilling a copy, they were priced out of the market for which they had been intended. Working men and women of the 1860's could seldom, if ever, afford to purchase new books. Those interested in literature relied almost wholly on the lending libraries and the ample supply of second-hand volumes to be found on the market stalls and in the bookshops. Philanthropists preferred to leave a little tract on their genteel calls at the homes of the lower orders, rather than hand out copies of *Fighting the Whales* or *Chasing the Sun*, no matter how well spiced with hints of hellfire and damnation.

Nothing more was attempted with the series for some years, but, with over a dozen short stories in hand, *Ballantyne's Miscellany* was revived by the publishers in 1869, but aimed this time at the middle-class market. Thirteen volumes, each handsomely bound in green cloth, and the whole set encased in a folding cloth box heavily blocked in black and gold, with a list of titles on the lid—this was a fine Christmas present for any boy, but at 15s. far beyond the reach of a working-class father. What was morally desirable had to give way to what was commercially expedient, but, perhaps as a sop, the volumes were still obtainable singly at one shilling each. At the beginning of the 1863 issue a note was printed giving details of the plan of the *Miscellany* and this read:

> There is a vast amount of interesting information on almost all subjects, which the working classes cannot attain to because of the expense, and in some instances, the rarity of the books in which it is contained.
>
> To place some of this information, in an attractive form, within the reach of those who cannot afford to purchase expensive books, is the object and aim of this *Miscellany*.
>
> Truth is stranger than fiction, but fiction is a valuable assistant in the development of truth. Both, therefore, shall be used in these volumes. Care will be taken to ensure, as far as possible, that the facts stated shall be true, and that the impressions given shall be truthful.
>
> As all classes, in every age, have proved that tales and stories are the most popular style of literature, each volume

of the series (with, perhaps, one or two exceptions) will contain a complete tale, the heroes and actors in which, together with the combination of circumstances in which they move, shall be more or less fictitious.

In writing these volumes, the author will earnestly endeavour to bear in remembrance those words of Scripture—'Whatsoever ye do, do all to the glory of God.'

In the opinion of Messrs. Nisbet & Company, this introductory note was having an effect other than intended, and the very class that could afford to buy new books for children were being repelled by the remarks made on the preliminary pages. Therefore, in the thirteen-volume edition of 1869, the emphasis of the first paragraph had been totally changed to read:

There is a vast amount of interesting information on almost all subjects which most people, especially the young, cannot attain to because of the expense, and, in some instances, the rarity of the books in which it is contained.

Having eliminated all reference to the working class, the publishers next prevailed upon the author to tone down his remarks about the Almighty, lest an intending purchaser should think that the religious bias was too strong. Confronted with commercial logic, Bob therefore altered the final paragraph so as completely to remove the Bible text. It now read:

In writing these volumes, the author has earnestly endeavoured to keep in view the glory of God and the good of man.

In its new style, and backed by advertisements in the literary Press, the *Miscellany* at last began to sell—and sell well. Before long the series became a real success and was enlarged by the addition of extra tales until it totalled eighteen volumes. New editions, in many different cloth styles and sizes, kept appearing through the years, continuing at least up to the start of the First World War, and *Ballantyne's Miscellany* finally proved to be one of Bob's most lucrative literary efforts.

Back in the early part of 1864 he had, of course, no idea of the eventual success of these little books—his immediate concern was to find sufficient funds to enable Teenie, John, the children and himself finally to leave Edinburgh in a solvent state. Somehow they had to raise eighty pounds to clear themselves, and on top of that an extra twenty-five or so to pay the removal expenses to London, but even then, although they could start with a clear conscience, something would have to be done pretty quickly, a picture sold or a book paid for, to enable them to find sufficient to meet the grocer's weekly bills. Bob, who had helped them on other occasions, had now not enough in hand to make John any further loan, and he wrote to Teenie to secure her approval of his making a tentative approach to his sister Mary's husband, Hector McKenzie:

Edinburgh. Friday. [*Jan.* 1864]

My dearest Teenie,

When this reaches you it will be the anniversary of your birthday—also of your marriage, I think. May God bless you and John, my dears, and prosper you in all your ways.

The lecture got on well; I delivered it well I think & with great ease. My throat behaved admirably. Afterwards I had a pleasant dinner with Dr. Williamson and an evening with the Lauders.

The attendance at the lecture was pretty good. They say 'better than usual,' but not full. They only gave me £2 10s. 0d. so that's the last I'll do for them. You see the management is in the hands of inferior folk. It would be the last, anyhow, for I'll not be here, I suppose, another winter. Still, I have had a notion of a professional Scottish tour!

A letter from Hector and one from Mary I enclose. I want you to tell me how much of John's affairs you wish me to explain to them in my reply. I must give to Hector as my reason for not complying [with his invitation to come and stay] that I cannot leave you and John at a time like this.

Shall I tell him that we have amongst us to make up to £80 or so, to clear us off here, and that we mean to borrow sufficient money to flit us? I would like to tell him this. He might offer to lend us what we require.

Your last letter was short. I'll forgive it if you write the next longer. I enclose a letter from the bairns.

Dr. Williamson says that my lecture was 'a great hit.' I wish it had been a great gain!

No more news and I must post this before it is too late. God bless you, dearest Teenie.

Your loving brother,

R. M. Ballantyne

As soon as Bob explained to him the financial difficulties which John was experiencing, Hector insisted on being allowed to help and wrote out a cheque for one hundred pounds without more ado. He had returned with his family from Hudson's Bay a moderately wealthy man—the rank of Chief Factor was well paid, and in addition, many legitimate sources of income inevitably accrued to a man who was in the fortunate position of being in sole charge of a large trading station in the backwoods.

On returning to Scotland he had purchased Gollanfield House, Inverness-shire, a largish, well-built property standing in about fifty acres of ground, and there he settled down with his wife and daughter to live the life of a retired country gentleman, spending his idle days in fishing and shooting, and entertaining his friends at weekend house-parties. Since their first meeting at Red River, he and Bob had been firm friends, while Mary, like the rest of sisters, dearly loved her youngest brother, feeling a motherly desire to cosset and care for one she considered an unprotected bachelor, whose generous nature and unsophisticated outlook made him an easy prey for designing females. In spite of her own kindly nature, it seems she could not help resenting the tight hold which Teenie exercised over her unmarried brother, and no sooner had Hector's cheque resolved John's present difficulties than Mary wrote to Bob offering him a permanent home at Gollanfield.

He received the letter while on a fortnight's visit to his friend James Cowan, who had invited him to his country house for a little shooting and fishing. No sooner did he reveal his address than Teenie started to bombard him with letters from London, full of complaints of his neglect of her and containing advice on everything from the treatment of his cold to the methods he should employ when writing his next book. This daily epistolary nagging finally stung Ballantyne into replying with a broadside of his own:

Glenesk House, Loanhead,
Near Edinburgh.
(Jas. Cowan Esq.)
29th January, 1864.

My dearest Teenie,

I am well used to be blown up, so I take it quite in good part, my dearie! At the same time you are used to getting a defensive reply—so here goes, as usual.

1st Count　I have *not* been telling stories about my health. Each time of writing I have been telling exactly the *facts*. One day my cold feels quite gone—another day it feels as if it were going to be bad. At present I have only a stuffed nose. Luckily no sore throat. Whether this will continue to Monday I do not know, but I think it will.

2nd Count　I've written you two or three letters *at least*, if not more, 'not in a hurry,' though no doubt the last line added to each has always been in a hurry, because of my anxiety to give you the *latest* news.

3rd Count　I have not 'begun' my new book here. When I left London I said to Mr. Watson that I would sketch the outline of the book for him; this I ought to have done long ago—and this is all I intend to do.

4th Count　Nelson's letter was not worth sending. It was a brief note asking me to go and see him, with a desultory remark or two on the subject of our dispute. All the facts connected with Nelson you know.

5th Count　I don't suppose my 'affairs are not interesting' to you—and I have no 'advice' at all 'where I am.'

6th Count　I don't agree either with you or Watson about Norway[1] being 'out at once.' It will be out time enough.

---

[1] Ballantyne had agreed to write a book about his experiences while salmon fishing in Norway, but the idea was abandoned when Routledges issued *Freaks on the Fells*, which dealt with Bob's adventures as an angler in the Highlands of Scotland.

7th Count I'm not trifling with my cold. I might as well tell a baboon that I am not well as tell that to James Cowan. You might know this, I think.

So now you are replied to. D'ye give in? No—very well—stick up—that's a fact. When found make a note of!

... I'm sorry to hear about the scrimp with cash. Use the money I sent you, and if you get into a real fix I'll always be able to keep the wolf from the door with Nelson's money. Mind, I look at it in two views. I am thankful to God for the *gift*—I am not particularly grateful to Nelson's for giving me a *small* portion of the money due to me in *equity*!

I'm sad about your constant difficulty in regard to money. Is there any word of Gambart or Flatto taking any more of the studios? Is the Nichols painting[1] near done? I fancy *that* will be sure money to the extent of £50 when finished. I've just written to Watson with the sketch of the plan of my new book.[2] I enclose a copy of it. Let me have your opinion.

Now dearie, I must stop. I have *not* written *this* in a hurry, although it is just possible that I may add a hurried line tomorrow!

God bless and prosper you and yours,

Ever your loving brother,
R. M. Ballantyne.

Had it not been for his loyalty to John and Teenie in their manifest and continuing money troubles, and the obligation he felt towards them in having provided him with a home for so many years, he might well have accepted Mary's offer of a room at Gollanfield House. He had stayed in Scotland after the rest of the family had moved south in order to tidy up their various business affairs in Edinburgh and see the remainder of the furniture safely despatched. John had spent most of 1863 in London and had been greatly helped in finding work by some of his old friends from the Royal Scottish Academy, many of whom were now figures of importance in the world of art. He and Teenie had

[1] A portrait of Erskine Nichol, A.R.A., on which John was then engaged.
[2] *The Lifeboat. A Tale of our Coast Heroes*, published in November 1864.

finally selected 13, The Mall, Kensington, as their new residence, a large Georgian edifice, three stories high, the top floor of which they hoped to convert into studios which could then be let to fellow artists. By January 1864 the family, with the exception of Bob, had settled in the new house, but her brother-in-law's continuing absence in Scotland made Teenie increasingly annoyed.

Instead of joining them immediately, he had asked permission to accept James Cowan's invitation to a fortnight at Loanhead, and then, at the end of this period, to his sister-in-law's horror, Bob had daringly written a delicately phrased letter telling of his decision to spend a few weeks with Hector and Mary in Inverness-shire.

By return of post he had a reply which left him in no doubt whatever of Teenie's furious anger at this change of plan. Shining greenly through her words was her flaming jealousy of his being cared for by any other woman but herself—even if that woman *was* his own sister. He received this literary tirade while sitting at breakfast at Gollanfield House, and enough of his reply has survived subsequent censorship[1] to enable one to glimpse the firm diplomacy he had to exercise in order to extricate himself from a situation which was more than likely to leave at least one of his doting sisters in tears, and probably cause a family rift that might take many years to heal.

[February, 1864]

. . . but if facts hit hard it is they, not I, who hit. I feel assured from former experience that you will misunderstand some of my meaning. I therefore guard myself in regard to what I said about 'home.'

I do not, I have no wish to, deny that yours has been my home in years past; that you have claims upon me which no other living mortal has, and that I will always gladly and *proudly* and openly acknowledge these claims. What I hold is that there are *exceptional* cases. There are times when a a man may temporarily prefer a stranger to a friend. I regard the claims of Hector on me in that light.

[1] A proportion of the letters have pages missing or portions cut from them.

Now, my beloved sister, I know not how you will take this letter, but I feel it necessary to suggest that you and I had better not write to each other for a few days. I do this on purely selfish grounds. The work that lies before me this week requires all my energies if I am to get away with an easy mind & I find that letters such as yours this morning totally unfit me for work.

I do not propose this, dearie, with the pitiful & spiteful idea of punishing *you*. It is fully as great a punishment for *me*. But I really think that God will not bless our correspondence as carried on just now. I think that we are both morally unwell & I recommend the silence of a few days as I would a disagreeable dose of physic.

My dearest sister, I love you, whatever you may think of this letter, & I will never cease to pray for you and yours. Again I assure you that your free comments on my intended course of action have *nothing* whatever to do with my sore feelings. If you say or think this it will be ungenerous. Moreover, I won't send the photograph. I'll bring it up and let you see it & remove your ignorance about the rose!

May God bless you, dearie,

Your loving brother,

R.M.B.

One would like to know more about the mysterious photograph mentioned in the last paragraph—and also the meaning of his cryptic reference to 'the rose'; but in this instance the past will keep its secrets, for the page quoted above is headed with the number '5', and the rest of the letter is missing. Whether he meant to defy Teenie and stay for as long as he wished is another question that cannot be resolved, for on the 13th February, Bob, Jane and Mary each received urgent telegrams summoning them to the bedside of their brother James, who had collapsed with haemorrhage of the brain after a bout of heavy drinking.

They arrived at his home in London to discover that he was now in a coma and critically ill, and they and the rest of the family gathered sombrely in the muted drawing room to await the inevitable summons to troop sorrowfully upstairs. On the 16th

February, at the age of fifty-one, Dr. James Ballantyne, oriental-
ist and man of letters, died peacefully without regaining con-
sciousness, his second wife, Annabella, his daughter Bessie, and
his brothers and sisters at his bedside. His son, Alexander, now
aged eighteen, was serving at sea and learned of his father's death
only several weeks later.[1]

Bob did not return with his two sisters to Scotland after the
funeral, but settled down once more under Teenie's care,
acknowledging that he ought to stay and help his brother until
he was sufficiently established in London to command a regular
income. John was only a slightly built little man, but something
like his brother in facial appearance, although the beard he wore
was merely a wispy ghost of Bob's thick, brown, carefully tended
mop which now swept down across his chest in true explorer
style. John had the self-depreciating mannerisms of a person one
would mark as a ditherer, his voice clogged with natural hesitation, and completely unable to make up his own mind or take
firm decisions unless pushed hard from behind. Yet he was
gifted with a kindly and generous nature and certainly thought
the world of his young brother, using him as a protection from
the realities of life by leaving all financial and business matters
in his hands.

On opening the post and finding a bill, John's usual habit was to
sigh gently and then wearily spear it on the iron spike that
graced the end of the overmantel—a spike that seemed rapidly
to become encrusted with a sheaf of similar demands. These
brother Bob would finally have to sift, sort into degree of urgency,
and eventually settle, usually by clubbing together all available
funds, and often just in time to prevent the duns knocking hard
on the old oak door. Teenie, with the embittered egoism of bad

---

[1] James Ballantyne was created Professor of Moral Philosophy in 1856.
His second marriage was to Annabella Georgiana Monck-Mason in 1854,
who bore him a son and daughter. The boy was named George Monck-
Mason Ballantyne, and was born at 50 Queen Street, Edinburgh, on the
3rd November, 1859. He became a schoolmaster and died in his early
twenties. I have been unable to discover the daughter's name. James's
second wife remarried in 1865; her second husband became Sir Edward
George Jenkinson, K.C.B., in 1888. Lady Jenkinson, as she then was,
died on the 15th December, 1915.

temper, used to rail and rant at her paint-bespattered little husband, making cruel comparisons between him and his successful young brother, until the constant nagging undermined his self-confidence and made him begin to doubt the quality of his own artistic ability. His work started to suffer, and the constant strain of finding clients, and then painting a portrait that would not displease the often comical figure before him, further increased his nervousness, until Bob realised that, unless something was done pretty quickly, a situation might be reached that would be disastrous for all concerned.

He took the initiative by inserting advertisements for pupils in the London papers, worded truthfully, but in such a way that it appeared that his brother was granting a favour by condescending to teach the young the mysteries of the pre-Raphaelite school of art. There was an immediate response, the interviews taking place in a studio which the brothers had carefully embellished with the best of John's work, plus several portraits borrowed for the occasion from some of his most distinguished former clients. The result was that he soon found himself with sufficient pupils to ensure a moderate, but steady, income. In addition, some of the young men later brought parents and friends along for a series of sittings, and John was extremely gratified with the success of the whole arrangement; his time was fully occupied, and even if teaching was not so lucrative as continual portrait painting, at least he appeared assured of being able once more to pay his way.

Before his brother left for London, Bob had worked out a plan to focus the public's interest on the works of John Ballantyne, R.S.A., in a way that would bring the maximum publicity and help to ensure that his name was not soon forgotten by people whose patronage could make him once again a fashionable name in the world of art. His brother was to try and obtain permission to paint a series of portraits of the more famous of his fellow artists while they were actually at work in their own studios. John could sit quietly in the background while the great painters of the day plied their own brushes at the easel; it would not be necessary for him to interrupt their labours in any way or request valuable time for sittings from men far too busy to gran it, and he should be able to capture intimate studies, full of revealing details, and with the subject shown in the most natural surroundings. He would be able to give the public a glimpse of their idols in the relaxed atmosphere of their own workshops, with none of the stiffness of a posed portrait, and an exhibition of ten or more of these canvases would be bound to attract a great deal of attention from the Press, filling the gallery with the curious, selling the pictures, and, the brothers hoped, firmly establishing John Ballantyne in the London market.

Both Teenie and her husband were enthusiastic, John in the knowledge that he again had a goal for which to strive and one that might result in the turning of his fortune, and his wife in the belief that the gradual deterioration in the family's standard of living that had taken place during the last few years might at last be arrested, the loans made by relatives repaid and times return when she could once again go shopping with a light heart and a full purse.

Bob had also formed a notion of his own plans for the future; living in London carried with it a number of advantages, including the opportunity for frequent visits to his publishers, James Nisbet & Company, where he was able to have many discussions with James Watson regarding subjects for his future books. Ballantyne had not been finding it easy to conceive settings for his plots without laying himself open to the charge of being repetitive, and the mistake he made about the coconuts in *The Coral Island* had made him realise the pitfalls surrounding any attempt to describe a locality of which he had no first-hand knowledge. He had now formulated a scheme which he believed would give him factual background material for every tale he wrote, ensuring that the details he used to colour the narrative were as correct as personal observation could make them.

He made the suggestion to Watson that in future he should live for a few weeks in the locality in which any new story was to be set, mixing with the characters who would later people his tales and absorbing the technical data needed to give an authentic atmosphere to the fictional adventures and excitements of the narrative. Three or four weeks at the site would be sufficient time for all the notes he required, and, in addition, he would be able to complete a set of illustrations from sketches made on the spot. If James Nisbet & Company would agree to pay his out-of-pocket expenses while he was away on location, he would leave immediately for the scene of his next story and guarantee to have it completed in time for publication by Christmas.

It could not have taken Watson long to perceive that the scheme meant paying the writer an extra ten or fifteen pounds for each new book produced, but he was also aware that Bob had the undoubted advantage of now being a well-established and well-loved author; the nine full-length tales of his which Nelson's had already published had all gone through several editions, and each time they reappeared they increased the fame of R. M. Ballantyne. This free publicity for an author whose name was already a household word amongst the junior members of the community was theirs for the asking, and his following of regular readers was ready made. Nevertheless Watson pointed out the poor showing that *Ballantyne's Miscellany* was then making, using this as an illustration of the difficulties of the times, and arguing that, although this scheme of Bob's was a sound one, he must ensure that the stories bustled with action and excitement, and that the moral preceptives which the author had used in previous tales must be kept to an absolute minimum.

Granting these conditions were accepted, he agreed to Ballantyne's request that his expenses should be paid by the publishing house. He would pay the author forty pounds for each thousand copies ordered by the booksellers, giving the additional benefit of odd numbers being calculated to the nearest hundred copies above, these terms applying to all editions published. With the copyright staying in his own hands, Bob was delighted to be able to sign a contract on these conditions. The documents to seal the bargain were exchanged after a celebration dinner at Watson's home, during the course of which a toast was drunk to the successful launching of *The Lifeboat*, the author's forthcoming book for boys.

This was the start of Ballantyne's long series of boyish escapes from everyday life in search of adventure images. In these translations of environment he endeavoured to emulate the heroes of his forthcoming tales, living in a variety of outlandish places and nostalgically recapturing some of the astringent excitements of his youthful years at Hudson Bay. That he thought of himself as a bold adventurer, a rather dashing sort of dog within the limits a Christian gentleman could permit, is made obvious by his continually disappearing into the wilds of civilisation, authentically dressed for the parts he hoped to play, and forever bracing himself for the tests of courage and heroism which would allow him to prove to the world that Robert Michael Ballantyne was as fearless and as brave as his young readers believed him to be.

The bearded figure from the backwoods that strode purposefully across the stage and sent the stuffed eagle crashing down with the first shot from his long-barrelled gun, was mirrored many times during the next twenty years in similar scenes of manly action. We find him dashing through the London streets in a fire-engine; disappearing beneath the waves as a diver; disguised as an Arab in the native quarter of Algiers; marooned in a lighthouse; speeding at breakneck speed as the driver of an express train; drenched to the skin on the Goodwin Sands; detecting crime in the General Post Office; deep underground with the Cornish miners; hauling the nets of a deep-sea trawler; and in many another precarious situation that called for fortitude and a complete disregard for bodily comforts.

The excuse the author gave for these dramatic forays was that he was seeking factual evidence around which to weave his fictional stories. This is patently true, but there lingers the strong suspicion that Ballantyne secretly longed to be recognised, not as a prosaic writer of popular juvenile fiction, but as the sort of figure revealed in the frontispiece—a ruggedly good-looking he-man, fearless and bold and the scourge of the ungodly. He had, after all, become an author by accident. If his mother had not carefully kept his Hudson's Bay letters, and if Miss Greig had not pushed him into publication, it is extremely unlikely that he would ever have written a book. There seems to have been no innate longing to be a writer, no compulsion to literary creation or feeling of having things of importance to say for the world to read; and, after the failure of his first published work, no real desire to repeat the experiment. But for the urging of his sister-in-law, *Hudson's Bay* might easily have been his swan song, for the feeling running through his letters, especially the early ones, is that his destiny would lead him towards a life in the open, an adventurous career under the stars that would ease his wander-lust and burnish his hunting skill. Having had these desires thwarted by economic circumstances, he indulged them as past-times and spare-time occupations, his leisure hours being spent in hunting, shooting and fishing, while he infused into his professional life as much action as the setting of his tales per-mitted.

Since the sinking of the *Royal Charter* before the eyes of the helpless onlookers on shore, who had found themselves powerless to assist because of the lack of even the most elementary life-saving equipment, Ballantyne had become determined to do all he could to remedy a state of affairs which permitted long stretches of coastline to be without either a lifeboat or even the most simple type of rocket-line apparatus. He hoped his new book would do something to arouse the public's conscience about this scandal, but he first had to acquire enough knowledge of the subject, and if possible experience a rescue under active conditions, to enable him to put pen to paper without revealing his ignorance of the technicalities and skills used by the lifeboatmen.

By the middle of March he was striding along the beach at Deal, clad in oilskin coat and sou'wester and no doubt struggling to subdue a most un-Christian hope that a gale of furious wind would lash action into the meadowy sea, sending the crew running, and the lifeboat out through the frothing surf, with himself pulling hard at an oar with the rest of the volunteers. But alas! the weather continued calm and Bob was forced to fill in his time with visits to the neighbouring ports, long walks along the cliffs, and discussions with the local coastguards and fishermen. His letters home gave details of the piteously small amount of equipment available to save lives from the countless wrecks which littered the coasts of Britain every winter, for the amount of money available was totally inadequate and many miles of rocky coast were without lifeboats or apparatus of any kind.

The scandal of our exploited and downtrodden seamen had stirred the conscience of at least one other man of purpose, al-though it was to be some years before his efforts on their behalf moved the Government of the day to make illegal some of the worst practices of the shipowners. Samuel Plimsoll, the Member of Parliament for Derby, was campaigning vigorously to gain seamen better conditions. His book, *Our Seamen—An Appeal*, did not appear until 1873, but he was already exposing the appalling circumstances under which the men worked, drawing attention to the rotten, leaking hulks in which they were so often sent to sea. But when Ballantyne visited Deal, public opinion had hardly been stirred, and five years later, the *Lifeboat Journal* could still print the following facts and figures of the toll the sea was taking:

1st November, 1870.

We have repeatedly, through the medium of this Journal, strongly called attention to the terrible and rotten state of many of the ships above twenty years old; in too many instances, on such vessels going aground, their crews perish before there is any possibility of getting the lifeboat out from the shore to their help.

Such is the notoriously ill-found and unseaworthy manner in which these vessels are sent on their voyages, that in every gale—even if it is only of a moderate character—it becomes a certainty that numbers of them will be destroyed, as will be seen from the fact that:

844 ships were lost in 1864
934 ,, ,, ,, ,, 1865
1150 ,, ,, ,, ,, 1866
1215 ,, ,, ,, ,, 1867
1014 ,, ,, ,, ,, 1868
1200 ,, ,, ,, ,, 1869

This gives a total of 6357 lost in only six years. It is overwhelming to contemplate the loss of life from these, in too many instances, *avoidable* wrecks.

These figures seem unbelievable today, but the greed of many of the shipowners in attempting to scrape the last ounce of profit from the weight of cargo carried caused constant losses from gross overloading. Undermanning, so as to keep the wages of the crew to a minimum; defective and cheap construction of new vessels; the designing of ships which were far too long, so that extra cargo could be stowed (often causing the vessels to break their backs in the first really severe storm they encountered): these and other contrivances all helped to swell the casualty figures. The criminal practice of over-insuring a leaking old hulk, fit only for the breaker's yard, in the hope that she, and usually the entire crew, would go to the bottom, was by no means unknown, but little had been done to prosecute the directors concerned. The vested interests of the shipowners did their best to stifle Plimsoll's cries for justice, but the scenes he caused on the floor of the House of Commons and his constant agitation outside, finally persuaded a reluctant Government to bring in the Merchant Shipping Act of 1876, which put an end to the worst of the evils perpetrated by unscrupulous profiteers. The publication of his book, three years before, did more to arouse the public conscience than anything that had appeared previously, and the maximum loading line which had to be painted on the sides of every vessel after the Act became law became universally known as the 'Plimsoll Line.'

Ballantyne's book, *The Lifeboat*, did much to make young people realise the debt the public owed to the underpaid fishermen and merchant seamen of the coastal towns and villages, and many of his juvenile readers were quick to persuade parents and friends to help the cause by sending a contribution to the National Lifeboat Institution. The story told of young Guy Foster, whose rascally uncle, a shipowner in the City of London, was determined to send his ill-found and rotten schooner, the *Nancy*, on a voyage from the Thames to Liverpool, skippered by the brave and stalwart John Bax, whose warnings about the ship's appalling condition the owner contemptuously ignores. With Guy aboard, the vessel loses her rudder in a gale and founders on the Goodwin Sands. Only the last-minute appearance of the Ramsgate lifeboat enables the surviving passengers and crew to be rescued from the wave-swept rigging of the sinking wreck. After his deliverance, Guy devotes himself to helping the Lifeboat Institution raise funds for another boat, a project to which his wealthy uncle refuses to contribute. But eventually the shipping magnate, too, is caught aboard a sinking ship, is rescued by one of the boats he previously refused to help, repents his meanness, but dies before his good resolutions can be put into effect. After further adventures at sea, Guy inherits his late uncle's business, provides life-saving equipment aboard all his boats, sends a hundred guineas to the Lifeboat Institution, marries a missionary's daughter, and he and his wife live happily ever after, surrounded by their grateful friends. The mixture very much as before, with the good triumphant and the wicked put to shame, but with Ballantyne's name on the title-page, a sure-fire winner in the juvenile market.

He had sketched the outline of the story while still at Deal, and before the end of April the sheets of the completed manuscript were in his publisher's hands, together with a promise that the five full-page illustrations[1] would follow before midsummer. Watson professed himself very pleased with the tale and Bob returned to the house in the Mall in high spirits. The first printing was to be of fifteen hundred copies, with payment to the author at the rate of forty pounds per thousand. Within a few days he had further cause for rejoicing, for Routledges, for whose magazine he had written a series of short stories dealing with his adventures while salmon fishing in the Highlands of Scotland, wrote to inform him that they were publishing the collection of tales in book form. Furthermore they agreed to pay him the sum of fifty pounds for so doing.[2] Everything considered, Bob must have felt extremely pleased with his future literary prospects and he chose this moment to broach to Teenie a plan he had long wished to put into action but which circumstances had previously intervened to prevent.

[1] The sixth illustration in the book was the pictorial title. This was drawn by F. Borders after a sketch supplied by the author.

[2] *Freaks on the Fells* appeared in December 1864. It was an autobiographical account of Ballantyne's experiences as an angler, but he used fictional characters to disguise both himself and his friends.

Chapter Nine

BALLANTYNE had long cherished the ambition of walking from
Scotland's capital to that of England's, recording on the way the
events of the journey in the hope of publishing them as a book
about the pleasures to be found in tramping through the countryside, a recreation which was becoming increasingly popular
amongst young people now that the railways had made distant
beauty spots more easily accessible. The wanderlust which
gripped Bob from time to time now impelled him to seize the
opportunity which the completion of *The Lifeboat* offered, although it meant that the trip would have to made in the reverse
direction from that which he had originally intended. He broke
the news of his decision to John and Teenie, telling them that he
proposed to start the journey immediately. He placated his sister-
in-law, who could never bear him out of her sight for long, by
promising her a letter every day, as well as the sheets of the
journal he intended to keep, and he agreed that she should take
some part in the editing of the manuscript before it was submitted for publication.

Clad in a thick woollen suit complete with buttoned waistcoat,
heavy shoes and a light-brown bowler, a knapsack on his back and
an ash walking stick, in which was concealed a small steel blade,
in his hand, he at last bade goodbye to the family and set off to
tramp the four hundred and twenty-six miles[1] which separated
him from his destination at Princes Street, Edinburgh. He
started on Thursday, the 28th April, on a bright but cloudy
afternoon, and was soon striding through the dusty streets of
central London with their clatter of horse-drawn vehicles, through
the hurrying bustle of home-going workers in Kentish Town,
through Hampstead and Finchley, with their country lanes and
fields of growing corn, until he arrived in the early evening at
Barnet, where he was to spend the night. No matter how weary
he happened to be, before going to bed his last task was always to

[1] This is the figure Ballantyne gives in the manuscript as being correct
'by the route I pursued.'

fill several pages of his journal, and the notes he made portray rural England in the mid-sixties of Victoria's reign, enabling one to sense the quiet solitude on the winding highways and the peace and tranquillity of the dusty country roads in those halcyon days before the first chugging, fuming horseless carriage topped the distant pastoral rise:

[1]The journey was the realisation of a dream wh. had haunted me from boyhood. To cast aside (not contemptuously, but independently) all the conveniences of modern times in the way of locomotion and depend entirely on my legs; to wander at will along the old coach-roads and among the shady lanes of Old England; to stop by the wayside & sketch; to fraternise with wayfarers & chat; to see, in short, my native land in a way in wh. it cannot be seen by those who travel by rail—this was the object & end of my journey.

I made the town of Barnet (only eleven miles from London) my first day's journey; and I contrived to stuff my 'little all' into a knapsack of MacIntosh cloth, wh. when full weighed exactly eleven pounds. . . The curious reader may desire to know what eleven pounds of wardrobe consisted of. If not, skip the paragraph—but if so, read the following exposé of the whole affair.

2 flannel shirts	1 pr. flannel drawers
3 prs. socks	1 pr. slippers
6 paper collars	1 necktie
1 pr. trousers	1 thin waterproof top-coat
1 water-colour box	with six inches of the tails cut off!
1 sponge	1 drawing book
1 very small brush & comb	1 tooth brush

1 portfolio with 4 quires 8vo note paper & a mass of uncorrected M.S. equal to 4 quires more, besides a moderate allowance of envelopes & blotting paper, a book of notes and memoranda & a thin copy of the Psalms of David.

Pushing on I soon left suburban London far behind, & began to inhale the pure country air . . . plunging into a

[1] This unpublished manuscript, with Teenie's pencil corrections and deletions, is now in the author's collection.

region of green fields, & trees, & hedgerows, & cattle, & larks; with, here and there, little gingerbread buildings that looked like the humbler class of cheap villas, or the wealthier class of almshouses. I began to experience my first *sensations* at this point (Highgate) in the journey, and feared that I would break down too soon. But they passed away—all except an insatiable thirst. Having read a book on training, however, which counselled abstinence from liquid on the road, I refrained, & was rewarded by meeting a travelling carriage and four with postilions in blue tights and a footman with a fat cook (doubtless) in the rumble, in company with a gigantic umbrella. The whole equipage was dusty & business-like; reminding me of the old coaching days so forcibly that I felt inclined to salute it as it rattled past & involved me in a cloud of dust.

Presently I came to a common—a small triangular bit at the junction of two roads. Here I found a veritable caravan. It was a travelling photographic establishment, 'Hammerton's Royal Photographic Saloon,' in sky-blue paint & mounted on wheels. The proprietor was a young man of a sandy complexion with strawy hair and moustaches & seedy garments. He was seated on a bank at the roadside. Near him sat a rather good-looking young woman clad in much-faded habiliments, some portions of wh. had once been fashionable. The aspect of the couple was somewhat disreputable but their bearing was polite & agreeable. Out of one of the windows of the caravan gazed the chubby face of a little girl.

On questioning the man I found that he was quite willing to talk, & without much pumping he gave me an outline of his career.

'Do you find this sort of thing pays?' said I as we jogged along beside the now slowly moving caravan.

'Pays? Yes sir, it pays well enough,' said the man. 'Anyway it pays better than doin' business in the towns. I've bin at it off & on for four years in these parts, an' I've never had no occasion to go further than twenty miles from this spot. But I've about worked the district out now, so I mean to give 'em a rest & try another round. When I comes back to 'em

again all the babies 'll have grow'd a bit bigger & so they'll
have to be took over again, d'ye see sir, an' then there'll
be a lot of noo babies. That's 'ow it is, sir. Why it don't pay
in the towns now. Taxes is too 'eavy. In Liverpool where I
took a small place once, I 'ad to pay £50 down the day I
entered, an' would you believe it, sir, the rates for the poor
come in the very next day—two pound ten! An' people in
towns gits impatient. If you chance to be out of the way
they goes right off to another shop.

'Now I hant got no taxes to pay except tolls. The feed o'
the 'oss don't cost me much—eighteen pence a day or so; &
the 'oss 'imself was cheap. (Looking at him I did not doubt
it!) He was £8 sir, but I got 'im for four. Why I run 'im forty
mile one day, sir. I built the waggon myself & the whole
thing only cost me £30. Its a cheap 'ouse it is—got a bedroom
in it, too! We just drive about from village to village. If it's
hiring times, I often get good work. Why, sir, I've took as
much as £20 in one day! But there's opposition at the hirings,
for the town houses send down & put up a booth. You see, if
they clear £5 it's worth runnin' down for.'

'Do you find the villagers generally quite ready to employ
you?' said I.

'Ho yes, sir. When I gits to a village, if I aint bin there
before, I puts up on a bit o' common an' puts the 'oss in the
stable of the Inn. Then I 'angs out my specimens and goes &
finds out the character o' the place. There's ginrally a character, sir, in most every village. Well, I does 'im & 'angs 'im
out, and the moment the people sees 'im—in they come so
fast I can scarce git 'em done. An' I never charge less than a
shillin' for anything—six cards for five shillin's.'

Meditating on the enterprise of the English nation I left
the photographer & his family and made my way to Finchley.
Here I have to remark that the baker dwelt (& displayed his
loaves) in a picturesque cottage with a porch adorned by
creeping plants. The gas-fitter & plumber dwelt in a similar
cot, with creepers surrounding the windows, in which leaden
balls & stop-cocks were displayed.

Cogitating on the rural felicity & luxury of the English I

came to a smith's forge, in front of which was a waggon loaded with upwards of thirty black wooden coffins! Aghast at the sight I asked the smith where they were going.

'To the asylum, sir.'

'What asylum?' said I.

'The mad-'ouse,' said he.

'Do they die so fast then?' I enquired.

'Well, if they don't die they kill 'em.'

The countenance of the smith induced me to forgo further questioning, so I passed on to Finchley Common.

Up to this point I had felt so strong & my knapsack so light that I began to grow vainglorious. I even regretted that my burden was not heavier. I was soon rewarded, however (for vice, no less than virtue, meets its reward), with a sensation in my back resembling the feeling that would probably result from a game of bo-peep played by a lancet & a darning needle up and down my backbone and through my heart. It did not last long, however, but acted the part of a moderator to enthusiasm. At seven o'clock I arrived at the town of Barnet & put up at the Red Lion—the which establishment might have been styled the Ravening Lion with propriety, its charges being exhorbitant & its attendance bad.

My first act was to call for the pot of 'Reid's Entire' which I had so resolutely denied myself all day, And let me tell you, reader, in confidence, it was nectar! I say this solemnly. I am not by nature given to malt. It comes from me therefore with some weight when I repeat—it was positive nectar! My next act was to have a cold bath; after wh. & tea, I went to bed & dreamed that I had rheumatic fever!

But before retiring for the night he had to sit down and write his promised letter to his sister-in-law.

Barnet

7.30

My dearest Teenie,

Here I am, fairly on my way. I have just had a cold bath and a *tremendous* tea (with two eggs) and feel quite refreshed & comfortable. I don't feel tired a bit.

During the walk I several times forgot that I had a knap-sack on! If I go on as I have begun I will do well. Of course I feel weak points all over me. My feet especially are very tender. But I have neither chafed or blistered them. My joints felt stiff till I got the bath. The walk was delightful. The country beautiful, even though the day was dull & rather cold; but a bright gleam of sunshine greeted me as I left London.

I don't know what sort of Hotel I'm in. There are no waiters—only chambermaids. But it is a good one—very old. The floor of my room is as rounded as an elephant's back. I must close this in haste to be in time for post. Put my small bible & *glazed* slippers in my portmanteau. The journal letter will be sent soon to you.

I thought of you often by the way. May God for ever bless you all.

Your loving brother,
R. M. Ballantyne.

The Hotel where I am staying is the Red Lion.

Next morning he was up early and started 'fresh as a lark' to walk the twenty miles to Luton. It was a sparkling, sunny day and by lunch time he had reached Harpenden where he was charged '1/- for two mutton chops & a pint of ale.' The evening was spent writing his journal and the following morning he set off for Bedford.

I was impressed, even at this point in the journey, with the solitude of the road. This was one of the great central high-ways of the Kingdom wh. must in former days have exhibited an absolute procession of vehicles & wayfarers of all sorts. It was now almost deserted. Few vehicles passed me except a cart or two, & no pedestrians save the labourers of the local-ities going to & returning from their work. So I found it all through England. The rail has thoroughly subdued the road & converted the great highways into mere byways.

The tramp I overtook was almost the only man I saw dur-ing a walk of several miles. He was a ragged, slipshod, dirty

fellow, with a listless shuffle in his gait that told of idleness &
dissipation.

'You,' thought I, remembering a country lad I had seen
walking in the opposite direction with a bundle on his
shoulder, 'have been to the great city to seek your fortune
& have *not* found it.' His naked toes were sticking through
his boots; his coat was indescribably ragged, patched &
greasy; his trousers, besides being as disreputable as his coat,
were torn up behind the right leg as far as the knee, displaying a red and unhealthy looking limb. A glance at his face
showed me that he was of the lowest type of humanity—not
excepting Hottentots or Australian natives.

In a broad Irish brogue he surlily told me how he had arrived in London the previous year, his hopes high from the
stories of easy, well-paid work he had been regaled with before leaving Dublin; but the few miserable jobs he found
around the docks had each lasted only a few weeks, and most
of the little wages he earned appeared to have been squan-
dered on gin and dissipation of the worst description, this
latter being something about which he seemed to have few
regrets. He was now making his slow and painful way back
to Liverpool in the hope of securing a free passage home. I
left him mumbling thanks for the sixpence I pressed into his
gnarled & filthy hand.

Having resolved before setting out on the journey that each
Sunday should be a day of rest, Bob spent the day quietly at
Bedford, attending church, doing a little sketching and, placating
his protesting feet. By Tuesday he had progressed as far as Kib-
worth in Leicestershire, but the strain of walking twenty miles a
day was beginning to tell.

> *Kibworth—Tuesday 3rd May* 64
> (*a small village* 16 *miles beyond*
> *Kettering.*)

My dearest Teenie,
    'How's your poor feet,' is no adequate enquiry in regard to
me at this present writing. I'm blistered and skinned & in
agony, but jolly!

Yesterday's 25 miles did up my feet, though not my heart —so I resolved to make this an easy day & walk to this place (16 miles). I have done so, but faix it was worse than yesterday. I did not feel energetic till the middle of the day—and all day I was walking on the tops of four blisters! I sewed them with worsted last night and mollified them with ointment this morning, but it was no go. I'll be very good to them tonight, however. On arriving here I felt positively inclined to limp.

The chief inn of the place (the Star & Crown) refused me (full), it sent me to the 'Lord Nelson' wh. was also full! But at the 'Coach & Horses' they took me in, & here I am. This is the oldest, poorest & funniest Inn I have been in. The village is a *mere* village—the Inn a roadside one, very old, very crooked & funny. I have to pass through 2 double bedded rooms to get to mine wh. is clean & comfortable looking.

Now I must close. I'll call at the post office in Leicester tomorrow in passing through it. It is 10 miles from this. I'm to sup here on beefsteak pie! How strange it seems to me to think I've been four days away already and been wandering on & on ever since I left you. I'll send a bit more of journal soon. I enclose a sketch tonight.

Your loving brother,
R.M.B.

Horrible, I've just discovered that I had forgot to post the *first* part of the journal to you! I post it now. Forgive me.

In spite of his blisters he managed to complete the twenty miles to Loughborough next day and by Thursday evening had arrived at Derby.

Derby. Thursday.

My dearest Teenie,

Here I am—toes & all. Och! but it's the heels now as well as the toes! The right foot little toe is in a melancholy state, but I think it's getting better. I had to limp, however, a great part of the day.

I made out 17 miles—from Loughborough to this. Tomorrow I hope to sleep in, or near Chesterfield, & on Saty at Sheffield, where I'll spend Sunday. My shoes bother me. There are lumps in 'em wh. I'm about to go out & get put to rights.

I overtook an old woman on the road today, very tired. She was going to Derby & I met her 5 miles out of Loughborough so she had 12 miles to do! I was very sorry for her and offered her my arm for a mile—when she said she wd. sit down again & wait till a cart passed—so I gave her 6d. and left her. While we were walking arm in arm together a smart lady and gentleman on horses galloped past. They looked & laughed at us.

I enclose more of the journal. Your letters are a *great* comfort to me. They enable me to bear up against the toes! I met an organ man today near the end of my journey, so I made him turn to and play me a tune while I rested on a gate! Gave him 3d. for the same. I dined for 7d. so I cd. afford to be liberal.

God bless you, dearest Teenie,

Your loving brother,
R. M. Ballantyne.

The pages of the journal he sent her contain a description of his meeting with one of the Duke of Manchester's mounted volunteers, who, with the rest of his squadron, was engaged in drill instruction in the lanes and fields near by.

I was enjoying the fine view, resting & listening to the innumerable & sweet country sounds that filled the still air, when the clatter of horses' feet startled me. The object that met my eye on turning round struck me with amazement & admiration. It was a magnificent warrior, mounted on a splendid charger, glittering in scarlet & silver & armed to the teeth. I would have as soon have expected to meet one of the Horse Guards in that quiet country road, as such a man.

He was six feet or more; wore a scarlet tunic, long black boots, tight corduroys, buff belts, a smart foraging cap, an enormously long sabre in a jingling scabbard of steel, a pair of massive pistols, a heavy moustache & prolonged whiskers. He was positively a resplendent object, and, as he came crashing towards me, I felt, despite the small sword in my walking stick, that I was at his mercy!

'Is't gone eleven yet?' he enquired, in the tones of a Marquis & the accent of a small Derby farmer, as he reined up at my side.

'No,' said I meekly, pulling out my watch, 'It wants twenty minutes to eleven yet.'

'Ah! that'll do—I'm first class; up to time; nothin' like it. You see *that's* the consequence.'

He pointed to a white good-conduct stripe on his right arm.

'You're going to drill, I suppose,' said I, sorely puzzled as to what arm of the service owned him.

'Yaas. Hit'll be squad drill this mornin', I expect.'

'The Militia,' said I at a venture, 'are out in in great force just now.'

'Yaas, but I aint in the Militia. I b'long to the Dook of Manchester's 'orse. I'm a volunteer.'

'Indeed!' I exclaimed with a glow of fraternal enthusiasm, 'I too am a volunteer—at least I was until a year ago.'

This piece of information appeared to have no interest whatever for the 'Dook of Manchester's' trooper, so I ventured to question him as to his regiment while he rode beside me. He told me there were 150 men in his troop, that all of them had not got good-conduct stripes, as he had, that the uniform was, in his opinion, a pretty good one, but that the ''elmet was too 'eavy,' and he was proceeding to tell me more when we came to a point where the road branched into two.

'This is my road,' said he loftily, pointing with his nose to the left.

'And this mine,' said I, pointing to the right.

And, putting spurs to his really fine horse, the trooper galloped away. The last words I heard him utter, as the hedge shut him from my view, were ' 'Allo! 'ow are ye?' and the individual thus addressed, appearing next moment, proved to be a butcher's boy on a grey cob with a basket on his arm.

He spent the next night at Chesterfield, then pushed on to the house of his friends, the Avelings, at Sheffield, where they persuaded him to stay for three days to give his blistered feet a chance to heal. By Tuesday, the 10th May, he was in Huddersfield, and he managed to average twenty miles a day for the whole of that week, arriving at Penrith in Cumberland on Saturday. He stayed in the Lake District for nearly a week, visiting Kendal and Ulleswater and occupying his time sketching and writing the pages of his journal. Many of the toll-keepers on the country roads were glad to earn a few extra shillings by selling refreshments, and the hot weather always brought out a crop of ginger-beer and cider stalls, although on the more lonely stretches of road these were rare.

I have seen gallons of ginger beer during my travels here, have had it forced on my attention & have drunk much of it —much more I fear than was good for me. In many places the toll-keepers sell it, & they have a way of putting it out on little tables & stands in the footpath on hot days wh. is absolutely irresistible.

Today I was marching somewhat languidly along in the hot sunshine, or under the shade of avenues of magnificent trees, when I came to a place where two roads met. It was far removed from the abode of man, as far as I cd. see—yet I came unexpectedly on a ginger-beer man. It seemed to me a vision! No village, no passengers (at this time, at least), a wide expanse of verdure, sheep & lambs—also cattle; but nothing whatever to warrant the entertainment of hope in the breast of man of ginger beer.

He looked at me. I looked at the ginger beer man & my mouth watered. The man saw at once that I was smitten. He spread a piece of canvas on the bank in the shade of a splendid elm and said—

'Sit down, sir.'

I obeyed, allowed him to draw a bottle & drank it. It was uncommonly bad, but delicious in the circumstances.

'Do you get much custom here?' said I.

'Ho yes, sir, plenty of custom. I've bin fifteen years 'ere.

I comes out every fine day to this 'ere spot and always sells it all hoff. Why, sir, I've had to go back 'ome three and four times for more "stuff," I 'ave—when it's uncommon 'ot weather.'

'And what do you do in bad weather?' I enquired.

'Oh! I stops at 'ome an' mends humbrellas an' takes care of the old missus wots bin bad with the chest for a long while.'

Observing that he had a large stone jar under the stand, I enquired if that contained more of the 'stuff.'

'No, sir,' said he, 'that's treacle beer. It's cheaper than tother. It's only a 'alfpenny a glass—tother's two-pence.'

I at once ordered a glass of the 'alfpenny beer (wh. was execrable—but cooling) & paid him 3d, much to his surprise, 2½d. being the legitimate charge.

'What sort of people drink that stuff?' I enquired, rising to go.

But the question was answered for me by the rough voice of a waggoner who was passing the stand.

' 'allo! old man. Give us a glass o' yer swipes an' look sharp —coom along!' and as I glanced back I saw that he was draining the pint at one continuous swallow.

A footsore and rather weary Bob Ballantyne finally reached Edinburgh on the 25th May, having worked out that he had 'only spent at the rate of 7/- a day, including purchases on the way.' He passed the next week or so in rewriting and editing the journal of his experiences in the optimistic hope of finding an immediate publisher at a handsome price.

These fond hopes were, however, doomed to disappointment. Bob was quite unaware when he set off on his journey that the story of a longer and more impressive walk was being published in London that very month. An American gentleman, Elihu Burritt by name, had recently accomplished a walk from London to John o'Groat's, and in late May the story of his journey, with copious notes on the towns and villages through which he passed and the famous people he had met, appeared in the bookshops. It was embellished with a photograph of the author showing him dressed for the trip, complete with tall silk hat, Gladstone-type bag, walking stick and umbrella. The tale gained the interest of the public and a second edition was called for the same year. When Ballantyne submitted his own manuscript, first to the editor of *Good Words* and later to other publishing houses, the answer was always the same, 'that in view of the recent appearance of a narrative of a very similar nature' they would not be interested. The account of his journey to Edinburgh was destined to remain unpublished until the printing of the extracts given in this present book.

He spent most of the month after his arrival visiting friends and relations and renewing acquaintances, seeming from his letters loth to return to London, although Teenie became increasingly insistent that he should come home. His letters to her give the impression that he was continually searching for excuses to prolong his stay in Scotland and expressions such as 'I must stay at least a few days with Constable's,' or, 'It would be discourteous to refuse Chalmer's offer of hospitality after his many past kindnesses,' etc., etc., occur amongst the pages of his replies to his sister-in-law's repeated summonses to return to The Mall. But in June, the sudden failure of one of the smaller Scottish banks left her two sisters, Mary and Elizabeth Hogarth, practically destitute, every penny of their savings being swallowed up in the crash. Bob seized on this calamity as another reason for delaying departure from Scotland, and immediately started to organise a relief committee to help the two spinsters in their distress, a course of action to which Teenie had to give unqualified approval. Once Ballantyne championed a cause he invariably supported it wholeheartedly and the present case was no exception. He wrote letters, pestered his friends, co-opted a band of helpers, and, within a few weeks had a team of middle-aged Edinburgh ladies as enthusiastic as himself. Before the end of the year over five hundred pounds had been subscribed, largely due to the efforts of these same formidable females, who had spent a happy summer and autumn in a welter of sales-of-work, fêtes, and rounds of personal visits to the wealthy with pleas and arguments as to the goodness of the cause. Bob composed an appeal of which several hundred copies were printed, adding at the bottom of the sheet:

Please address me care of T. Constable & Co., 11 Thistle Street, Edinburgh.

P.S. It is right to add that the ladies are not aware of the appeal which I am now making.

'This will ease their minds if it comes to their ears,' he wrote Teenie, 'but I warn everyone to take care of this—those I mean, who know the parties or are likely to guess them.'

With the bulk of the money the committee secretly purchased a small country cottage near Edinburgh, and Bob, under the pretence of taking the two Miss Hogarths for a ride in a hired gig, drove them both to their new home, where, in a tearful and dramatic scene of the type beloved by the Victorians, the key of the door and a cheque for the balance of the sum collected were handed to the gratefully sobbing spinsters by the ladies there assembled.

James Nisbet & Company (in the shape of James Watson) were more than pleased with the way Ballantyne's books were selling. By June 1864 *Gascoyne, The Sandal-Wood Trader* had topped the two thousand mark and within two months of *The Lifeboat* first appearing, a second edition had to be issued to fill the demand.[1] There had been many fearful wrecks on the coast of Britain that winter and the publicity the newspapers had given to rescues by the lifeboat crews had stimulated a tremendous amount of interest in the service. The book could not have appeared at a more propitious time and the sales were larger than for any other story Bob had written to date, Watson being quick to confirm that he would be happy to publish the author's next tale on the same terms as the last.

Ballantyne had inserted in the penultimate chapter of *The Lifeboat* an appeal for funds to help the National Lifeboat Institution, whose secretary, Richard Lewis, had been delighted with the response. Shoals of letters from the juvenile readers and a number of subscriptions from their parents had been received at the London headquarters and several new members had been enrolled to help in the good work. Lewis wrote to Bob, congratulat-

[1] Both the first and second editions were of fifteen hundred copies each. Two further editions were issued during the course of 1865.

ing him on the success of his book and thanking him for the aid he had given the Institution, but regretfully turning down the author's suggestion that the governing body should sponsor him for a lecture tour to raise funds for the Institution. However, he stated that the committee would be glad to help with the loan of various items of equipment should Ballantyne decide to proceed with the tour on his own account.

During the year Bob had delivered his 'Hudson's Bay' address at Falkirk, Largs, Melrose, Dunfermline, Ayreton, Gallowshields, Montrose, Dundee and Perth,[1] and any fears he once had of speaking before a large audience had long since vanished; in fact he confessed he enjoyed being able to hold the attention of several hundred people for an hour or more at a time and receiving the plaudits of the crowd at the end. He would have preferred that the Institution paid him a salary to defray his expenses and themselves reaped the benefit of the profit from the ticket sales, but, in spite of their refusal to sponsor him officially until a local committee had been formed to guarantee the expenses of a Scottish tour, he was determined to proceed with the scheme. Early in December 1864 he wrote to Teenie, giving his views on the subject.

> ... I think the Lifeboat will be a first-rate, serious, & weighty lecture wh. I shall not be ashamed to deliver before the most learned & fastidious society in the land! We shall see. I shall have my hands full when I get home for I mean to begin it at once. There will have to be rough diagrams & cartoons & models of boats as well as of apparatus, all of wh. I mean to exhibit in *operation*.

Although he spent Christmas with John, Teenie and the children in London, the new year found him once again hard at work in Edinburgh, endeavouring to enlist the support of both the poor and wealthy citizens for a fund-raising campaign to purchase a fully equipped lifeboat to be stationed on an unprotected stretch of the Scottish coast. He pestered the newspapers until they printed details of the local appeal he was

[1] Ballantyne kept a notebook giving a full list of the dates and places where he lectured.

making, coupling the story with excerpts from his book on the subject, and drawing attention to the many seamen who had perished on the rocky shores of Scotland for want of a boat to save them. Within a short time public interest became so aroused that,when his first two lectures were advertised to take place at the Queen Street Hall on the 23rd and 25th of February, the clamour for tickets was so great that all were sold within a few hours of their being offered and hundreds of disappointed people had to be turned away.

Both the lectures were an astonishing success, the room was packed to overflowing, and when at the conclusion Bob actually 'fired' the rocket (which he had contrived to work by means of a powerful spring) he sat down 'flushed but happy' to a standing ovation from the audience. A few days later he was addressing an even larger concourse in the Free Assembly Hall and as soon as the lecture was over he sat down to write to his sister-in-law and tell her the good news.

Thursday night.

My dearest Teenie,

The lecture tonight has been a *tremendous* success! It is perfectly marvellous to me. A quarter of an hour before the commencement the Free Assembly Hall was filled to the ceiling. There could not have been fewer than 2000 present. May God preserve me from vanity.

I cannot but be pleased, because I kept that vast assembly in the deepest attention for two hours, and they agreed *heartily* to my proposition & have formed an influential committee to work out the scheme. God has evidently made use of me to do good in this cause. I had Knox[1] in the chair. This time I hung the sailor from the roof by a rope in the cradle & it had a great effect, for it was powerfully comical. There was but little comedy in the lecture & I do think this was a useful relief. Tomorrow there is a committee meeting which I mean to attend. I have no doubt now that the boat will be produced by the artisans!

[1] Mr. Thomas Knox, J.P.

At first I was alarmed by such a tremendous concourse, but as I got on I warmed & became more earnest and enthusiastic than I ever felt before. Altogether I have reason to thank God and take courage. I resolved before going that as this was an unexpected success & my first great success in that way, that I would give the glory to God publicly & impressively. In accordance with this—before beginning the lecture I expressed my gratification at the manner in wh. my proposal had been received & *thanked God* for the favour that He had shown me in enabling me to influence the working classes so much. I wonder how much of pride there was in that statement! Still, I am glad I made it. It is by our *words* that we shall be judged.

God bless you, my dearest Teenie.

Yr. loving brother,

R. M. Ballantyne.

The next day a committee of the working people of Edinburgh solemnly pledged themselves to the task of raising sufficient funds to purchase and equip a lifeboat in the City's name, the vessel to be stationed at whatever part of the Scottish coast the Lifeboat Institution might think fit. Edinburgh and Leith were divided into districts, each with their own sub-committee. The rattle of the collectors' boxes was soon being heard at the doorsteps and street corners, outside the public houses on Friday and Saturday nights, and wherever the eager helpers believed they could prise loose a few coppers.

By the end of the year over four hundred pounds had been subscribed, mostly in pennies and sixpences from amongst the poorer members of the community, with Ballantyne giving all the proceeds from six Edinburgh and Leith lectures to the fund, as well as persuading Messrs. Nelson's, the publishers, to print, free of charge, several thousand copies of an appeal which he had written on the Institution's behalf.[1] In addition, he spent hours of his time at committee meetings, attending working men's clubs, sales of work, bazaars, writing letters of thanks, and the many other tasks needed to keep people enthusiastic for the cause

[1] At least one copy of this ephemeral single-page appeal has survived.

of saving life at sea. But at last, in the autumn of 1866, the target figure having been reached and exceeded, the shiny new boat arrived by train in Edinburgh, to be met at the station by a crowd of several hundred cheering people. At the formal ceremony of unveiling, carried out with due pomp by the Provost of the city, Bob had the honour of hearing the vessel named the 'Edinburgh and R. M. Ballantyne Lifeboat.' The name of the new craft had been kept a close secret from the chief person concerned, the final words of the title not being painted on the vessel until the day before the ceremony, and Ballantyne's amazed expression when the Provost tugged the concealing Union Jack away and read out the full name, caused a wave of good-humoured laughter to mingle with the applause.

While the station to receive it was being built on the coast, the vessel was exhibited on its carriage in many of the larger Scottish towns, with the object of raising further funds for its upkeep, until, on the 18th December, 1866, Bob handed the boat over to its crew at the lifeboat station at Port Logan, Wigtownshire. The vessel was launched several times the following year, the most dramatic occasion being in December, when the Scottish newspapers were full of a rescue she made of fifteen members of the crew of the barque *Strathleven*.

North British Mail. December 18th, 1867

Wreck of the barque 'Strathleven' of Glasgow

ON THE EVENING of Monday last, the barque *Strathleven*, (Captain Gilmour), 520 tons register, belonging to Mr. J. Ewing, Glasgow, and laden with sugar and rum from Demarara for the Clyde, was beating up the channel.[1] The night being dark, she missed stays when near the shore, and ran right in upon the rocks, when she capsized on her broadside, and the fore and main masts were carried away. This happened at the Heughs, about half-a-mile to the north of Float Bay, and as this is about the worst part of the coast here, it is a mystery how two of the crew (foreigners) man-

[1] The North Channel, between Northern Ireland and Scotland.

aged as they did to get ashore and scramble their way up the rocks at night.

After wandering about for two hours, they came upon the house of Mr. M'Culloch, of Float, who showed them every amount of kindness, and at once conveyed them to Mr. Campbell's, of the Laigh Float. Mr. Campbell immediately went to the scene of the wreck, and saw from the position of the vessel, that it was impossible to render any assistance without the aid of a lifeboat. He instantly despatched a messenger to Port Logan for the lifeboat, which was promptly forwarded.

During the interval the remaining fifteen of the crew, who were clinging to the side of the vessel, were continually crying for assistance as the water dashed over them, Mr. Campbell and others giving them every encouragement to hold on, with the prospect of speedy deliverance, which was happily realised. We may mention that Port Logan is about seven miles distant from the scene of the wreck, and great praise is therefore due to the crew of the lifeboat who went to the rescue. The lifeboat was the *Edinburgh and R. M. Ballantyne*, presented last year by the working people of Edinburgh.

One final postscript should be added to the story of this boat, and it is given in a letter which Bob wrote to the *Edinburgh Review*:

26th December, 1867.

Sir,

A curious and interesting coincidence has just been communicated to me by Captain M'Kerlie, of the Coastguard, Stranraer, which perhaps you will kindly make known through your columns.

Our lifeboat, it may be remembered, was exhibited in Glasgow last year on the 16th December. On the 17th she was placed on a railway truck and forwarded to her destination. The wife of the Captain of the *Strathleven*, accompanied by her children, went to see the boat, and put an offering into the subscription box. *Exactly* one year after, on the 16th December, 1867, the Captain's vessel was wrecked, and on the morning following (the 17th) he and his men were providentially rescued by the very boat which his wife had contributed to support.

I think that an event of this kind ought to encourage the ladies of Edinburgh to prosecute with renewed energy the good work of collecting for the fund with which this boat is to be endowed.

I am, &c.,

R. M. Ballantyne.

Meanwhile, in London, John was by no means out of the financial wood, and, amid all his social activities and agitation on behalf of the fund, Bob certainly could not afford to neglect his literary work. The continuing high sales of *The Lifeboat* convinced him that a story on similar lines could prove an equally great success, an assumption with which his publisher wholeheartedly agreed. But where was he to find a setting sufficiently varied to give an air of freshness to the tale and recapture the interest of his readers? Fortunately, this question was soon answered by his meeting, at one of his lectures, a keeper on leave from a lighthouse off the Scottish coast, and the conversation he subsequently had with the man first gave Ballantyne the idea of visiting one of these lonely structures and making it the location of his next adventure story. He lost no time in writing to the Board of Commissioners of the Northern Lighthouses and within a few weeks received their permission to spend a fortnight in the Bell Rock Lighthouse, twelve miles off the coast of Forfarshire.

The weather during his stay on the Rock varied between dead calm and a stiff breeze, so he was denied the spectacle of the full gale which he had earnestly hoped would occur. At low tide he would emerge from the lighthouse with his stand and easel to paint pictures of the massive tower with its base of slippery, sea-weed-covered rocks on which so many ships had perished in years gone by. When the tide was high or the weather rough he would sit in the library and work on the opening chapters of his book, varying this with spells of reading the books of reference he had brought with him, or writing his journal letter to Teenie. The isolation of his situation sometimes induced a wave of depression and melancholia amounting almost to a religious mania, coupled with morbid fears that he might succumb to the temptations of alcohol in the same way as his late brother, James. There is no evidence whatsoever in any of Bob's letters that he was at any time a heavy drinker, but, strict Presbyterian as he now was, Elder of the Free Church of Scotland and devout believer that sins of the flesh brought everlasting damnation if not repented and overcome, he resented and despised his own inability to resist the occasional glass of wine or dram of spirits. Smoking he had long since discarded, and his struggle to do the same with drink can be seen from these quotations from his letters home:

Saturday [6th *May* 1865]

My dearie, I find that when I have written the journal I have nothing left to write to you except chit chat & you must not look for much of that while I am so hard worked here. Every minute is precious. I am now going to make a sketch of the lighthouse—a section, showing the interior—for you; so I'll stop. Have only 3 more working days here. I do hope they will be good else I'll not get things far enough advanced.

Sunday 7*th*.

This has been a peculiar day. You will see by the journal that the great bell has been ringing all day on account of the fog. Poor Withers told me about his child's death. How I wish that I could speak to men about their souls. I read Hervey's Life & part of his Meditations. I like these old divines & their style—also their earnest love of our Saviour. This is our great want. Love that will cast out fear, & especially *sin*. Love that will make meditation on God, & Christ, & the Holy Spirit, & His works & especially His Word—and prayers, matters of *delight*; not merely duty. I am convinced that, until we arrive at this state, we are not in a right state, and that it is possible for us—you & me, darling Teenie,—to get to this state.

That *accursed* brandy that I brought with me has been a torment to me. It is a terrible snare. One is entangled more than he is aware. For the last four or five days I have not touched a drop & have been much better, body & mind, in consequence—aye—also in conscience. Well, I have been thanking God for this, but once or twice I have been sorely tempted. All my thankfulness fled—all my power of resistance seemed to fly—but, through God's blessing, by a great effort I held on. Today, however, I felt a *little* loss of appetite —a very little—yet here was an excuse. I went & took a nip. Shame on me. I do solemnly believe that I have been, & still am, on the verge of being a drunkard. It is absolutely appalling (at least it ought to be) to think that I have come to this *after* my beloved James's example and fate.

However, I have settled the question for the present, for I have poured the brandy out of the window & hurled the bottle into the sea! And thanked God for it. Don't blame me, dearie, for groaning to you. I groan to no one else. Besides I mean to do it no more. My groaning days are over. I am going to fight now, God helping me. . . Now, dearie, God bless you and goodnight.

On the Thursday morning following, the relief boat arrived from Arbroath. Bob was packed and ready long before it hove in sight. He left ten shillings and a copy of *Ungava* with the Chief Lightkeeper, with a promise to send more of his books later, including an autographed copy of *The Lighthouse* as soon as it was published. The journal of his visit concludes with the words:

As the boat pulled away from the Rock I turned for a last glimpse of the men who had been my fellow prisoners for two long weeks. They stood waving on the iron staircase at the base of the tower, then the gathering sea-mist rising slowly from the undulating ocean gradually thickened until they were lost to sight.

He returned next day to Edinburgh where he had to deliver a lecture and attend to some Lifeboat Committee affairs, but before the end of the month he was back on the coast, having rented the only spare room in the Waverley Inn, a tiny hostelry in the small village of Auchmithie, three miles north of Arbroath. Here he settled in peace and quiet to write the remaining chapters of his story, narrating how the Bell Rock lighthouse was constructed with immense difficulty by Robert Stevenson and his team of masons and carpenters on the dangerous reef submerged by every tide to a depth of twelve feet or more. He wove into this factual account of the beacon's erection his own fictional tale of the adventures of Ruby Brand and his companions, including the inevitable miraculous escapes from watery graves. In three weeks the book was finished, complete with a set of illustrations, and he returned to London to submit the manuscript for his publisher's approval. In November 1865 a first edition of two thousand copies appeared for sale, and, while not enjoying quite so great and immediate a success as *The Lifeboat*, the book sold well at five shillings, clothed in plum-coloured cloth and with an embossed picture of the lighthouse stamped in gold on its spine.

In December, Ballantyne received a letter from the Secretary of the Commissioners of the Northern Lighthouses, containing the following paragraph:

. . . They [the Commissioners of the Northern Lighthouses] have been so much pleased with the way in which you have combined the fiction of a tale, with the popular but correct account of the building of the Bell Rock Lighthouse, that they think it would be an interesting work to transmit to their lightkeepers and I have therefore to request that you will direct your publishers to transmit to me twenty-five copies.

Alexr. Cunningham.

He enclosed a copy of this letter when he next wrote to Teenie, and added the comment below:

. . . I wonder what Watson will say to the letter from the Commissioners of Northern Lights. Maybe they'll put the *Lighthouse* also on the Admiralty list.[1] I am very thankful to God for this answer to my prayers for the success of my books.

I have propounded an idea to Watson wh. he says he will

[1] The Admiralty had ordered that R. M. Ballantyne's *The Lifeboat* should be placed on the official list of books purchased for use in Her Majesty's Royal Navy.

talk of when we meet. It is that I shd. propose to Nelson to purchase back the copyrights of all my books with a view to a cheap edition & have them all in Nisbet's hands. I have hopes in regard to this. It wd. be a graceful thing for Nelson to do, *as a friend*, to let me have them cheap, and as a *publisher* he might think he had got a good enough return for the small sums he gave me for them. Besides, they cannot be of *much* value to him now, I should think.

Now, dearie, I must away to bed. I pray that God may direct me in regard to this as well as all other earthly things.

God bless you, dearie,

Yr. loving brother,
R.M.B.

But his visit to Nelson met with no success whatever; his old publisher was doing far too well out of reissuing *The Coral Island*, *Ungava*, *The Young Fur Traders*, *Martin Rattler*, and the rest of Ballantyne's books of which he held the copyright to let either friendship or sympathy pierce the tough sac of commercial expediency with which he surrounded himself.

Chapter Ten

In London, John had been toiling manfully to finish his series of pictures of famous artists at work in their studios. To his delight, John Millais[1] had granted him permission to visit his home at 7, Cromwell Place, South Kensington, where he was then engaged upon the 'Eve of St. Agnes,' a picture that created a sensation when it was first exhibited, and Ballantyne painted a fine study of Millais at work on this subject. Having successfully surmounted the hurdle of procuring his first celebrated sitter, John found little difficulty in persuading other well-known figures to give their blessing to his scheme, and, by October 1865, he had completed ten large oil paintings of some of the most distinguished artists of the day, including David Roberts, R.A., Thomas Faed, R.A., Holman Hunt, O.M., Erskine Nicol, A.R.A., and that darling of the Victorian public, Sir Edwin Landseer, R.A.

It was a particular stroke of luck for John to be able to induce this latter artist to co-operate, for Landseer's reputation for chronic bad temper, outbursts of wrath at what he mistakenly imagined were discourtesies, and extreme sensitivity to any criticism of his work, made him a very difficult person to approach for any favour. His irascibility had been considerably increased by a recent illness which bordered on a nervous breakdown and, to make matters worse, he had unfortunately been involved in a railway accident which had badly scarred his forehead and been the cause of frequent headaches. John's large painting of this most popular of all Victorian artists was to be the *chef d'œuvre* of the exhibition. It showed Landseer engaged upon the models of the lions which were later to grace Trafalgar Square and about which wide interest had already been aroused. The colossal bronze effigies which were to be placed at the base of Nelson's Column were to be cast by the Italian sculptor, Baron Marochetti, after

---

[1] In July 1885, at Gladstone's suggestion, John Millais was created a baronet. Other artists included in the series were Daniel Maclise, R.A., Thomas Creswick, R.A., Clarkson Stanfield, R.A., Sir Francis Grant, P.R.A., John Phillip, R.A., Baron Marochetti, and W. P. Frith, R.A.

Landseer had completed the design, and there had been much speculation about the form the monument would finally take. The picture John was to exhibit was therefore thought likely to draw considerable crowds and the *Art Journal* had immediately commissioned a set of engravings of the whole series of pictures, the sale of which, coupled with that of the original paintings, was hoped to return a handsome profit to the artist.

When all the arrangements had been completed, tastefully printed cards were sent to selected members of the Press, distinguished and wealthy patrons of the arts, and also the principal artists of the day, inviting them to the private view of John's pictures at the gallery of Messrs. Henry Graves & Company, at 6, Pall Mall, on the afternoon of Thursday, 16th November, 1865. But on the morning of the show, Ballantyne's hopes of a happy and successful day at the gallery were rudely dashed by his receiving a characteristically ill-mannered note from Landseer:

> *St. John's Wood Road, N.W.*
> *15th Nov. 65.*

My dear Sir,

I have received a card for the private view of your views of studios etc. As regards the scheme—I simply *assented* to the request and I am afraid made no conditions.

I now find that you have assented to Mr. Graves's hurry. Baron Marochetti knows we have refused to give any publicity to the lion business until the 4 lions take their place in Trafalgar Square.

If you are in nervous haste to turn a penny—let me know. I can only say the lion you saw and painted from no longer lives. The whole animal has been altered. I take leave to say it would have been better taste if you had consulted me in the matter. I now beg that the 'Lion Studio' be withdrawn from the list until the Nelson Monument is completed by the placing of the 4 lions at its basement—which is to be accomplished in a year or 14 months.

> Sincerely yours,
> E. Landseer.

It must have required considerable control on John's part to respond courteously to this last-minute demand by Landseer for the withdrawal of the chief exhibit and one that had been extensively advertised as being on view. Ballantyne's letters to his younger brother show that he had never imagined that the artist would impose any such restriction, being apparently convinced that Landseer fully understood that the picture would be shown with the others in the series as soon as they were completed. John's reply reveals little of the deep injustice he felt he had suffered, or the bitterness of his feelings at the mean trick he thought his wealthy brother artist[1] had played upon him:

The Mall, Kensington.
Novr. 16th. 1865.

Dear Sir Edwin Landseer,

It grieves me more than I can express to find that I have, most unwittingly, caused you annoyance in the matter of the Studios. As there are several points in your letter which call for a reply, will you kindly give me your patience while I make it.

First, in regard to my want of 'taste' in not consulting you in the matter—I was under the impression that I had your entire concurrence in the steps I was taking in order to give publicity to your studio, along with other in the series. In many conversations on the subject, both with Baron Marochetti[2] & yourself, the question of exhibiting the pictures in Mr. Graves's gallery was discussed, & as I understood, quite approved of by you; & I therefore thought that any further application to you might be deemed mere intrusion on my part, & the several calls that I made of late at Baron Marochetti's were more for the purpose of reporting the success

[1] The government of the day paid Sir Edwin Landseer a fee of £6,000 for designing the models of the four lions for Trafalgar Square. Baron Marochetti was responsible for the casting of the bronzework, and for this he was paid £11,000. (Information kindly supplied by the Ministry of Public Buildings and Works, London.)

[2] For the purpose of executing the commission for the Nelson Monument, Landseer and Marochetti shared a combined painting and sculpture studio.

of my arrangement with Mr. Graves than anything else.

But as I now find that your impressions & mine are at variance, I shall do all in my power to defer to your wishes. As the publication [of the series of engravings taken from the original paintings] will extend over a period of at least two years, will it be sufficient if I pledge myself that your picture shall be one of the last published instead of the first, as, from its being the most important and attractive, I had intended it to be? The picture has already been seen by a considerable number of people & the only difference in publicity now, is between my painting room and Mr. Graves's back gallery, where it is seen without any charge & by private card.

There are two expressions you have made use of which, in justice to myself, I must notice. As to my being in 'nervous haste to turn a penny,' why, I have been more than three years over the work & have been told over & over again by my professional brethren that the thing would 'hang fire' if I longer delayed exhibiting the pictures already completed, & in regard to its being a commercial speculation I can only say that it is as much (& not more) a commercial speculation as any of the productions of my brother artists.

It is not a speculation that I expect will ever yield me much profit (indeed after your restriction it is more than likely to be a heavy loss), but it is a work which I am proud to have achieved & the production of which has been a source of great pleasure to me, the only drawback now being the annoyance that it has unfortunately caused to you.

I remain,

Yours very truly,

John Ballantyne

Landseer replied the same afternoon,[1] but the note he sent did nothing to relieve John's dejection:

[1] A letter posted in the morning in any large town in the latter half of the nineteenth century could usually be relied upon to reach its local destination the same afternoon.

My dear Sir,

I am not well enough just now to enter into a discussion. You have jumped to a conclusion without remembering your pen and ink. I am always to be found by a note or letter.

The question has never been put *to me* about the immediate publication of the Lion. The colossal model was not finished when you came to the Baron's. I moreover told you, as soon as it was, and you wished a sitting from me, I would endeavour to meet your wishes. It now turns out that your unfinished picture of my unfinished Lion is to be exhibited as a true version of the combination studio and Lion as to be placed in Trafalgar Square. I have refused newspaper writers seeing the state of the model. I have refused all applications from photograph professors. You, without *consulting me,* yield to Mr. Graves and publish by exhibition an unfinished work. This I never dreamed of.

I have no objection to the picture being seen or published when complete—after the monument is *completed* in a year or 14 months' time—but cannot consent to this motley and *first impression* of the colossal bronze Lions being altered or interfered with.

Sincerely,
E. Landseer.

The next day, Ballantyne, having abandoned hope of receiving permission to display the picture or being allowed to sell the engraving, accepted the inevitable and wrote as pointed a letter as he dared to the man who, if once offended, could do his prospects in London immense harm. Landseer's remark about John's painting being 'unfinished' was a sarcastic reference to his not having had a formal sitting from the subject of the picture, knowing quite well that Ballantyne had worked from a photograph of himself which he (Landseer) had permitted to be taken. The last sentence in the letter quoted above seems to display some incoherence of thought on the part of the writer, as John had not requested permission to alter his picture or modify the painting of the model to bring it up to date, his reply to Landseer merely expressing his regrets:

The Mall, Kensington.
Novr. 17*th,* 1865.

Dear Sir Edwin Landseer,

I should indeed be wanting in both 'taste' and good feeling did I not act upon your wishes expressed in your note of this morning.

I have accordingly written to Mr. Graves to withdraw your picture from the exhibition. Of course I cannot expect your sympathy in the position of serious difficulty in which this places me, as you seem to think I have acted wrongly in the matter. I regret that you *do* think in this way, as I feel that the conclusions I arrived at & acted upon were based upon *most* reasonable grounds.

I was very sorry to hear of your accident & illness, but trust that you will soon be well & in working order again.

I remain,
Dear Sir Edwin Landseer,
Yours very truly,
John Ballantyne.

As soon as Bob heard from Teenie what had happened he wrote by return of post with emphatic advice to his brother John, but by the time his letter arrived in London the picture had been withdrawn from the gallery and the decision taken to close the exhibition several days before the intended date:

Royal George Hotel,
Perth,
[19*th November,* 1865].

. . . My opinion in regard to Landseer is that John ought to write firmly, emphatically, & plainly, as one gentleman is entitled to do to another, & put the case before Landseer & give him to understand that his conduct, if he perseveres, is unworthy of a gentleman—much more, of a brother artist.

If Landseer had been in ignorance of John's intentions, or if he had sat all along under protest, he wd. have had some excuse, but the plain *fact,* as it stands, is that Landseer has *permitted* John to waste his time, under false pretences, & in so doing he is a moral swindler & ought to be told so. Moreover he has swindled a *poor* brother artist, & in that view is mean. Truth is truth & there is not one sort of truth for the great & another for the small. The only difficulty in the whole affair is to 'bell the cat'—to give Landseer his true, *temporary*, character, for mind you, I don't believe that *he* sees it in this light. I believe him to be an honourable man, & *if* he saw it in this light he wd. at once give in; but he'll never see it thus if he is not told.

Oh! dear, how *much* I wd. like to tell him—either verbally or by letter! Think now—suppose John did—do you think it *could* do him any harm? Certainly not. I never heard of any harm coming from telling the *truth* to Queen, King or Beggar. On the contrary I believe that nearly all our miseries arise from humbug, deceit, false tenderness for the feelings of others—I say 'false' because, in nine cases out of ten, it is not the feelings of *others* that we fear to hurt but our own feelings & our own interests & our own prospects. I have seen it, I have felt it—therefore I know it!

Don't cite Tom Faed[1] as an argument against me. I uphold speaking *truth* to our fellows, & doing it (better let it alone if we cannot do it thus) in an honest, kind, gentle way. Tom, besides having much falsity mingled with his truth, is a passionate goose who thinks he can sway fate. He's very much like myself in *that* respect. It's a very different case here. Put it thus. If Landseer is right John is wrong. If Landseer is wrong John ought to tell him so, in the firm belief that honesty is the best policy. And it is dishonest to meet with Landseer as a friend and say *nothing* when he has done you the severest injury in his power.

Now, dearie, Goodnight.

Yrs. lovingly & truthfully,

R.M.B.

[1] Thomas Faed, R.A. (1826–1900), a painter who specialised in subjects depicting sentimental incidents in humble Scottish life. He had known John Ballantyne since the days when they were friends together at the Edinburgh School of Design.

John could attempt nothing further with 'The Lion Studio' for several years, but, after the placing in position of the four massive bronzes at the foot of Nelson's Column in 1869, he repainted the model of the lion to conform with the appearance of those in Trafalgar Square and submitted the finished canvas for Landseer's approval. Some years later the picture was purchased by Thomas Agnew & Sons, the London art dealers, one of whose partners, Sir William Agnew, presented it after Landseer's death to the National Portrait Gallery where it can still be seen.

Early in February, 1866, Bob returned to Scotland. By this time he must somehow have convinced Teenie that the house in The Mall contained too many distractions for an author intent on making his living by his pen, and that he needed absolute peace and quiet when engaged in the composition of a story. The numerous requests he had received from societies and associations North of the Border to lecture to their members must have provided another excuse for the trip, and the arrangements he had made with James Nisbet & Company about expenses when on location would have helped to remove further objections. But, whatever were the excuses and pleas advanced, he was eventually able to escape once more to his beloved Edinburgh, but with a firm determination, as he put it,[1]

. . . to let nothing deter me from writing & painting & painting & writing, until I have completed a sea-picture in oils worthy of a palace wall & have at last seen the final page of my new book crossed & dotted & delivered!

And perhaps if he had not let his friend James Cowan[2] persuade him to accept an invitation to a party at Leith, he might well have accomplished both his desires. But fate has a habit of ensuring that the best-laid schemes 'gang aft agley' and that night Bob Ballantyne met someone who, by the simple persuasion of her presence, caused him to forget his plans and jettison his resolutions, fixing his destiny on a course so different that his entire life was utterly changed from that day on.

[1] Letter to Teenie, dated 7th February, 1866.
[2] James Cowan of Glenesk, partner in the paper-making firm of Alexander Cowan & Sons.

The party the two men attended took the form of a musical evening at the home of Mrs. Grant, a widow in comfortable financial circumstances, who lived with her four grown children in a Georgian house in the best part of the town. Her late husband, the Reverend William Grant, who had been minister of the Established Church at Cavers, Roxburghshire, had been dead for nearly thirteen years.[1] Her income had just been sufficient to send her son James, now twenty-two, to the University to obtain a degree of Doctor of Medicine, and also to pay for her twenty-one-year-old daughter, Jane, to attend for twelve months one of the expensive Swiss schools conducted with the aim of imparting a final polish to the bearing and deportment of middle- and upper-class young ladies. Isabella and William, aged twenty-three and sixteen respectively, completed the family,[2] and they and the several guests gathered after supper around the piano in the lamp-lit drawing room that April evening, to sing the sentimental ballads so beloved by the Victorians and generally enjoy themselves. With the aid of Mrs. Grant's dumpy, black morocco diary, with its broken silver clasps, worn covers and crumbling spine, we can observe the events of the next few days and perhaps sense the warmth and intensity of this mid-Victorian romance as the yellow pages are turned again.

April 21st.
A splendid evening, altho' I found it a little tiring. All left the party at 11 after much singing and Bagatelle. Mr. R.M.B. in very great spirits & very fascinating.

April 27th.
Mr. B. to tea at 6. Uncle Andrew & Uncle David came late, very pleasant evening. They left before 10. Mr. B. remained till nearly 12. Much pleasant fireside talk.

May 2nd.
Nice note from Mr. B. this morning. He is an earnest Christian man.

[1] The Reverend William Grant died on the 26th September, 1853, aged forty-two, having contracted typhus fever through visiting sick parishioners during an epidemic of the disease.
[2] Her eldest son, Lewis Grant, was married and lived away from home.

May 5th, Saturday.

Mr. R.M.B. has been at Glenesk for four days with the Cowans. He came to tea & we all went out after it. Jamie & I to Powder Hill. Jane and he (B) with Isa & Willie were out till dark. R.M.B. and Jane lingered behind, when he told her of his deep attachment to her, but said he was never sure of her love. He was dreadfully agitated when he came in. Jane told me upstairs that she had told him his love was not hopeless. He had confided to her that he had never loved before. I was much put about.

The first pages of the letter in which Bob broke the momentous news to Teenie are unfortunately missing, but the final portion has survived:

. . . This new joy that has come into my life owes the *greater* portion of its strength to Him. It makes me happy to think of my dear Jane's sweetness, & loveableness, & prettiness, &c. but the thought that ever & anon sends a burst of *gladness* through me is, that she is a true, earnest follower of the Lamb.

I spent the afternoon, till 7 o'clock here & then went down to spend the evening with the Grants. The mother & sister alone knew of it last night—but the brothers had been told, so I shook hands *emphatically* with them! There is a boy boarder in the house who is not to be told at present so we had to be careful not by word or look to let *him* know.

I have arranged to go down tomorrow forenoon to have a business talk with the mother alone! I'm rather afraid of this, for I have not a brilliant prospect to lay before her. But the Lord is my help. He permitted the matter to go thus far & will assuredly carry me through. I did not go near Aunt Hunter today on purpose. Of course you can tell the dear 'bairns'[1] but for a few days they need not let it go any further.

Now, dearie, goodnight. God bless you.

Yr. loving brother,

R.M.B.

[1] John and Teenie's three children, Dot, Edith and Randal, all now in their teens.

By the way—tell me what necessary things will have to be done—for instance, what about an engagement ring—is there not something of that sort? Anything else you can think of tell me, for I'm awfully ignorant on the etiquette of such a situation!

Bob's fears about his future mother-in-law's reaction to his financial prospects proved to be groundless, for the next entry in her diary shows that he passed the test with flying colours:

May 7th.
I went up and broke the news to Uncle D. and Aunt A. Had a business visit from dear R.M.B., who told me all his means. Not great at present, but he has plenty of work as an author & can make good income. He was out at Currie in the evening but here afterwards till very late. Jane very happy.

May 8th.
Aunt Charlotte and Uncle D. at tea with R.M.B. They are very happy about the affair. He left at 9 for Lifeboat meeting.

May 9th.
J. & B. have been house hunting. Many beautiful letters to her from friends. She seems very fond of him.

May 11th.
Mr. Ballantyne came down bringing Mr. James Cowan, who gave me when alone such a fine character of his friend Bob, as they all seem to call him.

May 12th.
R.M.B. down early in a cab with a beautiful model of a lifeboat which had been sent to him by the Lifeboat Society. Jane has been given a beautiful ring by Mr. B.

The next day was a Sunday and Bob and Miss Jane Dickson Grant, to give his fiancée her full name, walked arm in arm to attend morning service in St. Cuthbert's parish church. She was a gently spoken, well-educated young lady, slim figured but with that rounded, teenage, feminine appeal that a male of Ballantyne's age must have found well nigh irresistible. Her face was well cut, and enhanced by soft, deep, brown eyes, which, combined with a near flawless complexion, won the heart of her husband-to-be to the extent of causing him to compose more than one deeply effusive poem in her honour. She wore her long brown hair either parted in the middle with plaits falling over her shoulders, or curled neatly around to form a bun at the back of her head. Photographs taken at the time show that these styles, coupled with her high cheekbones, straight little nose and well-formed mouth, suited her appearance admirably. The crinoline was still the height of fashion, and beneath her tight-laced and nipped little waist she wore huge, steel-hooped skirts, heavily trimmed with braid and fancy stitching, the whole massive bell of silk and taffeta swaying and dancing and rustling as she glided across a room:

> Her feet beneath her petticoat,
> Like little mice, stole in and out,
> As though they feared the light.[1]

She was a most attractive young creature, and beside the bearded, straight-backed, military-looking figure of her handsome companion, as they stood together in the family pew, enduring the interested stares of the remainder of the congregation, she must have caused a flutter in many a masculine heart.

But there was one young gentleman in the church that day who had eyes only for the great Mr. R. M. Ballantyne, a man he thought a giant in the world of literature and a hero on whose head it was impossible to bestow sufficient praise. Fifteen-year-old Master Robert Louis Stevenson, although he no doubt modified his assessment of Bob's ability as an author in later and more mature years, at that time apparently had no reservations to make about Ballantyne's genius as a story-teller, and moreover had decided to have the great man to himself for a few hours by inviting him back to dinner that very night. The story of the incident that occurred after the service that morning was often related to her children by Mrs. Ballantyne, who said that it was

[1] These lines, in Ballantyne's hand, are pencilled on the back of an envelope containing an early picture of his wife. They are taken from Sir John Suckling's poem, *Ballad Upon a Wedding*.

then, for the first time, that she realised that she was to marry a man who, at least to young people, was a famous and well-loved public figure.

As they left the churchyard to walk home, they were stopped within a few yards of the lych-gate by an eager young man, who raised his hat in greeting, said his name was Robert Stevenson, and begged to inform Mr. Ballantyne how much he enjoyed reading his books. Furthermore, having received permission to do so, he would deem it an honour if Mr. Ballantyne and his companion would take dinner that evening with his grandfather and himself at Colington Manse, where they were then residing.[1] Somewhat taken aback by the suddenness of the invitation, Bob rather embarrassedly introduced the lad to his fiancée, and, after thanking him, explained that as they had just become engaged to be married it was unfortunately impossible to accept his kind offer, a number of friends and relations being expected at Mrs. Grant's that evening and their presence would be required. He then asked which of his books Stevenson had liked best and was informed that the young man thought *The Coral Island* a wonderfully exciting story and that he had read it twice and hoped to read it twice more. After saying how pleased he was that the books he wrote brought pleasure to at least some of his readers, and hoping very much that they might meet again, Ballantyne and his bride-to-be shook hands with the thin and delicate-looking youth and bade goodbye to the future author of *Treasure Island* as they turned to walk home.

As far as is known, this is the only occasion when the two writers met, but the incident detailed above lends weight to the supposition that Stevenson's passionate love of the romantic islands of the South Seas, to one of which he eventually retired and died, may first have been kindled by his reading the adventures of Ralph, Jack and Peterkin as they fought the cannibals and braved the dangers of their remote coral strand. It seems probable that the wonderful romance of *Treasure Island*, unsurpassed as a straightforward adventure story for boys of all

[1] At this time Stevenson and his parents lived at 17 Heriot Row, Edinburgh, but young Robert spent much of his time at his maternal grandfather's house at Colington in Leith.

ages, perhaps itself owes some debt to the pages of Ballantyne's most famous book.

A week or so after the meeting with Stevenson, Mrs. Grant's diary recorded further progress in the arrangements being made for the forthcoming marriage:

May 21st.
Went about buying the house at 6, Millerfield Place, Edinburgh for my dear bairns. Agreed on the terms.

May 22nd.
Offered £900 for the house.

May 24th.
Jane writes every day and hears every day from dear R.M.B.

While he was in Edinburgh, Bob had been staying with his sister Jane at 6 Pitt Street, but he was now forced to return to London to collect his belongings from The Mall, at the same time informing his publisher that the book he had promised to have ready for midsummer would not now be in his hands until the autumn. Most important of all, he had to thank his brother John, and his sister-in-law Teenie, for the home they had provided for him during the previous twenty years, as well as answer the numerous questions with which he was sure to be plied by the lady who had looked after his moral welfare and well-being for so long. This must have been an ordeal to which he had looked forward with trepidation, but by June he was back in Scotland, no doubt with a feeling of immense relief. He passed the whole month at Aberdour, across the Firth of Forth from Edinburgh, where the Grants had rented a seaside house for the summer, his future mother-in-law faithfully recording the details:

June 5th.
Robert Ballantyne came by boat to Aberdour—in great spirits, dear man. He arrived from London this morning. We all had a very pleasant evening on the cliffs. Isa heard from S.G.B.[1]

[1] Isa was, of course, Mrs. Grant's daughter, Isabella. 'S.G.B.' were the initials of Stephen Balmer, the young man she hoped to marry.

June 9th.

Very wet day until the evening, but the boys got out the boat and we all had a great deal of nice music from Robert with the guitar.

June 22nd.

Robert and the boys had a long sail out to Carcrag and set it on fire. Put up my old shawl as a sail.

July 24th.

Mr. and Mrs. John Ballantyne and their children came from London and down here to lunch. Robert stayed afterwards to tea.

July 25th.

Mrs. Ballantyne and her two daughters and Robert to tea. All left at ¼ past 9. Dear Jane much excited; cried bitterly after they left. How devotedly she loves dear Robert.

Mrs. Grant informed Bob that she was providing her daughter with a tocher[1] of twelve hundred pounds, but of this sum nine hundred pounds had immediately to be spent on purchasing their new house at 6, Millerfield Place and much of the rest was needed to make it habitable. The ladies of the family spent the weeks before the ceremony in that flurry of excited activity which an approaching wedding always arouses in the female. The house had to be curtained, carpeted and furnished throughout so that all should be in order for the happy couple's return from their honeymoon; there were dresses to be bought, the wedding reception to be arranged, the cake to be prepared, and a thousand and one details attended to if everything was to be socially correct and in perfect good taste when the carriages of guests arrived.

As for the groom—shopping irritated him at the best of times and no doubt he kept well out of the way; but we do know that he was commanded by Teenie, on her arrival in Edinburgh, to attend immediately a reputable gentleman's tailor and order for himself an entire new wardrobe. That her orders were obeyed is evident, for the day before his wedding, with Jane demure and

[1] The word 'tocher' is used in Scotland to denote a marriage portion or dowry.

219

lovely by his side, we find him standing stiffly in an Edinburgh studio before a backcloth of painted trees and flowers, clad in his new velvet jacket with its piped lapels and pockets, smart sand-coloured trousers and black shoes, a plaid waistcoat around his middle and a fashionable silk cravat around his neck, his hair and beard neatly trimmed and with a brand new bowler hat by his hand, waiting patiently for the photographer to close the shutter.[1]

Members of the Free Church of Scotland, in the middle of the nineteenth century, usually had the marriage solemnized in the house where the wedding breakfast was held rather than the church itself. Mrs. Grant had therefore obtained permission from her sister Charlotte to hold the ceremony and reception in the large drawing room of her house in Park Place, Edinburgh, as being the only room big enough to accommodate the many guests who were expected to attend. Her diary records the day's proceedings:

July 31st. Tuesday.
A beautiful day with bright sunshine. My beloved Jane's marriage day. Isa went up at 10 with the luggage. Jane & I at 12. About sixty guests at Park Place. Dr. Glover very impressive. Everything went off beautifully, but dear Robert very agitated. They left at 4.40 for Carlisle.

The nervously happy pair, to whom the guests waved goodbye as the train pulled out of Edinburgh Station, were away for most of the month of August, travelling much of the time by coach and dogcart through the remote, mountainous districts of North Wales, their nights being spent at lonely village inns or the primitive hotels of small towns. When the sun shone and the weather was fine Bob fished the rivers and streams for trout, while Jeanie, as he now called her, sat on the bank and watched the bearded, forty-one-year-old figure of her husband as he flashed the line high over her head. Where the scenery was particularly inspiring he sketched and painted, his wife reading

[1] See Plate 4. This photograph was taken in Princes Street, Edinburgh, by a Mr. Moffat, whose studio was well known. Written on the back of the original, in Jane's hand, are the words, 'The day before our wedding.'

quietly by his side from works thought suitable for the eyes of a young lady just entering the matrimonial state. Sometimes it rained and they were confined to their hotel, but it is most unlikely that they were unduly perturbed.

With a wife to keep in the style to which she had been accustomed and a well-appointed home to maintain, Bob applied himself with vigour to the task of finishing his new book on their return to Millerfield Place. Several chapters had been written while he was on holiday with the Grants at Aberdour, and most of the background material he needed was already stored in his notebooks from previous sojourns at the coast. For this was to be yet another story of the sea, as usual littered with shipwrecks and maritime disasters of all kinds, to the repetition of which scenes more than one reviewer sarcastically drew the attention of his readers.

Ballantyne finished *Shifting Winds—A Tough Yarn* in less than a month, weaving the story around the activities of The Shipwrecked Mariners' Society and of The Sailors' Home, whose headquarters in Well Street, London, had supplied him with many of the facts and figures he required. However, after scanning the completed manuscript and illustrations, Watson ordered a printing of only fifteen hundred copies for the first edition, in contrast to the two thousand of *The Lighthouse*, most probably because he thought the theme had been overplayed. The author's notes show that the work sold only moderately well and both he and his publisher decided that a radically new setting was needed for his next tale if the interest of what Watson called his 'sea-sick readers' was to be maintained. A typical review of the book appeared in *The Northern Ensign* on the 20th December, 1866.

It is not many months since we had the pleasure of directing the attention of our readers to two admirable volumes from Mr. Ballantyne's prolific and popular pen, both connected with the sea, which is so much Mr. Ballantyne's element that we suspect the question is as applicable to him as to Dr. Guthrie,[1] 'What will he do when the vision of John of Patmos is fulfilled and there is no more sea?'

[1] Thomas Guthrie, D.D. (1803–73), famous Scottish preacher and one of the founders of the Free Church of Scotland.

We have no doubt that *Shifting Winds* will beguile the tedium of long voyages in many a cabin and forecastle, and that the yarn will be read with gusto by multitudes of our noble British tars.

From the time when he wrote *Snowflakes and Sunbeams; or, The Young Fur Traders*, Ballantyne always sent two sets of the printed sheets of each new title direct to Henderson and Barnard, the Edinburgh bookbinders. One set he ordered to be bound as a working and reference copy in a tough form of half-calf, with marbled boards, leather corners, and plain end-papers; but the other was always sumptuously clothed in full morocco over bevelled boards, the sides and spine heavily embossed in gold in an elaborate and ornate design, the page edges fully gilded and gauffered, while the end-papers were marbled and glazed. Before his marriage this latter copy was invariably given to Teenie, complete with a suitable inscription on the fly-leaf, but, from 1866 onwards, she had to be content with a signed presentation volume in the original cloth. The finely bound book was now reserved for his wife, the inscription usually reading—'To darling Jeanie, from her loving husband The Author,' followed by the place and date. He continued this practice until the mid eighteen-seventies, when it appears that the increasing expenses of a growing family made him dispense altogether with the services of a bindery.

After their honeymoon, Jeanie Ballantyne settled down to the domestic routines expected of a dutiful and loving wife and, with the help of Mamma, appears to have given every satisfaction both as a cook, a housewife, and the keeper of the family purse. From the letters he wrote to her Bob seems to have been more than pleased with the choice he had made, and entirely content with his 'darling Jeanie' in every way. Few of the letters he must have written to her during the first twelve months of their marriage have escaped destruction, but those that are left are deeply affectionate. In November 1866 he wrote her from Stirling:

> . . . didn't I miss you when I awoke this morning! God bless your sweet, innocent face, for I've been, more than I imagined, in the habit of looking at it when you are asleep. Well, it

won't be long, dearest, till I see it again. But I yearn for you and miss you so that you fill all my waking thoughts.

God bless you, my beloved wife,
Your own husband,
R.M.B.

During the first winter of his marriage, Ballantyne undertook an extensive and arduous lecture tour which embraced nearly every large town in Scotland. Each society or association to which he spoke had to guarantee him a fee of five pounds, plus his expenses up to thirty shillings, but he seems to have had little difficulty in filling halls up and down the country at least once or twice a week for many months, the subject of his lectures being either 'Hudson's Bay and the Frozen North' or 'The Lifeboat'. His familiarity with the work of the Lifeboat Institution and unrivalled knowledge of the part played by the coastal rescue services in saving life at sea was recognised in another quarter, for he had the honour to be requested by Adam and Charles Black, the publishers of the ninth edition of *The Encyclopaedia Britannica*, to write the article on 'Lifeboats' in volume fourteen, which was then in course of preparation.

Despite the lecture tour he managed to finish a somewhat inconsequential story called *Silver Lake; or, Lost in the Snow*, which he then sold to Messrs. Jackson, Walford & Hodder of London, who ran it during 1867 as a serial in a children's magazine called *Merry & Wise*, later publishing it in book form under its full title, and finally in *Old Merry's Annual for 1868*.

As usual, he reserved his main literary effort of the year for his annual full-length story for James Nisbet & Company. Watson had proposed cancelling their old agreement whereby he was paid location expenses, substituting instead a new flat rate of payment of forty-five pounds for each thousand copies sold. This offer Ballantyne accepted as being to his advantage; if two editions of a book gave a total of three thousand copies, it would now bring him one hundred and thirty-five pounds, whereas, calculated at the old rate, three thousand copies would have amounted to only one hundred and twenty pounds, plus about ten pounds expenses, giving him five pounds less. Any printing in excess of three thousand volumes would show an even greater advantage; the more popular the tale, the more he would earn, and the bonus would be a stimulus to greater effort.

As though determined to keep as far from the sea as possible, Bob chose the London Fire Brigade as his subject. Here was a body of men whose activities were filled with the most dramatic possibilities and far more modern in their outlook than any similar organisation in Scotland. He rejected using the local Edinburgh brigade, with their old-fashioned handpumps, and cumbersome equipment, as being far too archaic for his forward-looking young readers, who, like boys of every age, had an uncanny faculty for hearing of the latest mechanical contrivance within weeks of its invention, and moreover expected an author to be as bang up to date as they were themselves. In search of the technical information he required for the story, Ballantyne started a protracted correspondence with both Captain E. M. Shaw, chief officer of the Metropolitan Fire Brigade, and with Mr. Sampson Low, Secretary of the London Fire-Escape Society, who each gave him a great amount of help. Shaw's first letter promised full co-operation:

> *Metropolitan Fire Brigade,*
> *Watling Street, London E.C.*
> *June 15th, 1867.*

Dear Sir,

I shall be glad to do anything in my power for you, but I must tell you that the present Fire Brigade is a very different institution from that of 10 or 12 years ago. If you wish to know what it was then, you will find its exact counterpart where you are—in Edinburgh.

I think you will do well to call on Mr. Mitchell, & see for yourself how very different things were a few years since. In former times a fire here was attended with noise & confusion, such as one sees at a riot or in times of great political commotion. This was owing to the fact that the engines were worked by the crowd & that it was therefore necessary to admit a large number of noisy individuals inside the line of police. Now I am independent of the mob & have the pumps driven by steam, the consequence of which is, that all within the cordon of police is order & regularity, & that every one of my orders is instantly understood & promptly obeyed.

I do hope you will have an opportunity of seeing a few fires elsewhere, as otherwise it will be almost impossible for you to realise how great & complete has been the revolution in these matters.

I am, Dear Sir,

Yrs. truly,

E. M. Shaw.

In August, the author and his wife accepted an invitation from Teenie to stay for a month with John and her in London, and the visit provided Ballantyne with an opportunity to see the Fire Brigade headquarters and inspect the latest fire-fighting equipment. The first time he called, the officer-in-charge staged a display using the modern steam pump which was the station's pride and joy, following this with a demonstration of a rescue by means of a jumping sheet in which one of his men leaped from an upstairs window on to the taut canvas held by his comrades. However, the most memorable event was one in which Bob himself took part a few nights later, after arriving near midnight in the hope of being able to attend a fire. When nothing untoward had been reported by the early hours of the morning, Captain Shaw turned out the appliance for a timed practice run in which the author was allowed to take part. On the ringing of the alarm, Ballantyne and the rest of the crew made a dash for the engine, the boiler fire of which was kept continually alight, buttoning coats and donning helmets as they ran. The vehicle was pushed rapidly into the courtyard as the pair of powerful horses were trotted up. Quickly, the harness was adjusted, the fire damper of the boiler was opened and, in less than ten minutes from the moment when the bell first rang, the whip cracked and the fire-engine dashed away from the station amid cheers from the assembled crowd. Subsequent events are detailed in a letter the author sent to his sister, Jane:

. . . I was not unduly perturbed when I first took my place on the back of the vehicle, but we were soon proceeding at such a breakneck pace that I began to fear that the horses had taken fright and were no longer under the driver's control. I was on the back step, & unable to communicate with those on top, the violent ringing of the massive bell, the clatter of hooves & the shouts of the men, making any conversation quite impossible, while I became half blinded by the smoke from the steam engine. But I was too intent in retaining my hold on the swaying machine to risk clambering round to see if all was in order.

Twice, as the engine negotiated a corner, I feared we should topple over, for a wheel mounted a kerbstone with a terrific crash & the whole machine swayed alarmingly, while I then made the disconcerting discovery that my helmet was on backwards but was quite unable to remedy this at the time. I must confess to a feeling of great relief when the horses started to tire and we made our way back to the station. I strongly suspect that the fact that there was a layman aboard impelled the crew to redouble their efforts on this occasion, as they seemed tremendously amused by my appearance as I dismounted.

One can imagine that a smoke-grimed and dishevelled Bob Ballantyne was very pleased indeed to reach home again in the early hours still in one piece, but, to give him his due, his hair-raising experience did not prevent him volunteering for other rides on a later occasion.[1] He finished writing the story of *Fighting the Flames—A Tale of the London Fire Brigade* on the 9th September, 1867, the book appearing for sale at five shillings a copy in December the same year.[2] It seems to have been well received, for a second edition was published the following spring and the tale was re-issued several times in the next few years.

Soon after their return to Edinburgh an incident occurred which received a good deal of publicity in the Scottish papers and must have helped the sale of his book considerably. Perhaps what happened is best described in a report of the affair which the Deputy Chief Clerk of the city requested Ballantyne to make to him:[3]

[1] For a book he wrote in 1873, *Life in the Red Brigade*, details of which are described later, he spent two weeks at a fire station and went out with the appliances on several occasions.

[2] Ballantyne dated the last page of the manuscript of this story.

[3] Details of this letter are described from a fair copy he made of the one sent to the Deputy Chief Clerk of Edinburgh.

6 *Millerfield Place,*
Edinburgh.
29th October, 1867.

Dear Sir,

In reply to your note of yesterday, expressing the desire of the magistrates to know the details of my experiences of what came under my own observation at the recent fire in Canongate, I have to submit the following statement of facts.[1]

I arrived on the ground after the various cases of rescue from the windows were over, &, like many others in the crowd, stood looking on at the firemen under the impression that the matter of saving life was completed. From this mistaken idea I was aroused by hearing someone state that Mrs. Ferguson, who leapt from the window, had said that 'her bairn was in the garret' or words to that effect. I was strongly impressed with this, & felt convinced that the child must certainly be there still—perhaps other people also. At once I made enquiry of several persons (Mr. McPherson, the Inspector of Buildings, among others) as to whether anything was being done in the way of searching the upper floors & found that nothing was being attempted. Some appeared to think it wd. be useless, as any who were there must be dead by that time. Others said that the staircase was blown away & that it was impossible to get up. This was an error, but, believing it to be true at the time, I resolved to attempt to gain the attics by the roof & ascended the staircase of the adjoining house.

At the top I procured a table & a chair wh. enabled me to reach a skylight, from wh. I saw that the roof was much too steep to clamber along. Conceiving, however, that if I cd. get a sweep, or one accustomed to such work, to fasten a rope round the chimneys, we might by that means be able to reach the storm windows. I descended to the court & again spoke to Mr. McPherson, asking if he knew of anyone who cd. be got without delay. He immediately introduced me to Mr. Slater, who as first seemed to think that any attempt to gain the upper floors was either impossible or unnecessary. (I am

[1] The fire took place in a five-storey warren of slum houses in Chessel's Court, Canongate.

not sure which.) On my stating my strong convictions, however, he promptly volunteered to ascend the staircase if Mr. Mc.P. & I wd. follow him.

Accordingly, we at once went up, & Mr. Slater & I gained the upper floor, where, in the first room we entered we found Mrs. Ferguson's little child lying on its face. It showed signs of life when Mr Slater picked it up. Mr. S. carried it downstairs & while he was thus engaged I searched the rest of the flat, but found no one. Being somewhat confused by the smoke & the intricacies of the place I fancied that I had searched every place and then descended under the impression that all were got out. In this I was mistaken, for a Mr. Watson (I believe) & Mr. Slater, who had re-ascended, soon after discovered Mrs. Wilson & Mrs. Taylor in the attics. Mr. Slater ran down and called for assistance. I ran up the stair again with other men. We gained the upper floor, and I assisted two men (whose names I do not know) to carry Mrs. Wilson down to the court. She appeared to be dead at the time, but I heard one of the medical men afterwards say that he felt her heart still beat slowly. She died, as you know, & so did the little girl Ferguson, but Mrs. Taylor recovered.

This, sir, is all that I did, & all that I know in regard to the saving of life at that fire . . . but, from these facts I wd. argue that we in Edinburgh shd. not only have one or more fire-escapes, but also a body of men specially trained to save life at fires by all available means as well as the use of the escape —by means of jumping sheets, for instance, or blankets as extemporised jumping sheets, by rope ladders, by ropes fastened round chimney stacks whereby attic windows might be gained &c.

Trusting that the Magistrates will excuse my making these suggestions.

I am, Dear Sir,
Yrs. faithfully,
R. M. Ballantyne

Due note must have been taken by the City Fathers of the part he played in the rescue, for, in November the same year, *The*

Scotsman contained a long account of the presentation of silver medals to the individuals who most distinguished themselves during the fire, the name of R. M. Ballantyne being high in the list. The newspaper report of the ceremony also revealed the cause of the fire:

During the course of his speech the Lord Provost said:

'We are met to perform an interesting ceremony, that of conferring medals of honour on various individuals who distinguished themselves by their heroic efforts to save human life on the occasion of the disastrous fire in the Canongate on the 9th October last.

'The cause of that calamity is well known. It was the improper manufacture of fireworks in the street floor of a high dwelling-house, and bursting out suddenly, the fire very soon filled the staircase with smoke so as to render exit by it impracticable. Finding their egress by the stair cut off, some of the women threw themselves and their children over the windows; and it was mainly in attempts to save them by ladders, ropes, and blankets, that the heroism I speak of was displayed. These attempts were, I am glad to say, successful in several instances; but whether so or not, invited the approbation of the authorities, along with such marks of favour as was in their power to bestow . . .'

In presenting Mr. Ballantyne with his medal the Lord Provost said:

'I am delighted to admit you into this Legion of Honour. You have distinguished yourself on many occasions previously, both here and elsewhere, by your services in the cause of humanity; and it is gratifying to me, as Chief Magistrate of Edinburgh, to be able to present you on this occasion with one of our medals of honour.' (Applause.)

The same month saw the publication of *Fighting the Flames* and the newspapers were not slow in perceiving the news value of the coincidence, the publicity helping to swell the sales of the book in Scotland to a higher figure than any previous work of Ballantyne's had achieved. One might think that, having completed an arduous lecture tour, written two new books, and earned himself a silver medal, the author would have been content to rest content until the new year, but December ended with Bob trying hard to persuade his publisher to agree to revive his idea of *Ballantyne's Magazine for Boys*, and also to let him enter the field of literature occupied so successfully by Hans Christian Andersen and the brothers Grimm:

> *Draft of letter to Nisbet & Co.,*
> *Edinr. 26th Decr. 1867.*

My dear Mr. Watson,

Can you give me your ear for ten minutes or so? I have two points to remark on.

First. I am strongly inclined & impelled to make my next Christmas book a Fairy tale! This is a subject wh. has bulked very large in my mind for many years & one wh. I have always held, as it were, in reserve, until a fitting opportunity when I might hope to launch it under favourable auspices.

The idea that has haunted me is this. I shall assume that the open polar-basin (wh. is supposed to exist round the North Pole) is filled with lovely islands on wh. all the fairies that have ever existed shall be found dwelling—& not only fairies, but also such familiar friends as Sinbad the Sailor, Bluebeard, Cinderella, The Three Bears, &c. The chief of these I shall constitute the *dramatis personae* of the tale & cause them to go through innumerable adventures by land & sea, in wh. they will converse, of course, about things in general & sometimes about their former careers when they lived and acted in the parts of the earth (?) inhabited by ordinary human beings.

I need scarcely point out that the subject wd. afford unlimited scope for the union of the ludicrous & the sentimental, also for the application of many a moral, inasmuch as these beings might be supposed to take a calm & unprejudiced (&, in some cases, repentant) view of their deeds and feelings in previous years! The romance of the region might be brought out by the union of the fine climate (caused by the supposed warmth of the polar basin) with the presence of gorgeous fields & mountains of glittering ice wh. floats about & strands on these island shores. There would be plot & counter-plot—in short, a regular tale. What think ye of this? We might call it Fairyland discovered! or something of that sort.

The second point is a proposal wh. has been made to me by Blackie of Glasgow,[1] in regard to wh. I have not yet given him a reply, but the simple entertaining of wh. requires me to consult with you.

He wants me to edit, &, to a large extent, write an important work (as regards size at least) wh. may be shortly described as 'Scenes in Many Lands.' Descriptions of places & natives with manners & customs & anecdotes &c. The work wd. contain about 1600 large pages & wd. take up all my spare time for probably the greater part of 2 years. Now, I do not feel inclined to undertake this, even though he should pay me handsomely for it, because it wd. render the starting of our Magazine impossible for a long time to come, & a great deal of the material wh. I wd. be employed in collecting might be much more appropriately collected for ourselves!

In these circumstances I write to ask if you think we might start the Magazine (i.e. publish the first number) next December (1868) or January (1869). I have been, & still am, collecting material & preparing for it. If you do think so (I will not ask you to pledge yourself to it) I will at once decline to have anything to do with this work of Blackie's, without even taking the trouble to 'consider it.' Of course, I have no right to name it to you except in strict confidence.

Please let me have a reply as soon as possible, and, with the compliments of the season from myself & wife to you & yr. household, I am ever,

Yours sincerely,
R. M. B.[allantyne]

What Watson wrote in reply cannot now be discovered, but we do know that neither the magazine nor the book of fairy tales ever appeared; nor, for that matter, did the monumental work commissioned by Messrs. Blackie.

[1] John Blackie (1782–1874), the Glasgow publisher.

Chapter Eleven

BY 1868, Ballantyne's life had settled into a regular routine which was to vary but little for several years. During the winter he lectured as frequently as he could find audiences to fill the halls, spending the weekends away from home if the town in which he was to speak was distant from Edinburgh. The rest of his week would be devoted to working upon whichever story he was writing at the time, but a portion of his time was devoted to water-colour painting. Except for a few studies he made of his wife, he never attempted portrait painting, but the landscapes and views of coastal scenery with which he usually filled his canvases were competent and pleasing works and found a steady sale at a few guineas apiece.

On his return to Scotland he had rejoined the Edinburgh Volunteers and was soon confirmed in his old rank as captain. But his enthusiasm for the movement had waned and most of his leisure hours were reserved for his favourite sport of angling, or for the shooting parties at his brother-in-law's place at Gollanfield House, Inverness-shire. During the first few years of their marriage Jeanie usually accompanied her husband on these visits to Hector McKenzie's, staying indoors with his wife Mary and daughter Isobel, while the men set out with guns and beaters for a day on the windswept moors.

Bob's marriage was proving a very happy one, and his letters to Jeanie show him to be a devoted husband, although his increasing observance of the strict tenets of Free Church nonconformism distilled a highly emotional evangelical essence into nearly every letter he wrote to her. Even so prosaic a task as engaging a servant occasioned in him an outburst of religious fire.

[*circa* 1868]

My own darling Jeanie,

May the Lord bless your tender & forgiving heart.

I am very thankful to hear that you have engaged a servant who is good-tempered (apparently) & who, I hope with

252

you, will be a comfort to us. I am *sure* that she is an answer
to our prayers. But, don't misunderstand me when I say this.
If she turns out ill she will still have been the answer! Perhaps we need bad servants for some good end! *Whatever* she
turns out she will have been an answer. An answer to prayer
does not consist in our getting what *we want*; it consists in
the fulfillment of God's promise. *He* has said, 'Whatsoever
ye shall ask the Father in my name he will give it to you.'
Well—we unitedly asked for a good servant in the name of
Jesus. The answer is sure. We shall get a good servant *if such
will be good for us*. If not, we certainly will *not* get one. God
will not give us what will be bad for us, even though we ask
it in the name of Jesus. Can you not see this, darling, &
place the matter in His loving hands?

Love to you, my own sweet Jeanie,
Your,
R.M.B.

The happy-go-lucky airs of the carefree young lad of Hudson
Bay had by this time been almost completely submerged beneath
the conventional dignity expected from a forty-three-year-old
Elder of the Free Church of Scotland. Each day, when he was at
home, he and his wife stood together amid the cluttered nick-
nacks and heavily carved furniture of their dining-room, while
he offered prayers that their every action might be guided
throughout the coming twenty-four hours by a true understanding of God's will. The servant girl would attend these
prayers in her stiffly starched cap and apron, flitting below stairs
as soon as her master had finished intoning the blessing, there to
await the tinkling summons of the table-bell at the end of the
meal. With breakfast over and his mail and newspaper read,
the author would retire to his study, seldom emerging until the
gong summoned him to their midday meal. In the meantime,
Jeanie would busy herself with domestic affairs, or disappear for a
morning's shopping, returning in good time to supervise the
cooking of the family's lunch. Their afternoons they usually
managed to keep free for social calls on friends and relations, and
their day invariably ended with communal prayers after the

evening meal. And so to the candle-lit bedroom and the curtained privacy of the old four-poster that his father and mother had used before him.

The summer months most often found Ballantyne concentrating his talents on finishing the manuscript of his annual full-length adventure tale which James Nisbet & Company required in time to publish in November; hoping to catch the eye of the uncles and aunts or other generous-hearted relatives of the many hundreds of boys who would later give their excited thanks for the gift of a Christmas book by their favourite author. In addition to this major literary effort, he invariably completed at least one other book during the course of the twelve months, as well as sending a number of short stories and articles to children's magazines and annuals. Financially, the author was probably better off than he had ever been, for he was now reaping the benefit of owning the copyrights of the books he had written since leaving Nelson's. The five stories published by James Nisbet & Company brought him a regular and increasing income as they passed through new editions, and Messrs. J. B. Lippincott & Company of Philadelphia were re-issuing these works in America on terms Ballantyne described as most satisfactory.[1] Sometimes he could earn a few extra pounds by undertaking tasks one could only describe as hackwork, and February saw the appearance of *Photographs of Edinburgh*, an elaborate gift book offered to the public by Andrew Duthie of Glasgow, in which photographs of some of the most architecturally interesting parts of the city were accompanied by text from the pen of R. M. Ballantyne.[2]

In the late spring, his wife suffered a bad attack of influenza, and was in bed for several days, the illness leaving her with a persistent cough which stubbornly refused to disappear despite the application of embrocations to the chest and the dutiful swallowing of multifarious and evil-tasting concoctions prescribed

---

[1] The exact terms he received are unknown.

[2] This book was issued simultaneously in both quarto and octavo sizes at one guinea and half a guinea respectively. The photographs, which are pasted on the text paper, were taken by a Mr. Archibald Burns.

by her mother and her elderly aunts. For some time Bob was extremely worried, for he had the Victorian's well-founded dread of a cough of long duration presaging the onset of consumption of the lungs, having witnessed more than one of his close friends and relations being carried off by this insidious disease. He determined to give his dear little wife a long holiday in a more salubrious climate than the grey chills which Edinburgh commonly afforded and he wrote to Richard Lewis of the Lifeboat Institution, who was now a firm friend, asking him to name a locality where he could find material for a tale of coastguards and smugglers. 'I have in mind,' he wrote, 'a coast cut into by caves & inlets, with high cliffs and a wild landscape, that would suit a story of this kind & perhaps afford Jeanie leisure to enjoy a sandy beach, fresh air, & the blessing of God's warm sunshine, for the weather in Scotland has been depressingly dull & wet these several weeks.'

In his reply, Lewis suggested Cornwall as being suitable in every way, giving the address of a Mr. N. B. Downing of Penzance, as a person with a wide knowledge of the county and one eminently capable of arranging introductions and securing good but inexpensive accommodation. But it was August before Ballantyne and his wife arrived in the West Country, a series of unforeseen misfortunes having delayed their departure almost to the point of cancellation.

The first tragedy occurred soon after the long-awaited arrival of Isabella's fiancé, Stephen Balmer, on leave from his post in India, who disembarked in April suffering from a severe chill he had caught during the voyage home. His condition worsened rapidly, and to the horror of the family, within a few weeks he had died of congestion of the lungs,[1] leaving Jeanie's sister heartbroken and inconsolable. Mrs. Grant sold her house at 7 Springfield, Leith Walk, shortly after the funeral, moving with her two sons and her daughter to 1 Millerfield Place, only a few doors from her married daughter and son-in-law. Jamie, as her son James was always called, had taken his degree and was now a Doctor of Medicine, but he too had become increasingly unwell after appearing to recover from an acute attack of a mysterious

[1] Pneumonia.

and painful malady which had completely prostrated him in January. Seeing him going downhill so rapidly, his own physician called in an eminent consultant who confirmed what he and his patient both feared; that the complaint was chronic Bright's Disease, an incurable and progressive condition for which the prognosis was always extremely grave. This news threw a further blanket of gloom over an already downcast family and the departure of the Ballantynes for the sunshine of Cornwall was further delayed until Jeanie could be sure that her brother was in no immediate danger.

Their delayed arrival in Penzance coincided happily with a spell of fine, sunny weather and they were soon spending hours on the beach together, either relaxing in deck-chairs, or searching barefooted amongst the rockpools for specimens to inhabit the large glass aquarium which Jeanie tended so carefully in the parlour of Millerfield Place. They had accepted the hospitality of Mr. and Mrs. Downing on Richard Lewis's recommendation and found them to be a pleasant, friendly couple who treated them as members of their family for the length of their stay. They insisted on escorting their paying guests to social functions and arranged a musical evening in their honour to enable their Cornish friends to meet this distinguished Scottish author and his lady.

Despite the fact that he was officially on holiday, Ballantyne always retired to his room after breakfast to write a task of six or more manuscript pages, the end of the first fortnight seeing two chapters of his forthcoming book about the smugglers and wreckers of the Cornish coast almost completed. He confessed to his wife, however, that neither he nor his publisher were entirely happy that the tale was to be once again so strongly associated with the sea. Recent years had witnessed a positive spate of nautical yarns for boys. That prolific writer of sea stories, W. H. G. Kingston, had completed no less than nine in the last six years,[1] and a great number of other authors seemed to have followed his example. Ballantyne was well aware that he had himself already

---

[1] The list of Kingston's books fills eight pages in the British Museum Catalogue. He was nearly forty years of age when he wrote his first boys' adventure story.

used this theme in several recent books, a fact that had not escaped the notice of the reviewers. He had received a letter from Watson soon after his arrival in Penzance, in which the publisher had urged him to make full use of his imagination in seeking settings for his stories, using whenever possible radically new situations and localities to avoid staleness by too much repetition. He had also warned the author that adverse literary reviews could exert a considerable influence on booksellers already stocked with new editions of *The Lifeboat* and *The Lighthouse*. Of all this Ballantyne was well aware.

It was therefore with special interest that he learned from the Downings that one of their guests at their musical evening was to be Mr. S. H. James, the manager of the famous Botallack tin and copper mine near St. Just. Ballantyne admitted later to his wife that only the sudden realisation that here was the opportunity for an entirely new and exciting setting for his story prevented him from scrapping the work he had started and reserving any further composition until after their return to Scotland. Such a decision would almost certainly have resulted in the non-appearance of his Christmas book that year. During the supper interval Bob made a point of buttonholing James and acquainting him with his idea that a tin mine would make an excellent background for an adventure story, with the result that the manager invited both Bob and his wife to visit the Botallack and inspect the subterranean galleries and workings.

On the morning of the 18th August[1] they travelled over to St. Just by dog-cart, there to be entertained to lunch by Mr. and Mrs. James at their house at the foot of the steep hill leading up to the village; a house largely built of the granite which the miners had carved from the rocks with which they worked. Early in the afternoon the four of them made their way by horse and trap to where the tall, stone chimneys and ponderous grey buildings of the mine stood against a background of sea and sky. In those days, the Botallack was not only one of the most profitable, but had recently become the most celebrated of the Cornish tin mines.

[1] On the day of their first visit to the Botallack Mine, the Ballantynes signed the visitors' book. This book is now in the County Museum at Truro.

It owed most of its new-found fame to a visit made by the Prince and Princess of Wales in July 1865. Accompanied by an impressive retinue of West-country aristocrats, they had graciously consented to descend into the workings in order to observe how the men toiled with their hammers and chisels at the iron-hard granite rocks.

[1]It was a great day for St. Just and Botallack, that 24th of July on which the Royal visit was paid. Great was the expectation and preparation on all hands to give a hearty welcome to the royal pair. The ladies arrayed themselves in their best to do fitting honour to the Princess; the bal-maidens donned their holiday attire, and Johnny Fortnight[2] took care, by supplying the poor mine-girls with the latest fashions, that their appearance should be, if we may be allowed the word, splendiferous! The Volunteers, too, turned out in force, and no one, looking at their trim, soldierly aspect, could have believed them to be the same miners who were wont to arise each evening through a hole in the earth, red as lobsters,[3] wet, ragged, and befouled—in a word, surrounded by a halo of dishevelment, indicative of their rugged toils in the regions below.

Everywhere the people turned out to line the roads, and worthily receive the expected visitors, and great was the cheering when they arrived, accompanied by the Duke and Duchess of Sutherland, the Earl of Mount Edgecumbe, Lady de Grey, Lord and Lady Vivian, General Knollys, and others, but louder still was the cheer when the Princess rode down the steep descent to the cliffs in a donkey-carriage.

Perched on the very edge of the stark cliffs, the Botallack Mine's colourful history extended back to 1721, when digging for

[1] *Deep Down: A Tale of the Cornish Mines*, by R. M. Ballantyne, p. 77.
[2] 'Johnny Fortnight' was the name given to the local packmen who called every fortnight to offer trinkets, ribbons, clothing and other wares.
[3] The water which was constantly dripping from the roof and walls of the mine galleries was coloured a deep rust-red by the presence of iron ore, the miners emerging after a day's work with their clothes filthy and their bodies stained as if with a dye.

tin first started, the fever to find the precious metal gripping the local villagers to such a degree that before the end of the eighteenth century the workings had reached a depth of over six hundred feet. By 1778, galleries had been laboriously excavated until they extended for nearly five hundred feet under the Atlantic Ocean, often with only a four-foot crust of rock between the miners' heads and the crushing weight of millions of tons of surging salt water. Several lucky strikes leading to thick veins of ore had, by 1820, resulted in the mine becoming one of the richest in Cornwall, and when the Ballantynes made their descent down the new Boscawen Diagonal Shaft, which commenced near sea-level and dipped steeply to finish far below the ocean bed, the company which operated the diggings boasted that they employed well over five hundred workers.

The wild and rugged coastline on which the mine stood was owned by the then Lord Falmouth, who was in the fortunate position of receiving one-eighteenth part in value from every ton of copper raised, and from every ton of tin, one twenty-fourth part.[1] The Duke of Cornwall and the Royal Family took a one-third share in dues for all minerals raised under the sea, but, despite this constant drip of royalties, by the end of 1863 the company which had worked the mine for the previous thirty years had benefited by over £100,000, the profit for the year 1864 being no less than £16,000. The industry was later to fall on evil times, but in the 'sixties and 'seventies of the last century, tin mining in Cornwall was a highly profitable enterprise and made the fortunes of many of the speculators who had rushed to invest at the start of the boom.

To protect their clothes from the dirt and stains of the underground passages, the Ballantynes had the honour of being issued with the same overalls that the Royal Entourage had worn three years before, Jeanie being proudly informed that the cloak she borrowed had once graced the shoulders of a Duchess.[2] Clad in this attire they both boarded the small iron gig which had

---

[1] The information in this paragraph is derived from *The Mines of Cornwall*, by Thomas Spargo, published in 1865 and reprinted by D. B. Barton Esq., of Truro, in 1959.

[2] See Plate 5.

bumped and clanged its way up the steep slope from the bottom of the shaft as it was pulled to the surface by a steam-engine set high in the cliffs above. Before disappearing into the darkness, as they slid down the acute incline of the tunnel cut through the solid rock, each donned a heavy leather helmet on which had been a placed a lighted candle held fast by a lump of soft clay, this simple mode of illumination being quite safe as the mine was free from gas and other explosive hazards. This first descent was to be Jeanie's only trip below ground, for she confessed that nothing would ever again induce her to visit those Stygian depths with their eerie echoing rumbles and faint metallic tappings and the weird sounds of water falling into unseen caverns far below. But her husband was enthusiastic about the excellent possibilities of a story which the mine afforded, and as soon as they again reached the fresh air and sunlight of the surface, he made immediate arrangements to rent a room at Mr. James's house so as to be nearer to the scene of operations.[1] Once he and his wife had left Penzance for the rural surroundings of St. Just, Bob started to pass part of each day underground, exploring the maze of galleries and winding passages, sketching by the dim light of the flickering candles, and talking to the sweat-stained, weary men and boys as they chipped and blasted the dripping, steely granite in their never-ending search for the thin veins of elusive tin.

In the latter half of the nineteenth century the miners were forced by the economics of grim necessity to accept conditions that would not now be tolerated for an instant. They were treated more like slaves than free human beings, the mine owners grinding them by unremitting toil in underground warrens so unhealthy that a few years was sufficient to wreck their bodies and break the strongest spirits. Before they had reached the age of twenty-five, almost without exception they were infected with a type of hookworm which thrived in the damp warmth of the pit; but far worse than this endemic disease was an acutely painful form of silicosis, a killing sickness which gradually thickened and ulcerated their lungs as the years of

[1] Mr. S. H. James and his wife lived in Alma Villa, St. Just, a house he had built in 1854. It still stands at the bottom of Nancherrow Hill, but has been renamed 'Penrose House.'

breathing air laden with minute particles of abrasive granite dust took their toll. Of those who survived the many accidents and dangers of the mine, very few indeed lived to enjoy an old age free from chronic sickness and pain. Amongst those who had been lucky enough to reach the age of forty, it was difficult to find one man who was not incapacitated by silicosis and crippled by rheumatism, due to years of unceasing labour in the foul air and dank, insanitary surroundings in which he had been compelled to earn his daily bread. Payment was strictly by results— no tin! no pay! Many a hardworking man with a family of young mouths to feed was forced to exist for weeks at a time on a pittance as low as ten shillings a month, his wife ekeing out what little they may previously have saved by pawning their scanty belongings or borrowing from their more fortunate neighbours, the debts being repaid when her husband again discovered a 'keenly lode of tin' or a 'good bunch of copper.'

After eight or ten hours of heavy and exhausting labour in the bowels of the earth, the miner's only means of reaching 'grass', as they called the surface, was by climbing the seemingly unending series of perpendicular ladders which finally emerged through the small, square-timbered hole through which they had descended early that morning. This formidable and extremely tiring ascent could seldom be accomplished in less than an hour from the bottom of the pit, and the panting exertions of lungs silted with stone dust imposed a heavy strain on the hearts and blood vessels of men who had just finished a day of severe toil. The result was sometimes a tragic collapse before the topmost rung was reached, the gnarled fingers releasing their hold of the ladder and the unfortunate individual toppling backwards, bumping and crashing against the sides of the shaft, finally to hit the rock floor hundreds of feet below. Such accidents were by no means uncommon, and they and other disasters which at intervals swept whole gangs of men to their doom, were looked upon as occupational hazards, regrettable episodes for which the mine manager would convey the company's condolences to the bereaved but for which no compensation was payable except as an act of grace.

Ballantyne's fictional tales were always founded upon a solid substratum of fact and his story of the miners of Cornwall still has exceptional interest as being the only record we have which gives details of the everyday lives of these underpaid and over-worked men and boys, portraying vividly their struggle to wrest a precarious living from the grim and implacable granite rocks through which they chipped and hacked their way. He titled the book *Deep Down: A Tale of the Cornish Mines,* and the text of any edition is now sought at high prices by students of Cornish history, or those collectors who delight in stories of the West Country written during a period when few outsiders visited its wild and romantic shores. Here is a passage from the book in which Bob describes what he himself saw in the dilapidated stone cottages of the miners' families, written as being witnessed by one of the heroes of the tale, young Dr. Oliver Trembath.

[1]The first cottage he entered belonged to a man whose chest was slightly affected for the first time. He was a stout man, about thirty-five years of age, and of temperate habits—took a little beer occasionally, but never exceeded; had a good appetite, but had caught cold frequently in consequence of having to go a considerable distance from the shaft's mouth to the changing-house while exhausted with hard work underground and covered with profuse perspiration. Often he would do this in wet weather and when bitterly cold winds were blowing,—of late he had begun to spit blood.

It is necessary here to remind the reader that matters in this respect—and in reference to the condition of the miner generally—are now much improved. The changing-houses, besides being placed as near to the several shafts as is convenient, are now warmed with fire, and supplied with water-troughs, so that the men have a comfortable place in which to wash themselves on coming 'to grass', and find their clothes thoroughly dried when they return in the morning to put them on, before going underground. This renders them less likely to catch cold, but of course does not protect them from the evil influences of climbing ladders, and of bad air. Few men have to undergo such severe toil as the Cornish miner, because of the extreme hardness of the rock with

[1] *Deep Down: A Tale of the Cornish Mines,* by R. M. Ballantyne. London, 1868, pp. 158 *et seq.*

which he has to deal. To be bathed in perspiration, and engaged in almost unremitting and violent muscular exertion during at least eight hours of each day, may be said to be his normal condition.

Oliver advised this man to give up underground work for some time, and, having prescribed for him and spoken encouragingly to his wife, left the cottage to continue his rounds. . . At one cottage he found a young man in the last stage of consumption. He lay on his lowly bed, pale and restless—almost wishing for death to relieve him of his pains. His young wife sat by his bedside wiping the perspiration from his brow, while a ruddy-cheeked little boy romped about the room unnoticed—ignorant that the hour was drawing near which would render him fatherless, and his young mother a widow.

This young man had been a daring fellow, whose animal spirits led him into many a reckless deed. His complaint had been brought on by racing up the ladders—a blood-vessel had given way, and he never rallied after. Just as Oliver was leaving him a Wesleyan minister entered the dwelling.

'He won't be long with us, doctor, I fear,' he said in passing.

'Not long, sir,' replied Oliver.

'His release will be a happy one,' said the minister, 'for his soul rests on Jesus; but alas! for his wife and child.'

He passed into the sick-room, and the doctor went on.

The next case was also a bad one, though different from the preceding. The patient was between forty and fifty years of age, and had been unable to go underground for several years. He was a staid, sober man, and an abstemious liver, but it was evident that his life on earth was drawing to a close. He had been employed chiefly in driving levels, and had worked a great deal in very bad air, where the candles could not be made to burn unless placed nine or ten feet behind the spot where he was at work. Indeed, he often got no fresh air except what was blown to him, and only a puff now and then. When he first went to work in the morning the candle would not keep alight, so that he had to take his coat and beat the air about before going into the level, and, after a time, went in when the candles could be got to burn by holding them on one side, and teasing out the wick very much. This used to create a great deal of smoke, which tended still further to vitiate the air. When he returned 'to grass' his saliva used to be as black as ink. About five years before giving up underground work he had had inflammation of the lungs, followed by blood spitting, which used to come on when he was at work in what he called 'poor air,' or in 'cold-damp,' and he had never been well since.

Oliver's last visit that day was to the man John Batten, who had exploded a blast-hole in his face the day before. This man dwelt in a cottage in the small hamlet of Botallack, close to the mine of the same name. The room in which the miner lay was very small, and its furniture scanty, nevertheless it was clean and neatly arranged. Everything in and about the place bore evidence of the presence of a thrifty hand. The cotton curtain on the window was thin and worn, but it was well darned, and pure as the driven snow. The two chairs were old, as was also the table, but they were not rickety; it was obvious that they owed their stability to a hand skilled in mending and in patching pieces of things together. Even the squat little stool in the side of the chimney-corner displayed a leg, the whiteness of which, compared with the other two, told of attention to small things. There was a peg for everything, and everything seemed to be on its peg. Nothing littered the well-scrubbed floor or defiled the well-brushed hearth-stone, and it did not require a second thought on the part of the beholder to ascribe all this to the tidy little middle-aged woman, who, with an expression of deep anxiety on her good-looking countenance, attended to the wants of her injured husband.

'Your husband is not quite so well to-day, I hear,' said the doctor, going to the side of the bed on which the stalwart form of the miner lay.

'No, sur,' replied the poor woman; 'he has much pain in his eyes today, but his heart is brave, sur; I never do hear a complaint from he.'

244

This was true. The man lay perfectly still, the compressed lips and the perspiration that moistened his face alone giving evidence of the agony he endured.

'Do you suffer much?' inquired the doctor, as he undid the bandages which covered the upper part of the man's face.

'Iss, sur, I do,' was the reply.

No more was said, but a low groan escaped the miner when the bandage was removed, and the frightful effects of the accident were exposed to view. With intense anxiety Mrs. Batten watched the doctor's countenance, but found no comfort there. A very brief examination was sufficient to convince Oliver that the eyes were utterly destroyed, for the miner had been so close to the hole when it exploded that the orbs were singed by the flame, and portions of un-burned powder had been blown right into them.

'Will he see—a little, sur?' whispered Mrs. Batten.

Oliver shook his head. 'I fear not,' he said in a low voice.

'Speak out, doctor,' said the miner in a firm tone, 'I ain't afeard to know it.'

'It would be unkind to deceive you,' replied Oliver sadly; 'your eyes are destroyed.'

No word was spoken for a few minutes, but the poor woman knelt by her husband's side, and nestled close to him. Batten raised his large brown hand, which bore the marks and scars of many a year of manly toil, and laid it gently on his wife's head.

As Ballantyne had thought fit to include these sad and moving factual descriptions of what he had himself seen when visiting the miners' cottages at Botallack, one might have expected a thundering denunciation of a society which permitted men to work for a mere pittance in such appalling conditions. But except for a few homilies regarding the necessity of the miners abstaining from strong drink and the need to keep themselves as fit as possible so that their working life could be prolonged, the author makes no comment about the rapacity of the owners and the absent shareholders. He describes a dinner given by the management to these gentlemen in the account house at Botallack,[1] in which the adventurers, as he terms the shareholders, are informed of the flourishing condition of the mine. The average wage of a Cornish miner at this period was fifteen shillings a week.

At the next Botallack account-dinner, Mr. Cornish gladdened the hearts of the adventurers by telling them that the lodes which had been promising for such a length of time had at last got to the length of 'performance,' and that he had now the pleasure of announcing a large dividend—which he paid them there and then.

Mr. Cornish afterwards congratulated the adventurers on the success of the mine, and the splendid prospects which were opening up to them—prospects which, he had no doubt, would be fully realised ere long. He referred also to the condition of the miners of the neighbourhood, and alluded to the fact that the neighbouring mines, Wheal Owles and Levant, were also in a flourishing condition; a matter, he said, for which they had reason to be profoundly thankful, for the distress in the district had been severe and prolonged. The manager's voice deepened at this point, and he spoke with pathos, for he had a kindly heart, and his thoughts were at the moment with many a poor miner, in whose little cottages the effects of gaunt poverty could be traced in scanty furniture, meagre fare and careworn brows.

As a story of adventure, the tale is well told. Ballantyne had retained the first two chapters he had written in Penzance, interweaving the start of the smuggling story into the fabric of his tale of the Botallack Mine, this unusual combination of situations giving him full scope for a most exciting yarn of mysterious underground explosions, daring rescues and escapes from the flooding galleries of the pit, followed by the final defeat of the smugglers after a tremendous fight against heavy odds. His publishers were extremely pleased with the reception the tale received from his youthful public, and in February 1869 the

[1] The old account-house of the Botallack Mine is standing to this day, and is now known as 'The Count House.' At the time of writing it is the headquarters of a flourishing folk-singing society, and is visited by many thousands of devotees to the art every year.

author was able proudly to show his wife a cheque for one hundred pounds on account of the sales of *Deep Down*.

Notwithstanding this piece of financial good fortune they were not to have a summer holiday that year, for on the 25th June a considerable domestic upheaval was occasioned by the long-expected arrival of Master Frank Grant Ballantyne, a healthy, bouncing baby boy, who was to engross the entire attention of his doting mother and the greater portion of the leisure of his proud and happy father for many months to come. Bob's letters to Jeanie were now invariably full of advice on the correct up-bringing of an infant as unique as their remarkable young son. Some of his hints on child care must have amused both his wife and his mother-in-law. In October he was a guest of Hector McKenzie's for a week's shooting before the start of his winter lecture tour, and he wrote Jeanie as follows:

Tuesday night.

My own darling Jeanie,

I'm distressed about our beloved baby. Surely it's too soon for teething! I envy you so much of the opening of the bud all to yourself—no I don't, but I regret losing so much of it myself.

Besides, I think you wd. not be the worse off for a little of my philosophic advice now & then. For instance, wd. a guttapercha ring not be better than his own little fist to bite? But I'm very thankful to hear he keeps in such good health. I'm glad, too, that you are so also, dearie, and. . . [Here a page is missing.]

Today we came in at 2.30 & I snored and read the Scotsman till five. Tomorrow Mr. Fraser is to go with us & we shall probably be out *all* day. Well, sporting is good & useful, & I'm very fond of it, and take a heavy lift of it, but I wd. not lead the life Hector does for £1000 a year.—Now, there's the tea bell.

No time for more than to say good night. I kiss your photograph every morning!

Love to all—specially Frank.

Ever, darling Jeanie,

Yr. loving husbd.

R.M.B.

Staying at home that summer did not prevent him completing his annual book for Nisbet's, and this time he drew on his knowledge of Norway, gained during his salmon-fishing expeditions with the Cowans,[1] to write *Erling the Bold; A Tale of the Norse Sea-Kings*, a book which competed successfully with the second edition of his previous tale, for which there was a renewed demand as Christmas again drew near.

Despite growing competition from other authors (some of whom had been quick to emulate the successful formulae he had evolved), by 1870 Ballantyne was acknowledged by the reviewers in the literary columns of the Press to be the foremost writer of books for boys, only W. H. G. Kingston approaching anywhere near his output of full-length volumes produced solely for the enjoyment of juvenile readers. The man who was later to be Bob's most serious rival in this field, George Alfred Henty, was only just embarking on his new career as a writer of adventure stories, and his first tale for boys, *Out on the Pampas: or The Young Settlers*, was not due to appear until the following year.[2]

Ballantyne's business relationship with James Nisbet & Company was proving a most lucrative association for both parties, and an estimate of the author's income from his literary work reveals that he was now earning between four and five hundred pounds per annum, this sum being supplemented by his lecture fees and the value of any water-colour paintings he sold. In the 'seventies this was considered quite a handsome income on which to maintain a middle-class family, more than sufficient to cover the expenses of a much larger household than the one Bob commanded and one calculated to ensure a surplus for occasional luxuries and even the gradual accumulation of a moderate bank balance, provided the master of the house shunned the more expensive vices with which his path might happen to be strewn.

[1] In an interview printed in *The Boy's Own Paper*, vol. XI of 1888/9, Ballantyne states on page 499, 'Four salmon fishing visits to Norway produced two literary fish in the shape of *Freaks on the Fells* and *Erling the Bold*.'

[2] Previous to this, Henty had written an unsuccessful three-volume novel entitled *A Search for a Secret*, published in 1867, and some books dealing with his experiences as a war correspondent for a daily newspaper.

Fortunately for his dependants, the author was a pillar of Free Church society and as such believed most strongly in the utmost moderation in all things appertaining in any way to the sordid pleasures of the flesh, even the infrequent partaking of a dram of spirits now occasioning a self-condemnatory outburst of remorse for the weakness of character he thought this sinful indulgence displayed.

His affectionate letters to Teenie ceased abruptly from the day of his marriage, all communications after that date being addressed to his brother John or to the family in general. Things had not gone well for his artist brother during the last few years, and the Landseer episode had come as a stunning blow. Increasing financial difficulties had forced the family to vacate the large house in The Mall and move out to Totteridge, where they had found a smaller, less expensive residence. During the latter part of their stay in Kensington they had experienced increasing difficulty in collecting the rents for the studios they let in the upper storeys of their house; many of the hopeful young artists who took the accommodation being quite unable to earn any sort of a living with the brush, and often disappearing with several months' rent still outstanding. John himself had had little real success as a portrait painter, his only regular income being derived from what he was able to earn as a teacher, and here, as in most other fields, competition had become fiercer for the pupils available. Another worry was the conduct of the children for, as far as their parents were concerned, this had gone from bad to worse. His son, Randal, was now leading a life of such dissipation in the seamier haunts of the West End that he was now well on the way to becoming an alcoholic; Dot, his eldest daughter, had shocked the family by embracing the Roman Catholic faith and had even threatened that she might 'take the veil'; while Edith, after a violent quarrel with her mother, had left home vowing never to return.

The future seemed a sorry prospect for the dejected little painter, and he also had to endure the constant nagging of a domineering wife, now no longer physically attractive, who could never forgive herself for having married a failure; something she reminded her long-suffering husband about at every available opportunity. After visiting them both at Totteridge to broach the matter of the raising of funds for the education of his sister Williamina's illegitimate child, Bob came away depressed at the example of masculine subjection he had just witnessed, and wrote his wife that no financial help could be expected whatsoever:

[April, 1870]

. . . I have spoken to John about Williamina's child. There is no hope of his doing anything. He has more than he can manage in keeping himself and his family square.

Since my last visit to Totteridge I have had my conviction tremendously deepened of the unutterable evils that result from a wife attempting to *unduly* lead her husband. Poor John gave up the reins immediately after his marriage—wh. was a sin against his young &, at that time, ignorant wife. Small blame to her that she took them. One cannot expect an old head on young shoulders! But the sin is visited very heavily on him now. He is utterly powerless. All he can do is to kick & wriggle under his misery. God help him. I did not find it difficult to do them harm, but oh I find it awfully hard *now* to do them good . . .

Ballantyne had come up to London to visit his publisher and, during their discussion, Watson had revealed that he had now been forced to change his mind regarding the continuing popularity of sea stories. The demand for new editions of *The Lifeboat* had convinced him that another tale in the same type of setting would not now come amiss. Two days later Bob had left for Ramsgate, having first obtained permission from the Elder Brethren of Trinity House to spend a week aboard *The Gull*, a lightship which guarded one of the channels through the notorious Goodwin Sands. He arrived with a formal introduction to Captain Vaile, The District Superintendent of Trinity House, who was asked to render him every assistance, and another to Captain F. Shaw, the Harbour Master.

He spent a week ashore before going aboard the lightship, and here he again met Isaac Jarman, the celebrated coxswain of the Ramsgate lifeboat, with whom he renewed the friendship started when he was at Deal writing his book *The Lifeboat*. Jarman and his crew had been responsible for many dramatic rescues from sinking wrecks on the dreaded Goodwin Sands in the storms that swept the coasts every winter, and the newspaper reports of their heroic exploits had made his name, and that of the lifeboat he commanded, famous throughout the land.

The following Saturday Ballantyne accompanied Captain Vaile aboard the steam tug *Aid*, which was used both as a relief vessel and for the maintenance of the many buoys and markers which plotted the navigable channel through the shifting sands. Soon afterwards he was deposited with his gear upon the deck of the Gull Stream lightship, to be welcomed aboard by the mate, John Leggett, and the rest of the crew. In spite of a bad bout of sea-sickness, Bob stayed on the pitching, rolling ship for seven days, swapping yarns with the men, making copious notes on the methods used to keep the huge, clockwork-driven oil lamp flashing its warning signal across the waste of sea and sand, and sketching the scenes aboard the ruggedly built little vessel as it bobbed and tugged at the massive cable secured to its anchor bedded deep in the sand below. Ballantyne was lucky in that he caught one glimpse of the lifeboat in action as it swept past on its way to a sinking ship:

[1] A 'dirty' day had culminated in a tempestuous night. The watch on deck, clad in drenched oilskins, was tramping overhead, rendering my repose fitful. Suddenly he opened the skylight, and shouted that the Southsand Head lightship was firing, and sending up rockets. As this meant a wreck on the sands we all rushed on deck, and saw the flare of a tar-barrel in the far distance. Already our watch was loading and firing our signal gun and sending up rockets for the purpose of calling off the Ramsgate lifeboat. It chanced that the Broadstairs boat observed the signals first, and not long after, she flew past us under sail, making for the wreck.

A little later we saw the signal-light of the Ramsgate tug looming through the mist like the great eye of the storm-

[1] *Personal Reminiscences in Book-Making*, by R. M. Ballantyne, London, 1893, pp. 70-1.

fiend. She ranged close up in order to ask whereaway the wreck was. Being answered, she sheared off, and as she did so, the lifeboat, towing astern, came full into view. It seemed as if she had no crew, save only one man—doubtless my friend Jarman—holding the steering lines; but, on closer inspection we could see the men crouching down, like a mass of oilskin coats and sou'westers. In a few minutes they were out of sight and we saw them no more, but afterwards heard that the wrecked crew had been rescued and landed at Deal.

One suspects that Ballantyne was more than pleased when the time came for him to say goodbye, for he suffered terribly from sea-sickness every time he left dry land. Before the relief vessel called to collect him at the end of his stay, he left an order for one of the beautifully carved and inlaid work-boxes on which some of the men spent hours of their off-duty time, leaving directions that it was to be posted, as soon as completed, to his wife in Edinburgh.

His first night back in London was an extraordinary one, and the letter he wrote home to his wife reveals much about the deeply hidden side of Ballantyne's character. After visiting his publishers and having dinner in the evening with Richard Lewis of the Lifeboat Institution, he set off to meet his nephew Randal. This appointment he did not keep and instead he finished the night tramping the gas-lit streets of central London in an apparently sudden and spontaneous endeavour to spread the Word of the Lord amongst the prostitutes who lurked in their hundreds in the darkened doorways and alleys of the metropolis:

Having arranged that Randal was to meet me at Barnet Station at 10.30 p.m. I left Mr. Lewis at 9.30 & took a cab for King's Cross; but, before I had gone far, I began, as the horse is said to do, 'to snuff the battle from afar.' Soon I saw smoke and flames & my old familiar brazen helmeted charioteers dashed by. At once I dismissed my cab—threw Randal & all other considerations to the dogs & made for the flames. It turned out a poor affair after all. I made myself known to one of the men; got within the cordon of police, into a neighbouring house whence the hose was playing on the burning building, but cd. see nothing but smoke & sparks, so I came down again & chatted with the men beside the engine. This machine turned out to be my old friend the engine of King St. of Regent Circus, but alas! none of the old faces were there. All were scattered or dead. Soon they were ordered home, the fire having been got quickly under, so one of them said, 'Have a ride, sir.' 'Yes,' said I jumping up, and away we went through the streets as of old—a drive of about a mile. Not quite as furiously, however, as they were returning, not going out. Still, they went at an inspiriting rattle and I could not help fancying that once or twice they made an unnecessary spurt just to please me!

Arrived at King St. & spent more than half an hour with them. Then said goodnight & sallied forth—I knew not wither! It was past 12 midnight by this time & I did not know what to do, so I resolved to walk down the Strand & see the streets of London by night. All was as quiet & orderly as Edinbr. after 1 p.m. I saw however, many of those poor forlorn waifs everywhere & was accosted frequently, but as usual took no notice of them. But it suddenly occurred to me 'You might try & save some of these.' Immediately I prayed to God to lead one to me, & then walked on, taking no notice of those who merely made a remark in passing.

Presently one came up & boldly took my arm & tried to stop me. I turned & looked her full in the face. 'Where are you going, my dear?' said she. I gave no reply. 'Can't you speak?' said she. 'Yes,' I said, 'I can speak. Come, take my arm & walk with me.' She took it & I walked for an hour with her telling her of Jesus & urging her to repent & turn to Him. She was rather hardened, made light of it at first, but when I left her was a good deal softened.

I then walked up Oxford St. & another took hold of me. The moment I began, as before, she cried, 'Oh, sir, don't pity me!' & tried to withdraw her hand, but I held her & talked earnestly of the possibility of escape for her & a life of love if she wd. turn to Jesus. She did not seem to be hardened. Was new to the life I am sure, but she tried to get away & refused to take money wh. I offered to her. At last she fairly

broke down, laid her head on my breast & wept! I pressed
Jesus on her—kissed her cheek—& went away. As I looked
back I saw her like a statue in the moonlight gazing after
me.

I had no intention of doing more, but still another came
to me. She seemed to be only 17. God help her. I left her
weeping. Then I walked to Totteridge where I arrived about
six in the morning.

> God bless you, my own darling.
> Yr. loving husbd.
> R.M.B.

Reading this smug and self-righteous letter, one may arrive at
the conclusion, that at the expense of these unfortunate females,
Ballantyne chose a needlessly cruel way of proving that he could
openly embrace temptation after the enforced celibacy of a month
without the company of his young and pretty wife; emerging
from the encounter without one lustful chink showing through
the moral armour with which he had encased himself. Large
numbers of working-class women were annually driven, by the
economics of the stone-hearted *laissez-faire* of the church-filling
Victorian Establishment, to join the ranks of the tarts and good-
time girls of the London streets, hoping to supplement their
starvation wages or the pittance their husbands brought home,
by the hard-earned pickings derived from dreary commercial sex.
At frequent occasions, their conduct, and that of their more
professional competitors, occasioned thundering outbursts of
hell-fire and damnation from the pulpit and the correspondence
columns of *The Times*, followed by forays of tract-laying evan-
gelists into the gin-palaces and coffee shops of the metropolis.
Late-night visits to brothels by illustrious figures of the Church and
State, in an effort to reform the abandoned young ladies in the
very place where they were called upon to perform their sordid
duties, became an increasingly popular pastime for those whose
high position in society made their moral purpose clear. Not
least amongst those who stalked menacingly through the darkened streets of the West End and the back-alleys of the dock
area, with flies laced tight with cobbler's thread, growling

reprovingly each time he fixed sexual vice in his sights and urging the participants to give themselves to Jesus, was none other than the Queen's ageing Prime Minister, the Right Honourable William Ewart Gladstone, Esquire. Ballantyne was one of the many who followed in his distinguished footsteps.

Perhaps condemnation of the author's attitude of patronising condescension towards the prostitutes of London's West End should be tempered by the knowledge that the art of self-analysis as revealed by Sigmund Freud was not to be propounded for many years to come; and that the warm euphoria which seemingly surrounded Ballantyne on his walk back to Totteridge that night was no doubt thought to be honestly and sincerely earned by deeds well done.

Chapter Twelve

IN ORDER TO BE ABLE to write in peaceful, uninterrupted seclusion, the author now rented a small room overlooking the sea in the scrubbed, off-season tranquillity of Mrs. Theobald's Lodgings in Marine Parade, Yarmouth, returning to London in less a month with the all but completed manuscript of his latest literary offering to his youthful readers safe in the small leather suitcase which accompanied him on all his trips. He stayed in the capital only long enough to draw a set of illustrations for the work direct on the wood for the blockmakers to cut,[1] leaving for home by train immediately these were finished, with the pleasurable knowledge that *The Floating Light of the Goodwin Sands*, as he had called the tale, was now completed and in his publisher's hands.

The book appeared in the shops in November, priced, as usual at five shillings a copy, this time cased in bright orange cloth on which a picture of the masthead of the Gull Stream lightship, surmounted by its massive warning light, was blocked on the spine in gold. Watson had given orders that the initial printing was to be stepped up to two thousand five hundred copies, but within a few months the whole of this first edition had been sold and in the following autumn a second had to be printed to satisfy the renewed demand. 'Let us give thanks that our prayers regarding the success of this work have been answered,' Bob wrote to Jeanie while away on yet another lecture tour, stating that he was continuing his round of the halls 'with a light and gladsome heart.'

The following May their second child was born, a healthy young son whom they christened Edgar William McKenzie Ballantyne, but who was soon known to everybody as plain 'Ted.' The invasion of his home, both before and after the birth of the baby, by his wife's mother and sister from a few doors up the street, who insisted on taking full charge of all domestic affairs,

---

[1] The author was paid an extra two pounds for drawing direct upon the wooden blocks.

drove Bob to write jestingly to his brother that he was sometimes glad to escape to the comparative peace of Edinburgh Central railway station, a location he had chosen for seeking information for his next tale for boys. He had obtained permission from the board of directors of the railway company, whose true identity he hid under the pseudonym of the 'Grand National Trunk Railway,' to travel on the footplate of the Edinburgh-to-London express in order to gather technical data for his forthcoming book. In June he made the exciting but exhausting trip both ways, at times helping the bearded fireman and driver shovel coal into the firebox of the tall-funnelled engine, and being permitted on the last part of the return trip, when he was as dirty and smoke-begrimed as his two companions, to take charge of the train and operate the controls over several miles of the fastest part of the track.

The title he finally chose for the tale was *The Iron Horse, or Life on the Line*, and the author did his best to see that boys who were ingenious enough to persuade uncles, aunts or parents to part with five shillings on their behalf, or paid over their own hard-saved money to purchase the book, received full value for their pains. He packed into the volume's four hundred pages a vast assortment of dramatic incidents, including the detection and arrest of thieves who preyed upon the goods the trains carried, the outwitting of bogus claimants on the company's compensation resources for passenger injuries, frantic last-minute rescues from the path of oncoming engines, the loss and recovery of a valuable diamond ring, and several fatal railway accidents of varying degrees of horror; all woven into a factual account of the working of the British railway system and its effect upon the nation's economy. The tale was at least as successful as its immediate predecessors, and at the rate of forty pounds in royalties for each thousand copies sold, Ballantyne found himself one hundred pounds in pocket within three months of its first appearing in the bookshops.[1]

His wife's brother, Jamie, had become increasingly unwell during the last twelve months and was obviously going downhill

[1] *The Iron Horse* was published in November 1871 in a first edition of two thousand five hundred copies.

very fast indeed. A doctor relative in Tasmania, who had been informed of his complaint, wrote to the family saying that the local water, assisted by the climate, had curative properties for liver diseases that were little short of miraculous, a claim that subsequent events did nothing to substantiate. But when the family received the communication from Tasmania it did appear to offer at least some hope in a situation where there seemed little to do but wait for the inevitable end, and, with the consent of his medical adviser, young Dr. James Grant prepared to leave the shores of Scotland for ever. Before his brother-in-law sailed, Bob wrote him a goodbye letter, penned it seems, in a mood of sombre depression, in which his own past misdeeds, real or imaginary, are held up as a warning to others of the rocks on which he had 'hit and received great damage. . .'

Sunday, 6th Augt. '71.

My dear Jamie,

One line before you start to say goodbye once more—and God speed you.

I always find that when I part with a friend I wish that I had made more of him when I had the chance. So it is with you. I wish very much that we had seen more of each other, but it's too late to wish that now. Perhaps God will spare us to meet again some day when we have more leisure.

I wish, too, that we had had more converse about religious subjects. Does it not seem strange that men should find time to talk on all subjects except that of religion? I blame myself, dear Jamie, for not doing so. Don't fancy that by this I mean to insinuate that you needed such converse more than I. God knows, if you knew me, Jamie, you would not think that. But we might both have encouraged each other by talking more about that Eternity, into wh., when we have entered, this Time will at last appear in its true relative insignificance.

And we might have talked about that blessed Saviour whose chief glory *to me* is that he can save to the *uttermost*. If God ever lets you fall as low as I have fallen (may He forbid it), you will be better able to appreciate that idea. Oh

Jamie, stick to the Lord Jesus. Love to Him implies hatred of sin. Acceptance of Him insures salvation. There is a mistake that we fall into—viz. that Salvation *in eternity* is what we get from Him chiefly. But it is more. If I had accepted Christ sooner & had loved Him better & followed Him closer, I should have escaped many sorrows that have already embittered the most of my life & that will (I fear) embitter it, more or less, to the end. (Perhaps not. There is no limit to God's mercy & power.)

I make these confessions in order that I may indicate the rocks on wh. I have hit & received great damage before you reach them. I have sailed over the course wh. you are about to traverse & wd. show you my chart. I would have you escape *temporal* troubles as well as eternal—and there is only one way of escape from both—through 'Him that loved us & gave Himself for us.'

Wherever you go may God's best blessing—His love & Holy Spirit—rest upon you—body & soul.

Your affectionate brother,
R.M.B.

P.S. Believe me, there is not formality, but a strong impulse in my heart, when I say, once more, God bless you, my dear brother.

When he wrote this letter Ballantyne was well aware that young Dr. James Grant, although still in his early twenties, was dying from an incurable disease, and this unhappy knowledge must have contributed towards the depression of mood which led to his gloomy review of his own past sins. This guilt complex, which quite often damply blanketed his spirit, may have been caused by some secret past indulgence, or trait of character, which now appeared deeply sinful to one who believed in a code of conduct strictly regulated by the austere doctrine of the nineteenth-century Free Church of Scotland, with whose Calvinistic ethics regarding spiritual and bodily behaviour the author did his best to comply. He certainly lost no opportunity of religious observance. Except in the case of incapacitating illness, he and his wife invariably attended church for both morning and evening services on Sunday, a day which was always treated as one of rest with none but the most essential work being performed by any member of the family. It was a day during which he would not even travel unless the trip appeared to be absolutely vital, and at home he always laid aside the book on which he was working, not touching it again until the following Monday, no matter how pressing the urgency of the task.

His day always started and finished with prayers in which the whole family joined, and he and Jeanie read some part of the Bible together every evening before retiring for the night. And yet, in those mid-Victorian years when puritanical conduct was considered socially elevating, and it was almost unthinkable for a middle-class family not to attend church at least once on the the Sabbath, and to be seen attending, the Ballantynes would certainly not have been classed as especially devout members of the congregation by their Presbyterian neighbours who also wended their way to the Free Kirk, wet or fine, every Sunday morning and evening. As a husband and a father, Ballantyne had a duty to his wife and children and a part to play as head of the family, in which respectability and social standing were as important as earning their daily bread; and he seemingly thoroughly approved, and enjoyed conforming to, the mode of conduct laid down as correct by the Elders of the Kirk.

That he was sincere in his belief in an Almighty but forgiving God, and in his wish to live what he considered to be a Christian life, there can be no doubt. References to his faith in eternal salvation and his unshaken conviction that there was 'a life of unspeakable happiness awaiting after death' for those who truly repented their sins here on earth, frequently occurred in his letters to his wife. In the pages of his books he seldom missed a chance to stress to his young readers the necessity of true repentance and the joys to be found by 'giving oneself to the Lord Jesus Christ,' urging them to shun, as being snares of the Devil, such temptations as smoking, strong drink and the taking of the Lord's Name in vain.

He confessed on more than one occasion that he felt far happier when engaged on a work which he believed might stir the public's conscience to good deeds on behalf of themselves and others, and amongst these he classed such books as *The Lifeboat*, *The Lighthouse*, *Fighting the Flames*, and *The Floating Light of the Goodwin Sands*. In these volumes he considered that perhaps he had done something to help humanity by drawing attention to the needs of the Institutions concerned for funds to maintain the services given, or to aid their extension to areas where the facilities to save life did not already exist.

At the end of 1872 he was presented with an opportunity to write on a subject about which he felt a passionate desire to arouse the anger of his readers, and through them a large section of the community, against the cruelties and barbarous treatment of the slave traders on the east coast of Africa towards the miserable captives which they sold in their thousands every year. It was a subject into which he could really flash the fire of his evangelism to help right a grievous wrong, and he set about the task with an enthusiasm that he had not felt since the days when he was campaigning for funds on behalf of the Edinburgh lifeboat. Since the publication of *The Iron Horse* a further three full-length tales had appeared from his pen; *The Norsemen in the West*, an adventure story about America in the days before Columbus first set foot on the shores of the West Indies;[1] *The Pioneers*, in which he retraced the footsteps of a famous explorer, Sir Alexander Mackenzie;[2] and *Life in the Red Brigade*, a quick-moving yarn about the London Fire Brigade, similar in style to *Fighting the Flames*.[3] But none of these approached anywhere near the success of *Black Ivory—A Tale of Adventure among the Slavers of East Africa*, which appeared as Ballantyne's annual Christmas book in September 1873.

His interest in the subject had been quickened by reading a report of an anti-slavery meeting to which the newspapers had devoted some space, and he wrote immediately to the Reverend

---

[1] *The Norsemen in the West; or, America Before Columbus* was published at five shillings in October 1872.

[2] *The Pioneers; A Tale of the Western Wilderness* was issued in June 1872, priced at two shillings and sixpence.

[3] *Life in the Red Brigade* appeared in September 1873, with the imprint of George Routledge and Sons. The copyright of this volume was registered in his wife's name. It was reissued by James Nisbet & Company in 1887.

Dr. Ryan, then Vicar of Bradford, but until lately the Bishop of Mauritius:

6 *Millerfield Place, Edinburgh.*
3 *Decr.* 1872.

[1]Dear Sir,

I have just read, with much interest, the report of the Anti-Slavery meeting held in Leeds on the 16th of last month, and venture to hope that you will not deem me intrusive if I ask you to do me the favour to point out what you consider the best sources for obtaining detailed information on the subject of East African slavery.

I contemplate devoting my next Christmas tale for young people to the exposition of this subject. The report of the speeches delivered at the meeting in Leeds is very briefly given in the *Mercury*, and only shews me that there is probably a mass of information somewhere to which I might be directed by men, who, like yourself, have had practical acquaintance with the country in wh. the horrible traffic is carried on.

East African slavery is prominently before the public just now & will doubtless continue to be for some time to come. All of the speakers & writers on the subject call on men & women to do what they can to bring about its abolition. I heartily sympathise with the effort & pray God that He may accord success to it. I would also respond to the call by doing what lies in my power to further the good cause in the way indicated.

Trusting that you will excuse the liberty I take in thus addressing you.

I remain, Dear Sir,
Your obedt. servt.
R. M. Ballantyne.

The manuscript was completed by the following May[2] and the author prefaced the work with this comment:

[1] Quoted from the draft of the letter sent, which Ballantyne retained as a copy.

[2] To enable him to write the book in peace, in March 1873 he rented a room for six weeks at Mrs. Poole's, Merville House, Llandudno, Wales.

In writing this book, my aim has been to give a true picture in outline of the Slave-Trade as it exists at the present time on the east coast of Africa.

In order to do this, I have selected from the most trustworthy sources what I believe to be the most telling points of 'the trade,' and have woven these together into a tale, the warp of which is composed of thick cords of fact; the woof of slight lines of fiction, just sufficient to hold the fabric together. Exaggeration has been easily avoided, because—as Dr. Livingstone says in regard to the slave-trade—'exaggeration is impossible.'

I began my tale in the hope that I might produce something to interest the young (perchance, also, the old) in a most momentous cause—the total abolition of the African slave-trade. I close it with the prayer that God may make it a tooth in the file which shall eventually cut the chain of slavery, and set the black man free.

R. M. Ballantyne.

No book which the author had so far produced enjoyed such an immediate success. The first edition was of three thousand copies, greater as an initial issue than that of any previous work from his pen; but by early December 1873, less than three months[1] after the book was published, Watson was forced to order from his printers an additional three thousand volumes so as to satisfy the unprecedented demand from the booksellers. 'If things continue in this fashion,' the author wrote to his wife, 'we shall soon find ourselves in "easy circumstances." '[2]

The year 1873 had been one of chequered fortunes for the Ballantynes. In the very first month tidings had arrived from Tasmania that Dr. James Grant was dead, having at last succumbed to his long illness. Once again the family appeared in

[1] The first edition was dated 1873, but the second three thousand copies, which were issued in December of that year, were dated '1874' on the title-page. The printers were Messrs. T. & A. Constable of Edinburgh, who printed nearly all the books which James Nisbet & Company published.

[2] From a letter to his wife, dated 13th March, 1874, written when he was in Algiers.

public in the black regalia of mourning which Victorian convention demanded of the bereaved. But on the 23rd of April, Jeanie gave birth to her third child, a daughter, Jean Randall Howard, and the sorrow she felt at the loss of her brother was at least partly forgotten in the joy which the arrival of the little girl brought to her and her husband.

Even with the assistance of a housemaid and her mother's anxious help, Jeanie must occasionally have found difficulty in coping with three children all under the age of four; and although none of her letters to her husband during this period have survived, those he sent her in reply sometimes reveal that she complained, that with Bob away from home, the two boys lacked his restraining hand and watchful eye. Often they proved more than a handful to a nursing mother with other cares to attend to, and her husband was on the receiving end of several irate outbursts of temper. 'I do sympathise with you, dearie, in your continuing troubles with the bairns,' he wrote her while on a visit to his publishers in London, 'but how Frank opened the bureau & secured the ink I am at a loss to understand, for I am sure I left it securely locked, remembering our previous upset in this direction.' No other details are given of what must have been a peace-shattering drama conducted in the study of Millerfield Place, but one can imagine that Jeanie, perhaps suspicious of the prolonged silence of inquisitive and usually noisy Master Frank, finally opened the door of the room to discover him and his brother happily engrossed in the newly found pleasures to be derived from an open bottle of their Papa's lovely black ink. R. M. Ballantyne Esquire, probably found himself in considerable trouble on his return home that weekend.

Shortly afterwards, the parents were dismayed when first their eldest son, Frank, and later two-year-old Ted, both developed whooping-cough. With their dread of a disease to which members of the Ballantyne family seemed particularly prone, it is little wonder that the anxious mother, with an infant only a few weeks old, should have worried herself into a state of mind where she became convinced that the boys in their weakened condition would most surely succumb to tuberculosis of the lungs, or that her darling baby daughter would also contract whooping-cough

with possible fatal results. In a letter to his brother, the equally
worried father did not disguise his own anxiety:

[*June,* 1873]

. . . I fear that Jeanie is making herself ill with the extra
work & worry & sleepless nights she has had to endure by
tending the two bairns; at present the baby continues well—
let us say no more! Frank was blue in the face with whooping
last night & poor Ted [is] not much better. We can only pray
that God in His infinite mercy will preserve us all through
this time of trial. I confess that we are at present downcast
by this turn in our fortunes & can but pray that our Father
in Heaven will see fit to lift this burden from us and restore
our dear bairns to health. Join your prayers with ours, dear
John and Teenie, that our boys may not be taken from us, for
to lose either would surely break poor Jeanie's heart.

. . . I am now utterly determined to heed this warning &
move as soon as they are well, which, please God, will not
be too long delayed.

Ballantyne had by this time finally resolved to leave Scotland
and move to a more friendly climate, and although an absence of
other letters renders it impossible to learn the full reasons which
prompted him to take up residence abroad, it is permissible to
conclude that his fears about the health of his wife and children
were probably the prime motive for his removing them all to
Switzerland. His knowledge that, as an author, he was not tied
by his work to any particular locality, and that he could as
easily write his books on the Continent as at home, must also have
played a part in persuading him to move, and his love of travel
and the excitement of starting a new life in strange surroundings
may have finally tipped the scales. For when next we hear from
him in September of the same year, the whole family are
happily ensconced in the Pension Mooser, Canton de Vand,
Montreux, the whooping-cough apparently long since forgotten,
and the two Ballantyne boys bouncing with the sturdy resilience
of robust young men who are thoroughly enjoying the intriguing
complications of growing up.

Ballantyne was now at the peak of his fortunes as a writer,

with a following of young readers that cleared each new book from the shelves within weeks of its first appearance. His income must now have been in excess of eight hundred pounds per annum, for besides the fresh tales his pen produced, further editions of many of his previous works were re-issued at regular intervals.

With his financial affairs better than ever before, he stayed long enough to see his family comfortably settled in Montreux, and then lightheartedly departed for the warmth of Algiers, returning after several months of extended holiday with the completed manuscript of *The Pirate City*, a cut-throat yarn set in the seething squalor of the disease-ridden port in the first quarter of the nineteenth century. This was a period when the lawlessness that had characterised so much of the city's history had reached new depths, caused in large measure by an influx of deserters from the navies of the powers engaged in the Napoleonic Wars. Desperadoes and criminals of all nationalities used the town as a hide-out, banding together to conduct daring piratical raids on shipping sailing near the north coast of Africa, until the sweltering collection of mud-brick houses and winding, narrow streets had earned for itself the infamous title of the 'Pirates' Nest' amongst the seafarers who were forced to voyage in the southern half of the Mediterranean. The author made the most of this sinister setting, and some of the scenes of blood, torture and execution which he describes in the pages of his book, must have chilled the nerves of the more timid of his readers. Nevertheless, the young men of the day must have lapped up these horrific episodes with relish, whetting the appetites of their friends to do the same, for the work went through several editions during the course of the next few years.

The family moved to the Château d'Oex near Montreux in the spring of 1875, the shawl-wrapped addition to their numbers being Robert James Grant Ballantyne, a new baby, whom Jeanie had insisted should bear his father's name. In later years she confided to her children that she regarded Switzerland with a particularly warm affection, as being the country that had witnessed some of the happiest months of her married life. She was no stranger to this sternly beautiful land, for she had spent over a year at a finishing school near Geneva before she met her husband, and, by the time she left home, had become fluent in both the French and German languages. She much preferred the Swiss to any other continental nation; the climate, the magnificent scenery, and the high standard of living which British residents of only moderate income were able to enjoy, made life there a very pleasant one for those in the Ballantynes' position in society.

The author's continuing success in the world of literature now enabled his wife to employ both a housemaid and a full-time nanny to care for their four bairns. After interviewing a short list of applicants for this latter post, she engaged a German-speaking Swiss girl, Elise by name, a big-boned, big-hearted creature, with a bland, good-humoured personality that nothing could ruffle, and which soon endeared her to all the Ballantyne children. She promptly dubbed the new baby 'Hans,' a name which stuck to him for the rest of his childhood, and it was not long before she, with 'liebe Hans' tucked safe in his bassinet and the other three children strung in a hand-linking crocodile behind, became a familiar sight in the rustic streets of Château d'Oex. Despite a somewhat lethargic disposition, she proved herself a capable and intelligent young woman, relieving her mistress of many domestic chores, and enabling her to accompany her husband on trips to remote valleys which it was his practice to visit on fine weekends. Jeanie's letters to her mother reveal that they passed long days far away from the world's affairs in these peaceful and isolated spots; she contentedly searching the grassy slopes for Alpine flowers, while her bearded, fifty-year-old husband sketched and painted, or filled page after page of his pad with descriptive passages for inclusion in his forthcoming book.

At least twice a month, provided the weather appeared settled and the sun shone from a bright blue sky, they would kiss the three elder children goodbye and board the horse-drawn diligence which they used as a coach; the baby swaddled with shawls 'with nothing but a little pink face showing from the cocoon,' as they waved from the creaking, swaying vehicle as it jerked away from the door. Surrounded by Bob's battered strap-bound suitcase, a picnic-basket, a small portable easel, and a couple of hat-boxes, they would happily disappear for a few days alone in the wilds.

They rented their double-bedded room at one of the log-built village inns which nestled high up in the passes, overshadowed by the towering, snow-capped peaks which serrated every horizon, and knew that they had escaped until the following Monday.

Early each morning, with the baby sometimes carried pick-a-back in a knapsack on his father's shoulders, they would leave the little cluster of broad-roofed houses with their wooden balconies and brightly painted doors and windows, climbing steeply winding paths to the stillness of slopes that viewed a fairy-tale world. Only the misty tinklings of cowbells and the occasional muted distant barking of a farmer's dog reminded them of the village set in its chequered fields below. High above the valley they would spend the long sunlit hours, the baby fed and peaceful in his wicker basket, his father stretched on the grass as he mused and wrote, or slept after lunch with his hat tipped over his eyes, while Jeanie sought the elusive edelweiss and made bouquets of tiny mountain flowers.

A few days later they would reappear at their pension in Château d'Oex,[1] Bob with water-colours to show the children, and his wife with a posy of specimens for pressing and a small present for each of them. Ballantyne usually brought back a chapter or two of his new story to add to those he had already completed, his latest tale being set, as might be expected, amid the snows and glaciers of the Swiss Alps.[2] *River of Ice*, as he called this most recent addition to his adventure stories for boys, proved no less successful than his other productions, the second edition being issued only a few months after the volume first appeared.

Ballantyne had now reached a position where his finances allowed him to realise a dream he had cherished for many years: that of gratifying his wanderlust by making an extended visit to South Africa. He had now managed to salt away over eight

[1] Their address was now the Pension Rosat, Château d'Oex, Canton Vand. At that time, Château d'Oex was a small town of some two thousand three hundred inhabitants, a few miles from Montreux.

[2] *Rivers of Ice* appeared in October 1875, priced at five shillings a copy. The second edition, with the title-page dated 1876, was published the following April.

hundred pounds in the Savings Bank, and was the recipient of a regular and increasing income. In addition he owned the house in Millerfield Place, which brought in a rental of fifty pounds per annum, and his future prospects seemed rosy. The only obstacle was his wife's objection to being deprived of the company of her husband for several months; but her protests about being left alone for so long were overcome by his agreeing to pay for her mother's travelling expenses to Switzerland and the cost of her residence there until his return. With the obedience expected from a Victorian wife who loved and respected her husband, Jeanie finally acquiesced to his trip, being informed that the visit would give her spouse an unrivalled opportunity for gathering material for several books, and having extracted a promise that he would write every few days of his experiences amongst the settlers and natives of the Cape of Good Hope.

On his arrival in London to make final arrangements for the journey he was informed by his publishers that they had arranged an experiment which might result in his gaining information that would be of value for a new adventure story; one that he could write on the voyage out and would ensure his Christmas book appearing the following year, even if he wrote nothing else until his return. James Watson, of Nisbet's, had met a Monsieur Denayrouze of Paris, the owner of a firm that manufactured underwater equipment of various kinds, and during the course of conversation had been invited to try for himself the latest of the firm's diving suits. This offer he had declined with thanks, but the invitation was still open if Ballantyne would care to take advantage of it. Whether the author demurred has not been recorded; but that he finally agreed to take the plunge there is no doubt.

Apparently arrangements were made for Ballantyne to descend in a diving dress, first in a large, glass-sided tank which the company had erected in Alexandra Palace, and later in more realistic surroundings in the River Thames. Everything went well indoors, as the author jubilantly explained to Jeanie:

[*September*, 1875]

. . . I've got up nearly all the information I require now

269

about Diving. Been down in the diving-bell at the Politechnic, and also, yesterday, I went down in a diving dress at the Alexandra Palace!

It was comical work. I *had* to do it in public! The regular diver was down with me. I did not stay long—not quite a quarter of an hour, but that was enough. It put me quite up to the feelings of the diving dress at least in shallow water (about ten or twelve feet) & showed me a mistake or two that cd. be made. I shook hands facetiously with the diver when I got to the bottom of the tank & poked him on the head; then sprawled about the bottom & nodded to people at the windows of the tank; after wh. I let out nearly all the air from the dress by mistake & let in a few drops of water wh. induced me to return to the world above. Again I descended, &, after a few minutes once more came up. The sensation was by no means unpleasant, except when I let out too much air, and I was none the worse, but rather the better of my dip. It will enable me to write much more effectively, I expect...

Had he left his experimenting at this stage, all would have been well; but, spurred by this success, he found himself, a few days later, on the deck of a barge moored in the Thames, surrounded by the paraphernalia of what he was assured was absolutely foolproof diving equipment of the most modern type. Encouraged by his playful exploits in the tank, the author needed little persuading to strip to his woollen vest and long underpants; allowing himself to be encased in the thick rubbercloth diving suit, complete with lead-soled boots, massive breast and back plates, and a large brass helmet. With the face-piece screwed into place, he shook hands with the assembled company and descended the ladder at the barge's side, disappearing beneath the waves in a cloud of little bubbles. For a time all went well. He wandered about on the muddy bed of the river, shouting reassuring comments through the speaking-tube and appeared to be thoroughly enjoying himself in his strange surroundings. Under the watchful eye of the inventor, the two men at the pump rhythmically turned the handles of the large wheel which worked the piston to compress the air, and a continuous stream of bubbles broke the surface of the river.

What happened next is not very clear. As Ballantyne related it to his wife, he remembered trying to bend double to retrieve an object he had felt in the mud, but seconds later felt his suit dilate to an unbearable degree, his feet left the bottom and he shot to the surface like a gas-filled balloon, emerging with a bounce that frothed the Thames with foam for yards around. Consternation and alarm ruled on the deck of the barge, with the Frenchman dancing around screaming imprecations at his assistants, while poor Bob was rapidly hauled aboard the vessel feet first, the face-piece removed with a hiss that deflated the suit, and the unfortunate inmate, red-faced and gasping, was pulled unceremoniously head foremost out of the rubber casing. Soaked and filthy, his beard bedraggled and the blood pounding in his ears, Ballantyne lay on the oily deck in his underclothes, brandy being forced down his throat and smelling-salts thrust under his nose until he revived sufficiently to stagger drunkenly to his feet. His remarks to Monsieur Denayrouze, when at last he was able to speak, have not been recorded, but one imagines that his powers of self-control must have been taxed most severely.

He was fully recovered in the course of a few days and made good use of his frightening experience in his story *Under the Waves, or, Diving in Deep Waters*,[1] the frontispiece of which shows an unfortunate diver suffering much the same fate as the author of the book. He wrote a preface to the work, but was gentlemanly enough to content himself with only a formal comment on the Denayrouze equipment:

> I have to acknowledge myself indebted to the well-known submarine engineers, Messrs. Siebe and Gorman, and Messrs. Heinke and Davis, of London, for much valuable information; and to Messrs. Denayrouze, of Paris, for permitting me to go under water in one of their diving dresses.

Whatever else he might have liked to add, he was charitable enough to leave unsaid.

[1] *Under the Waves* appeared on the 15th October, 1876, priced at five shillings a copy.

Chapter Thirteen

His holiday in South Africa resulted in the production of two new books, of entirely different types. *The Settler and the Savage* was a fictional adventure story set in the period immediately after the Kaffir Wars, the sort of tale that had an appeal for boys of all ages. But *Six Months at the Cape* was an autobiographical account of the author's travels around the Colony and was aimed primarily at an adult readership. Under the guise of a series of letters to 'Periwinkle,' a fictional friend he invented for the purpose, Ballantyne wrote an account of his experiences in the bush and at an ostrich farm where he stayed for several weeks. Today, the story makes interesting reading, giving us a picture of the life of the settlers in the harsh conditions that prevailed at the Cape in the mid 'seventies, but the volume was almost ignored by the reading public and had only a small sale. The failure of this book must have confirmed Ballantyne in his conviction that his *forte* was in writing books for boys, and that to aim any higher was to court almost certain disaster. He could have had few illusions by this time as to the scope of his literary talents, for he never again attempted anything more serious than adventure stories until, in the last few months of his life, Archibald Constable persuaded him to start writing his autobiography.

On his arrival back in England in June 1876 he went immediately to join Jeanie and the children in Switzerland. Most of the next three years the family spent together in either Montreux or Nice, Ballantyne disappearing at intervals to seek information for fresh books. In September 1877 he was the guest of Admiral Wilson in H.M.S. *Thunderer*, an ironclad battleship of the latest type which was then in Portsmouth harbour, and for two weeks was aboard the warship while he made notes of life in the Navy for his book *In the Track of the Troops: A Tale of Modern War*. Twelve months later, in the guise of an amateur detective, he passed a fortnight amongst the sorters and delivery men at the General Post Office in London while writing *Post Haste, A Tale of Her Majesty's Mails.*

His family was growing in both numbers and size and now comprised three boys and two girls, the youngest daughter, Alice Christina Hogarth, having been born in Nice on the 23rd March, 1877. The fact that the family so often moved from place to place meant that the children's education had been woefully neglected, but Jeanie was determined that the boys should receive the benefit of attending an English public school. When the Ballantynes returned to London in 1879, their eldest son Frank was nearly eleven years old and his brother Ted only two years his junior, but neither had ever been given any regular schooling; what little they had learned had been taught them by their mother or the various governesses she had employed. This was a state of affairs that Jeanie was now anxious to remedy, and that winter she and her husband selected a rented house in London Hill, Harrow, not far from the famous school.

Not long afterwards, to their parents' great satisfaction, the Headmaster of Harrow School provisionally allocated places for their younger sons to attend as day boys, while Frank was accepted at Sedberg School in Westmorland as a boarder. The eldest daughter, and the rest of the girls in their turn, were sent to a local private school. Mrs. Ballantyne now set about trying to curb her husband's restless spirit in the hope that the family could at last settle down and make Harrow-on-the-Hill their permanent home. She had already been successful in persuading him to have a small holiday chalet built near the beach at Wimereaux, not far from Boulogne, a resort they had discovered on a previous occasion, and here they always spent their holidays when the children were free from school. But she had set her heart on their owning a home of their own in England, a place that would anchor the family while the children were being educated and give their parents some security for their later years. Matters came to a head in 1881, when Jeanie discovered that she was expecting yet another baby, and she now positively insisted that her husband should take steps either to build or buy a house.

Whatever arguments Ballantyne may have advanced against this outlay of capital must soon have been overcome, for the following January he was writing to his friend John Gifford, the manager of the National Bank in Edinburgh, in a somewhat lighthearted attempt to borrow the necessary money:

London Hill, Harrow.
17th January, 1882.

My dear Sir,

I want to raise £1,500 on good security. This being so, I, not being a business man, come to you for advice as to how it is to be done.

My object is to build a house. Yes, sir, a house! (My bosom has been fired with the same ambition that animated a certain 'Jack' well known to fame.) I have more than sufficient possessions to warrant my ambition, but these are partly invested and unavailable.

In Edinr. Water Trust 6 per cent	200
Loan to Scottish-American Water Trust, 5 per cent	250
House No. 6 Millerfield Place wh. is valued at	1050
Insurance on my life, now worth	572
In Edinbr. Savings Bank	628
TOTAL	£2700

Prospects unlimited—to say nothing of a mine of copyrights that wd. make a millionaire envious, besides land in France—land, sir, observe that. (It's only a quarter of an acre, no doubt—but no matter), and a chalet thereon, as well as—but enough! Why, when these facts are considered it is a marvel that men do not run to me to borrow, instead of I to men. But so it is, and such is life!

Now, will the 'National' lend me the money? If so at what rate & will the period be definite or indefinite (because I want it the latter, to pay back in instalments as I can.) If not—who will agree to be the victim? Are there not building societies? Are they safe?

Give me your advice on these points, my dear sir, & believe me,

Yours ever,
R. M. Ballantyne.

The manager of the National Bank had no hesitation in coming to the rescue, and soon afterwards the family found themselves in a turmoil of builders, plasterers, decorators, plumbers, landscape gardeners, and the rest of the promise makers and promise breakers who descend in droves on the prospective occupiers of any new house. Ballantyne and his wife had selected a partially wooded piece of ground on which to have their home-to-be erected, a site of just under one acre of gently sloping hillside in Mount Park Road, Harrow. Having at last signed the contract and embedded a golden guinea in the still wet mortar of the foundations in order to bring them luck, they were delighted to learn from their architect that he had every confidence that they would be able to take possession of their new home in time to celebrate Christmas around their own fireside. But it was well into May 1883 before the last of the interminable workmen had left 'Duneaves,' as they christened their imposing new residence. In the meantime, the costs of construction had unaccountably risen by a sum in excess of two hundred pounds over the original estimate. 'Never mind,' said the proud owner in a letter to his brother, 'the house is built to last a century.'

Duneaves was to be the family home for the next twelve years, a place they all grew to love and where Mrs. Ballantyne would have been quite content to pass the rest of her days. She delighted in once again having a garden of her own to tend and care for, and persuaded her husband to sanction expenditure on a far higher scale than he had originally intended. There was a series of gravel walks, edged with ornamental blue bricks, that wended their way to a little summer house, and she talked him into having a patch of ground levelled in order to do duty as a tennis court. A wide terrace was constructed around the house, a shrubbery was planted and a lonicerna hedge to give privacy from the road, and the following spring the grass under the trees was bright with the golden heads of several hundred daffodils. By the autumn they had been forced to enlist the services of a part-time gardener. He came to join a staff of two, composed of a housemaid and a nanny, which latter post had been filled since the birth of Miss Isobel McKenzie Ballantyne, who had arrived the previous March. 'Belle,' as the family came to call her, was the last child of their marriage, a fact for which her father must have been profoundly thankful, for he had celebrated his fifty-seventh birthday a few days after she was born.

During the whole of this period the author continued to churn out books in a never-ending stream. Amongst them was *The Lonely Island*, a tale dealing with the Bounty mutineers, which appeared in December 1880. The next three years saw the publication of *My Doggie and I; The Giant of the North, or Poking Round the Pole; The Battery and the Boiler, or Adventures in Laying Submarine Electric Cables; Battles with the Sea;* and *The Madman and the Pirate.*

But the tale that gave most pleasure to his own children, and proved one of the most successful of his later works, was *The Kitten Pilgrims*, which appeared in quarto form in glazed pictorial boards in November 1882. The story was based on John Bunyan's *Pilgrim's Progress*, but Ballantyne had wisely simplified the tale so that it had an instant appeal to young children. For the pious figure of Mr. Christian, he had substituted two comical kittens and a fierce little dog called Trusty, who quickly became involved in a series of battles with various monsters that attempted to bar their way to the promised land. The book undoubtedly owed much of its popularity to the twelve full-paged coloured illustrations, all of which were from Ballantyne's hand, and for the author's fearsome and bloodthirsty descriptions of the way in which the monsters were despatched. Much of the slaughter would have done justice to a modern horror comic. Here is the manner in which the kittens Dick and Flimsy helped the dog Trusty to remove from their path the Octopus Untruth, who had wickedly attempted to impede their progress:

'That's the way, Dick!' cried Trusty. 'Go at him, Flim! Don't spare him. You must cut him up till not a morsel is left, for he's a low, mean, wicked, abominable monster! Cut out his beak, my boy! Well done, Flim. Stick your foot in his other eye! Cleverly cut, Dick! Slice off his nose next! That's the way! Out with his tongue! Hurrah!'

And on to the next bloody execution.! But the book quickly became a firm favourite with younger children and was reprinted several times in different formats during the next few years. It rivalled in popularity the series of 'Kitten' books which Ballantyne had written some twenty-five years before.

The next few years at Harrow passed peacefully and comparatively uneventfully. They entered into the social life of the town, entertained a little on their own account, and Ballantyne was elected to membership of several local clubs. He became interested in the work of the newly formed Salvation Army, and this, coupled with an uneasy fear that one day he might possibly suffer the same fate as his late brother James, prompted him to sign the pledge and become a total abstainer. Thereafter he wore a small blue ribbon in his buttonhole to proclaim to the world his rejection of alcohol in all its forms. He felt so strongly about the subject that, although he was a firm supporter of Mr. Gladstone's radical policies, he resigned from Harrow Liberal Club in 1886 when the committee carried a resolution permitting the club bar to sell intoxicating liquors.

He also had an uncompromisingly hostile attitude towards the use of tobacco; but despite this, and his latest stand against the consumption of any type of spirits—'except where deemed necessary as a medical stimulant'—he still retained a strong sense of humour. He also had a keen appreciation of anything that turned humdrum formality or dramatic posturing into something that could be termed hilarious. Two incidents occurred about this time which illustrate this trait, revealing that behind the mask of censorious virtue that too often hid the real Ballantyne, there still lurked a man who could dissolve into laughter like any schoolboy if the comical side of an otherwise solemn situation became a little too much to bear.

One such incident happened in a provincial town where the author and his wife stayed for the night after a lecture he had given in the afternoon. In the dining room of their hotel they met Percy Fitzgerald,[1] a short-story writer and newspaper correspondent whom Ballantyne had known for some years. Fitzgerald was staying there alone and was delighted at having found someone with whom he was already acquainted. He invited them

[1] Percy Fitzgerald relates the incident in similar terms in his book *Recreations of a Literary Man*, Chatto and Windus, London, 1883.

to dinner and insisted that they should accept two spare complimentary seats for a performance at the local theatre that night. All three were pleased that what they had expected to be a dull and probably boring evening should be enlivened in this way, and as soon as the meal was over they set out for the theatre.

The officers of the local garrison and their ladies had hired the hall for the performance, on the understanding that time would be allowed between the acts for some of their own amateur performers. All went well for a time, but the third of these non-professionals turned out to be a lady who taught elocution, and who had kindly allowed herself to be persuaded to come forward to recite Edgar Allen Poe's dramatic poem of 'The Bells.' The piece describes the effect of various types of bells with considerable power, the first verse being devoted to the sensations aroused on hearing the gay ringing of bells after a wedding. The theatre was crowded and a hush fell over the audience as the angular figure of the performer strode purposefully to the edge of the stage to recite the first strophe:

> Hear the music of the bells,
> Wedding bells, etc., etc.

The lady imparted to these lines a sort of tender nuptial tone, coupled with a kind of conjugal grace, and when she came to the chorus she chimed out:

> Bells, bells, bells,
> Bells, bells, bells, bells.

appearing to peal them as if she was a bell-ringer herself. Her voice fell into a sing-song and she lightheartedly raised her hand to her ear as if to try and catch the distant chiming. At that moment Mrs. Ballantyne was horrified to hear from her husband a distinct and very audible titter. They were sitting about six rows from the front of the stalls and several people craned their heads to view the offender, who by now had somehow succeeded in turning the sound into a fit of coughing, a sharp nudge from the elbow of his wife finally bringing a strained and red-faced silence.

The next verse commenced, this time dealing with the solemn

tolling of funeral bells. The lady on the stage, who was a spinster in her late forties, now attempted to turn from being a blushing bride into a ghoul-like figure with contorted face and palsied hands. The effect was odd to say the least; and when she came to the burden of the poem, she shrank back as though hearing the muffled knell issuing from a mortuary tower:

> To the pealing of the bells,
> Bee-yells, bee-yells,
> Boles, Boles—BOWELS! BOWELS!

Between each 'toll' of the 'BOWELS' there was a long pause. She boomed out the words, oblivious of their meaning, while her hands, as though holding an imaginary rope, slowly and sadly drew it down at every peal. This was too much for Ballantyne. With tears streaming down his face he collapsed into helpless laughter, Fitzgerald doing the same, while from every part of the theatre came gusts of uncontrollable mirth. Half the audience turned to hush the rest, wives started pummelling husbands, husbands were shaking wives, but all to no avail. The infection had spread and a good fifty per cent of the crowd were shaking with unsuppressible laughter. But worse was to come! When at last some sort of order had been restored, the fair elocutionist, her face now suffused with a look of deep reproach and wounded sensibility, bravely began to recite the final verse.

In this she attempted to depict the alarm of a fire, with the sweating horses galloping through the deserted streets, and the wild ringing of the fire bells rousing the sleeping population. With an icy glance which Jeanie always maintained was directed solely at her husband, the grim-faced performer began calmly with the opening words:

> Hear the music of the bells,
> Fiery bells, fiery bells,

But as the conflagration spread, her agitation increased, the peals of the bell following short and fast. When she reached the refrain:

> Bells, bells, bells, bells!

her arms started to work with frantic energy at the rope, up and down! up and down! for all the world like someone trying desperately to flush a faulty toilet. And with every stroke came the word 'BELLS'; but drowning this were shrieks of laughter from all parts of the hall, some of the audience falling backwards in hysterical agonies, while Ballantyne, his silk hat irreparably crushed, was on his knees between the seats positively sobbing with mirth.

Throughout all this pandemonium the middle-aged spinster could still be seen madly tolling her imaginary rope, her hands flying up and down with ever-increasing speed, although not a word she spoke could be heard. Finally, amid scenes of the utmost confusion, a row of seats having fallen backwards with their occupants, injuring the legs of those who sat behind, the unfortunate lady, wounded to the very heart, retired in a fainting condition into the wings, not to be seen again. In the cab, on the way back to their hotel, Ballantyne and his friend were thoroughly chastised by an indignant Jeanie who realised the tragedy of the affair for the person most concerned; but the night of the 'Pealing Bowels' became a legend from that day forth.

The attraction which the evangelism of William Booth and the Salvation Army had for the author led him to attend several meetings addressed by the fiery General. Ballantyne was most impressed by his compelling personality and mastery over the rowdy gatherings in the East End of London. The two men were introduced after one of these meetings and Ballantyne was successful in persuading Booth to come down to Harrow for lunch with his family and discuss the good work the newly formed Army was accomplishing amongst the poorest members of the community.

The younger members of his household had been carefully schooled as to their conduct when in the presence of the great man, and everyone was on their best behaviour when they at last sat down to the magnificent lunch. It had cost Jeanie and her plump and jolly little maid many hours in preparation and the hostess was on tenterhooks that all should go well for the occasion. Before the fire in the dining room, as they took their places, lay a fat little pug dog. This they had agreed to board for one of the boys at Harrow School, and during the preceding weeks it had become a family pet, spoilt and pampered, and grossly overfed. Now, having recently gorged itself on scraps left over in the kitchen, it slept heavily on the fireside rug, oblivious to the world. As course followed course on the mahogany table, all appeared to go as planned; the conversation ranged over a wide field, with the eldest daughters occasionally being permitted to comment on the affairs of the day. Ballantyne proposed the health of the founder of the Salvation Army, which was drunk in tumblers of water by all assembled at the board. The author had said grace before they sat down to the meal, and, as the maid brought in the coffee, Booth rose to his feet to pronounce the final blessing.

'Let us give thanks to the Lord for His bounty of which we have just partaken,' he said, as the family stood with closed eyes around table. And it was at that precise moment, in the dead silence that followed his words, that the pug dog chose to break wind in a high-pitched rasping note that echoed round the room like a trumpet. The effect was electrifying. Mrs. Ballantyne swayed as though about to faint, while her husband cast his eyes to the ceiling as though imploring a merciful Heaven to open the floor and swallow him up. Meanwhile the dog had risen stiffly to its feet, and, glancing suspiciously at its tail, stalked slowly through the door into the hall.

So far nobody had spoken, but the unfortunate maid, unable to contain herself any longer, suddenly blurted, 'Oh Gawd, Ma'am. I can't help it!' and collapsed into hysterical laughter, throwing her apron over her head and fleeing from the room, from whence her cries could be heard growing fainter as she stumbled down the stairs to the kitchen. The three Ballantyne girls had become convulsed with giggles and their father's shoulders were shaking in a most suspicious way; but all waited for any reaction from the General, who could turn what was an uproariously funny situation into one of the utmost embarrassment. Turning to the author, who could no longer conceal his mirth, Booth permitted himself a pent-up chortle of the most surprising vigour, saying amid gasps of laughter, 'We may take that, I think, as a fervent Amen.'

The day was saved: the children were quickly ushered from

the room, to their profound relief, and the tension evaporated relieving the Ballantynes of any further embarrassment. But it was a long time before the pug dog was forgiven his perfectly timed interjection.

It was seldom that Ballantyne now left the family home in search of new situations in which to set his tales. As the years went by he drew more and more on his experiences in the past for subjects for his books. One of the last of his forays in search of adventure was in 1884, when he spent a fortnight in a fishing trawler in the North Sea to enable him to write a story about the work of the Mission to Deep Sea Fishermen. He was horribly seasick for nearly the whole period, but he emerged, as he put it, 'looking pale and positively cadaverous, but with a sheaf of salt-stained notes for the book'.[1] *The Young Trawler. A Story of Life and Death and Rescue on the North Sea*, was published in October 1884, the author having written to his wife when he finally docked at Yarmouth:

> It was an experience I do not wish to repeat. Even after coming ashore the pavements and buildings of the port continued to sway in the most alarming manner, and the nausea prostrated me for the remainder of the day. Soon after we had put to sea I began to wish that I had not left the safety of dry land & I have more than once thanked God for bringing me back to the welcome shores of England. I shd. never have made a sailor, of that fact I am certain.

In the six years between 1884 and 1890 his prolific pen produced no less than fourteen full-length adventure stories.[2] and,

[1] From a letter to his wife, posted in May 1884, when he landed from the mission smack *Cholmondeley*.

[2] The dates of these books are as follows: *Dusty Diamonds Cut and Polished*, 1884; *The Young Trawler*, 1884; *Twice Bought, A Tale of the Oregon Goldfields*, 1885; *The Rover of the Andes*, 1885; *The Island Queen*, 1885; *Red Rooney, or The Last of the Crew*, 1886; *The Prairie Chief*, 1886; *The Fugitives, or The Tyrant Queen of Madagascar*, 1887; *The Big Otter*, 1887; *Blue Lights or Hot Work in the Sudan*, 1888; *The Middy and the Moors*, 1888; *The Crew of the Water Wagtail*, (1889); *The Eagle Cliff*, (1889); and *Blown to Bits, or The Lonely Man of Rakata*, 1889. In addition to these works, Ballantyne contributed several short stories to magazines and annuals.

THE

Rover of the Andes

A TALE OF ADVENTURE in

South America

R. M. Ballantyne

J. Nisbet & Co. London.

Title page from *The Rover of the Andes*, first published in 1885

Quashy in Danger

despite fierce competition from other authors in the same field, the majority of these works enjoyed sales almost as high as the more popular of his early books. But if one reads these later novels, it becomes obvious that his large output was affecting the quality of his writing. His plots, never the strong point of any of his tales, were now having a very threadbare look, while too many of his descriptive passages were suffering from the repetition of situations that he had employed on more than one previous occasion. Ballantyne was now using too much fact and far too little imagination, and his well-tried formulas were becoming soiled and mechanical, with the most implausible coincidences littering the pages. His young readers must frequently have been able to predict the result of the dramatic situations he contrived long before they read the end of the tale. But his name on the title-page was still sufficient inducement for them to part with their shillings for a new adventure story by the great R. M. Ballantyne.

It was shortly after his sixty-fifth birthday in 1890 that he first began to experience giddiness and vertigo on occasions when he was obliged to stand upright for more than a few minutes, but for some months the symptoms were of only short duration and caused him merely minor inconvenience. But while on a fishing trip in Scotland in the late summer, accompanied by his son Frank, he lost his balance and fell heavily on the rocks at the water's edge. Badly bruised, he found himself unable to rise and his son discovered him twenty minutes later lying half in and half out of the water, soaked to the skin and nearly petrified with the cold. The lad hurriedly dragged his father up the bank, but Ballantyne was quite unable to walk and had to be left, propped against a tree, while Frank ran to the village for assistance. The unfortunate author was later brought back in a very woebegone state to the cottage where they were staying, lying prostrate on a field-gate carried by farm labourers, and was immediately put to bed to await the arrival of the local doctor. It was imagined at first that he had suffered some kind of a stroke, or perhaps fractured his skull in the fall, but the absence of any paralysis or head injury, and the fact that the patient appeared to recover completely within a few days, made the physician advise that a specialist should be consulted as soon as Ballantyne was fit to return to Harrow.

This proved to be the start of serious attacks of vertigo, although he would sometimes be free of the symptoms for months. He was examined by doctors and specialists in nervous diseases, but although several different diagnoses were made, each in turn proved to be incorrect. Mrs. Ballantyne began to suffer an increasing fear that perhaps a malignant tumour of the brain was the hidden cause of her husband's loss of balance and giddiness, but time mercifully proved this idea to be erroneous. On the advice of his doctors, several weeks were spent in bed, diets were recommended and faithfully adhered to, he was leeched on the temples, forced to swallow a nauseous mixture of evil-tasting medicines, and was even secretly tested for locomotor axtaxia in case his ailment might have a syphilitic origin—but all without avail. His dizziness kept recurring, but fortunately with periods of intermission that enabled him to continue writing with almost undiminished vigour, although the quality of his work suffered to an increasing extent.

In the autumn of 1891, after weeks made miserable by vertigo, he departed to take the curative waters of Bath, in the hope that a course of treatment at the famous spa might at least alleviate the worst of his symptoms. But two months of tasting the waters at the Grand Pump Room Hotel seemed to have absolutely no effect on his complaint and he returned home at the end of December in a worse state than when he left. It was now obvious to the family that the disease, whatever it was, must be a progressive one, for the attacks of giddiness which blurred his vision and caused him to reel were gradually becoming more and more frequent and he was soon forced to rely on a walking-stick. His illness threw a blanket of gloom over the Christmas festivities at Duneaves, and this depression was not lightened for his wife by the absence abroad of their two eldest sons. Frank, now twenty-two, had departed to the United States of America to seek a post with friends in Washington. Ted, after completing a successful course at Sandhurst, was now a subaltern in the Army and on his way to join his regiment in India. Their uncle, John Ballantyne, after being forced to abandon his career as an artist, due to failing eyesight, had taken the post of curator at the Royal Academy of Arts Schools at Burlington House, but had retired in poor health after some years, and was now living with Teenie at Seend, near Melksham, in Wiltshire. They were both in very straitened circumstances, having only a small pension to live on, and there is no doubt that had it not been for financial help from his brother (on a scale which Jeanie did not discover until after her husband's death) the impoverished painter would have been hard pressed to maintain any semblance of a middle-class standard of living.

In February, after the author had been forced to pass a particularly miserable week in bed, the whole room swirling round each time he opened his eyes, his specialist advised a radical change of air and climate as holding out the only hope of a complete cure. As soon as the attack had subsided and he was once more on his feet, Ballantyne made immediate arrangements to take a holiday in Egypt, and, with the blessing of his wife, he embarked on the *Hydaspes* at the end of the month. After an uneventful trip he arrived in Cairo and went by previous arrangement to the house of a Mr. and Mrs. Lawrence at Mex, a lakeside resort near Alexandria. But after nearly two months of rest and sunshine he could only report to his wife that 'In some ways I feel better, but cannot say that the vertigo has abated. Still, to be better in any degree is a matter for wh. I thank God.'

During the periods when dizziness left him he worked on the manuscript of *The Hot Swamp, A Romance of Old Albion*, a tale he had set amongst the hot springs of Bath in the days before the Romans came to Britain. He finished the book on his return home in May, and later in the year commenced yet another, this time entitled *The Walrus Hunters*. But the effort to complete what was to be his last book for boys taxed him to an exhausting extent and several times he was forced to lay aside the manuscript when writing became impossible. Walking any distance was now out of the question unless he had an arm to hang on to. He had fallen several times in the house and his wife had become frightened to leave him alone for more than a few minutes at a time. 'Poor Bob staggers like a drunken man,' she wrote to her sister-in-law, 'and we are now obliged to take a cab to go the short distance to church. He is often unable to come downstairs without assistance and I grieve to see him in such a condition. Pray God that his mind is never affected—this would be more than I could bear.'

In November 1892 he received a visit from Archibald Constable, the publisher and printer, and a man with whom the author had been on intimate terms of friendship for a great many years. It was a fine, late autumn afternoon and Ballantyne decided to honour the occasion of his friend's visit by taking a short walk with him in the garden, a place into which he had not ventured for several weeks. He swayed as he walked and had frequently to be assisted by his companion before they finally reached the rustic seat in the shrubbery at the end of the lawn. There they sat for a few minutes and the physical contrast between them must have been marked. The sparse, upright author, cloaked like Holmes against the chill, his thin fingers crossed on the top of his cane, with his now wintery beard and lined face making him look considerably older than his sixty-eight years; and the portly, red-faced publisher, gold-chained and sovereign-weighted, in whose father's office Ballantyne had worked and chafed as a young man on his return from Hudson Bay. It must have been obvious to Constable that not for much longer could that slight figure by his side continue to turn out his yearly, bow-stringed adventure books, so eagerly awaited and devoured each Christmas by expectant boys.

In a letter to *The Scotsman*, written a few years later, Constable recalled this meeting at Harrow:

> While he walked with me in his garden he used a stick, and even so he sometimes tottered. He told me that he had fallen once or twice; but in his chair, he said, he was still able to work. And work he did—to the end.[1]

The publisher had become increasingly dismayed by the reports he had received regarding the rapid decline in the author's health, and had purposely journeyed down to Harrow both to comfort his ailing friend and to urge him to keep a promise he had made some years before. On that occasion Ballantyne had stated that he might one day write the story of his own full and

[1] This letter appears in the issue for the 2nd March, 1894.

varied life, and Constable had extracted from him a firm promise that he would definitely do so. But nothing more had been heard of the projected work. His friend now strongly urged him to make the effort which an autobiography would require, so that he could preserve his memories of a life chequered with incident for the generations who could never know him as a man. In this way, perhaps he might help future writers by revealing the rewards he had gained and the disappointments he had suffered, pointing out to them the pitfalls to be avoided in the career of a writer of juvenile fiction. These were some of the arguments the publisher used, according to the story of the conversation which the author later related to his wife. They must have been persuasive, because, before Constable left for home that evening, Ballantyne had given him a fresh promise to start the story of his life as soon as the book he was engaged upon was finished.

There is little doubt that he must have been well aware that time was now running short, for the spells of dizziness from which he suffered were becoming more frequent every week, and he was finding it almost impossible to concentrate and invent. But his memory was almost unimpaired, and although the monotonies of his past were sometimes lost in the mists of forgetfulness, dramatic incidents and the important events of his long career were still etched bright and vivid in the eye of his mind. There were days when the giddiness, which made his life so wretched, left him completely, and he now seized every such occasion to narrate passages of his memoirs to his nineteen-year-old daughter Jane, who acted as his amanuensis whenever writing became too difficult. With her help, and the encouragement given him by his wife, he began to enjoy the task of stringing the threads of his past existence into a coherent design, trying to weave a self-portrait of a Victorian author for whom fame and the publication of over a hundred separate books had brought with it no more than very moderate financial success.

Because of the nature of his illness his study chair had been specially fitted with a wooden board which formed a desk across the arms, and, safe in this device, he slowly dictated the first chapters of what was to have been his life story. But a prolonged attack of vertigo, which prostrated him for several days, brought the work to a sudden halt, and his wife forbade any further attempts at writing until he had made a complete recovery. Unfortunately, any faint hopes they may have cherished of his regaining his former vigour were doomed to disappointment. The disease was progressively weakening an already frail constitution, and as the months went by it became increasingly obvious to his family that he had written his last book.

Young Jane Ballantyne now found herself faced with the prospect of seeing many hours of painstaking dictation and copying completely wasted. Rather than accept this, she determined to salvage as much as she could from her own and her father's efforts. Hunting through the drawers and pigeon-holes in his study, she collected together as many of the author's published and unpublished short stories as she could find, and sent these, together with the completed chapters of his life story, to his usual publishers. One wonders that Nisbet's agreed to accept them for publication, for the resultant book was a most rambling and disjointed volume. Ballantyne had called it *Personal Reminiscences in Book-Making*, in itself an unfortunate title, and it turned out to be a mere hotch-potch of unconnected incidents from his past, strung together more like rough notes for a later, full-length book. At the end of chapter six the 'personal reminiscences' cease abruptly, finishing with the remark that 'bad health is not to be denied, and I find that I must hold my hand. Perchance this may be no misfortune, but possibly the "garrulity of age" is descending on me! Before closing this sketch, however, I would say briefly, that in all my writings I have always tried—how far successfully I know not—to advance the cause of Truth and Right and to, induce my readers to put their trust in the love of God our Saviour, for this life as well as the life to come.' There then follow seven short stories, under such diverse titles as 'The Burglars and the Parson'; 'Rescue the Perishing'; 'Jim Greely, The North Sea Skipper', etc., none of which are in any sense autobiographical and have been merely added to pad out the volume to about two hundred and forty pages.

Needless to say, the book had a very poor reception. Much had been heard about the promised autobiography in literary circles, and its publication had been impatiently awaited by many of his readers. But the work, when it finally appeared, was admitted to be a great disappointment by even his closest friends.

That same summer Ballantyne was shocked to learn that the firm that owned the copyrights of his earliest books, Thomas Nelson & Sons, had decided to drop the price of these volumes to only half-a-crown a copy. For many years they had been continually re-issuing *The Young Fur Traders*, *The Coral Island*, *Ungava*, *Martin Rattler*, *The World of Ice*, *The Dog Crusoe*, *The Gorilla Hunters*, and the whole series of 'Kitten' books, in large editions, without paying the unfortunate author a single penny in royalties. Literally tens of thousands of copies of these and other titles from Ballantyne's pen had appeared in the bookshops under Nelson's imprint, comprising for the most part the most popular stories he ever wrote, and now they were proposing to slash their price to only half what his current books were sold at. The author was naturally most distressed at the news. In an effort to put a stop to a scheme that would obviously have a serious effect on the sale of the works published by James Nisbet, and in which he still retained a financial interest, Ballantyne wrote Nelsons with a plea that they should revert to their old price:

Harrow.
27th July, 1893.

Messrs. T. Nelson & Sons,
Edinburgh.
Dear Sirs,

I have a request to make of you, an unusual one I admit, but I hope you will not refuse to grant it on that account— namely, that you will return to the old charge of 3/6 (instead of 2/6) for each of the seven volumes of my works wh. you possess.[1] For it is quite impossible for me to compete satisfactorily with you when the books wh. you now sell at 2/6 are similar in size & get-up to those wh. I have been selling up to now at 5/-.

I base my request chiefly on the fact that for thirty-eight

[1] This statement refers to the seven volumes listed above. Nelson's also owned the copyright of the series of nursery books, such as *The Three Little Kittens*, and several other lesser-known titles.

years Nelson & Sons have reaped the whole profits of these books (except the £99 wh., on an average, including several honorariums, I received from each of them.)

For over thirty years of that period you have undersold me (at 3/6) while during the same period I have advertised your seven volumes—1st by bringing out one or two new books every year, & 2nd by including the names of some of your volumes in the list on the title pages. I never complained of this underselling, because I had no right to do so, but don't you think it seems hard that after you have made thousands of pounds out of my books, while I received only a few hundreds, you shd. further reduce them to the unremunerative price of 2/6—a price wh. will, I fear, take the wind out of my sails altogether.

I have no claim to make in this matter. I merely put the facts before you and ask the return to the old price as a favour. I wd. also ask you to consider whether—now I am nearing the close of life & unable to fight the battle with my wonted vigour—it wd. not be a generous, as well as a reasonable act on the part of the wealthy House of Thomas Nelson & Sons, to relieve me from such ruinous competition.

Yours faithfully,
R. M. Ballantyne.[1]

A few days later came a reply expressing Messrs. Nelsons' regret and pointing out that 'decisions of policy are made some months ahead and that therefore it is quite impossible to accede to your request.' Their letter ended with a polite hope that Ballantyne would enjoy many fruitful and healthy years in the future. And that was that. Business was business and the seven volumes continued to appear at half-a-crown.

It was a miserable year for the ageing author. He was now plagued by vertigo and nausea even when lying down, and for days at a time he was unable to leave his room. Every type of medical treatment had been tried; several different specialists had been consulted, but not one had been able to say what it was that

[1] Quoted from the copy of the letter which Ballantyne sent to Messrs. Thomas Nelson & Sons.

was affecting his sense of balance. All he had to show for months of expensive treatment was a long list of doctors' bills which ate into his savings and added one more worry to the cares with which the family were afflicted. He was now prepared to grasp at any straw which offered hope, and when he heard that a Mr. and Mrs. Searle, who conducted a nature-cure clinic at Tivoli near Rome, had successfully treated others with similar complaints, he received his doctor's permission to make the journey and made immediate arrangements to depart.

It was decided that his daughter Jane should accompany him to act as nurse, as Jeanie still had the younger children to look after. There was no thought at that time that his illness, disagreeable though the symptoms were, was in any way a danger to life. His grey hair and almost white beard, and the fact that he had lost considerable weight, made him look much older than of late, but his appetite was as sharp as ever, his general health remained reasonable and his eyesight was still keen in the intervals when the giddiness left him. His hearing had been affected to some degree, but not enough to make him be considered deaf; only his sense of balance had deserted him during the period when he was suffering an attack. The new hope that each so-called remedy or treatment held out (and they had heard great things about the nature clinic) made his wife say goodbye with a lighter heart than for many months past. With her daughter to take care of him she looked forward to her husband returning the following spring, if not completely cured, then certainly refreshed by the Italian climate and perhaps well on the way to recovery.

But Ballantyne and Jane were sadly disillusioned on their arrival in Tivoli at the end of October. The 'quiet, intimate establishment, set in beautiful surroundings, in which Nature is gently assisted to soothe and heal the ailing,' to quote from the brochure which the owners sent to Harrow, turned out to be the intact section of an old monastery, which the Searles had converted into an austere type of hotel, pleasant enough, no doubt, during a hot Italian summer, but a draughty, medieval old cloister in a cold Italian winter.

They were given beds in two of a corridor of small stone rooms that had once done duty as monks' cells; gloomy, ill-lit places with tiny, slit windows set high up in the walls, and were then apologetically informed by Mrs. Searle that due to cancellations they would be the only guests until the commencement of next season's bookings. As neither young Jane nor her sick father could speak more than a few words of Italian, this meant that the only chance of conversation they had during their entire stay was with their host and hostess, a fussy, middle-aged couple whose well-meaning little attentions and petty disciplines Ballantyne soon found unbearably irritating, and with whom all topics of mutual interest were quickly exhausted. Notwithstanding a strictly vegetarian diet, the damp and depressing surroundings, and the fact that the Searles' course of treatment called for the patient to undergo the ordeal of taking three tepid baths every twenty-four hours, the ailing author stubbornly persevered with the 'cure' for over two months, by which time his daughter had been driven to tears by the utter boredom of weeks of isolation from society. But in January, after Jane had been forced to write a worried letter to her mother reporting a worsening in her father's condition, he managed to scrawl a single sheet to his wife admitting that the treatment had failed.

San Antonio,
Tivoli,
10 *Jany.* 1894.

My dearest Jeanie,

   This place is doing me no good, I fear. The house is cold & I cower over the fire with hot hands & toes and cold calves! We all dine in top coats & cloaks.

   I must come home soon—if God will.

   Dearest Jeanie—I can no longer hope—but I pray for & with you continually.

Yr. loving,

R.M.B.

His handwriting had now deteriorated to such an extent that this letter can be read only with difficulty, and looking at the sloping lines of wavering pencil one can visualise the blurred vision and shaking hands of the old author as he strove to complete this last letter to his wife. His vertigo had become so bad in the last two or three weeks that he now had to be supported by both arms whenever he attempted to move, and a particularly severe attack a few days before they were to leave forced them to postpone their departure until the end of the month.

Both Ballantyne and his daughter were now longing to be home, and no sooner did his latest attack show signs of subsiding that they thankfully said goodbye to the Searles and their 'nature clinic,' and left Tivoli for Rome on the first stage of their journey back to Jeanie and the family at Harrow-on-the-Hill. Jane had written and engaged rooms at a Madam Smith's, a lady who conducted a small *pension* at No. 7 Via Corso, in the centre of the city, where they meant to stay quietly for a few days before attempting the rest of the journey to Naples and a boat bound for England.

After five days of wet, blustery weather, the 8th of February dawned fine and sunny, and as her father declared himself to be feeling much better, Jane ordered an open, horse-drawn carriage so that they could take this fleeting opportunity of viewing the sights of the Eternal City. Ballantyne was assisted to the vehicle and warmly tucked in with travelling rugs, while his teen-age daughter took her place dressed in a new Italian gown which her father had insisted she should purchase as a reward for her constant care of him during the preceding months. Soon after midday they were driven off to view the wonders of the capital, the hopeful driver pointing out with his whip the magnificent fountains, St. Peter's Square, the Forum, innumerable statues, and a host of other classical antiquities as the horse clip-clopped through the sunlit streets. About five o'clock they finished an enjoyable tour with afternoon tea at a small but exclusive restaurant much favoured by English tourists before being driven back to their lodgings.

Although confessing himself more than a little tired, Ballantyne seemed in good spirits when he was helped up to his bedroom at nine o'clock, and when Jane retired for the night about two hours later she found him sound asleep and breathing deeply. About half an hour after she had gone to bed, she heard through the partly open communicating door the sound of two heavy sighs, as though her father had suddenly gasped for breath. For a few moments there was silence and then came a soft thud as though a book had fallen from his bed. There was no further sound from his room, but Jane had become sufficiently worried to light her bedside candle and call out to see if he had awakened. Receiving no answer, she slipped out of bed and hastily tiptoed through the door into her father's room. By the light of the candle she saw him lying as though asleep, his eyes closed and one hand touching the wooden floor where it had slipped from the coverlet. She sensed instinctively that he was dead, and shortly afterwards the weeping girl had her fears confirmed by the hastily summoned doctor, who came downstairs from the bedroom to announce formally that the life of Robert Michael Ballantyne was over.

Chapter Fourteen

TIDINGS OF THE AUTHOR'S DEATH were received by telegraph in London next day, and within twenty-four hours all the leading newspapers had reported the event and the majority carried obituary notices, extending in some cases to over two columns in length, mourning the passing of 'that prolific and excellent writer of tales for boys,' as *The Times* put it.

His wife received the news *via* a telegram which her daughter had been careful to send to their next-door neighbour at Harrow, a close and intimate friend of Mrs. Ballantyne, whom Jane knew could be relied upon to convey the ill-tidings in a gentle and sympathetic manner. This lady came hurrying round with the doleful information just as Jeanie and the children were sitting down to lunch and she stayed to comfort the grief-stricken family for the rest of the day. The shock of her husband's death was the greater as this event had been totally unexpected and Mrs. Ballantyne had the sorrowful task of informing her absent sons. Frank returned immediately from Edinburgh, where he had been studying for a medical degree, and as young Isobel had just gone down with measles, it was decided that he should represent his mother at the funeral and he left at once for Rome.

Up to the time of his arrival poor Jane had found herself having to cope with all the funeral arrangements, although she received energetic assistance from Madam Smith, whose desire to see her *pension* freed from the mortal remains of the author stimulated her to an almost embarrassing helpfulness. Because of the sudden-ness of Ballantyne's death, the authorities required that an autopsy should be performed. This revealed degenerative changes in the structure of both inner ears, a condition now known as Menière's Disease. This is now recognised as a chronic complaint causing paroxysmal attacks of intense giddiness lasting from minutes to several hours. In most cases there is progressive deaf-ness and the fact that Ballantyne's hearing was only slightly impaired had made diagnosis much more difficult. But in addition to this disease, the pathologist discovered that the cervical plexus, a large group of nerves forming the top of the spinal cord, which help control, amongst other things, the working of the diaphragm, had become inflamed as the result of infection of unknown origin, and this in itself could have caused sudden collapse by interfering with the action of the lungs. Death was officially ascribed to heart failure, the doctor telling Jane that the constant effort to maintain his balance must have imposed considerable strain on the heart of a man in his seventieth year.

Frank arrived in Rome the day before the funeral, and with his sister followed his father's mortal remains to the last resting place in the Protestant Cemetery. In this most beautiful of Italian cemeteries the author lies buried to this day. His grave is within a few yards of the casket containing the heart of Shelley and close to the spot where the body of the poet Keats lies.

By his Will, probate of which was granted in May of the same year, Ballantyne left his entire estate of £2,601 2s. 3d.[1] in trust for his wife's sole benefit during her lifetime, after which the capital was to be equally divided amongst his surviving children. The fact that one of the most popular boys' authors of the period, with over one hundred books bearing his name on their title-pages, should have left such a comparatively small sum, points, amongst other things to his impoverished brother and sister and other needy relations having not appealed in vain.

Within days of learning of Ballantyne's death, a movement started amongst the boys of Harrow School to raise money to erect a monument to the memory of their dead hero. This story was quickly taken up by the newspapers, and the fund gained so many youthful supporters that a committee of distinguished names was formed to take charge of the subscriptions and decide what type of memorial would best perpetuate his name. Among the well-known literary figures who willingly promised their support was that of Robert Louis Stevenson, who wrote to the treasurer with a plea that the money should be used for the benefit of the author's family.

[1] The value of his dwelling-house at Harrow was, of course, included in this sum.

W. Scott Dalgleish, Esq., LL.D.   *April 24th,* 1894.
Dear Sir,

It will give me great pleasure to have my name appear on the representative committee of the many grateful readers of the late Mr. R. M. Ballantyne. I shall request my lawyer to send my subscription.

At the same time I cannot allow this to go without entering my protest in a limited extent to the proposals (as I understand them) of the Memorial Committee. It appears to me that when a writer who has given us all great pleasure and made childhood charming for so many, but who seems to have been in far from wealthy circumstances—when such a man dies and leaves a widow and family, the proper object of our little subscriptions is indicated beyond doubt. Mr. Ballantyne would, I am sure, be vastly more gratified if we added to the prosperity of his wife and family than if we erected to him the tallest monument in Rome.

I am aware that the public think otherwise; but the public are not all men of letters. What I have to press upon you is to keep the memorial small—'the primary object—the monument,' inexpensive; and to devote as much as possible to the funds collected to what was doubtless Mr. Ballantyne's 'primary object,' his wife and family. It seems to me that a simple tablet would suffice with our benefactor's name, dates of birth and death, the indication that he was the author of many works, and some words to this effect: 'Erected to his cheerful memory by a grateful generation.' This would not cost much and, with taste, it may be as elegant as you please; taste costs nothing; and Ballantyne's 'primary object'—the subject probably of his most anxious dying thoughts—can then be carried out in a manner suitable to his wishes, and honourable to our gratitude.

Excuse me to have detained you so long, and believe me,
    Yours faithfully,
      Robert Louis Stevenson.[1]

---

[1] Stevenson's letter was printed in the *Scottish Daily News* on June 9th, 1894, and in many other leading daily papers during the same week.

Before the end of the year over six hundred pounds had been subscribed, mostly in pennies and sixpences from the thousands of boys to whom his books had given so much pleasure. Stevenson's letter had an undoubted effect on the deliberation of the Memorial Committee, for they finally decided that only forty guineas should be spent on the actual memorial and presented a cheque for the balance to his widow.

A white marble tombstone was placed on his grave, on which the following words were cut.

IN LOVING MEMORY OF ROBERT MICHAEL BALLANTYNE,
THE BOYS' STORY WRITER.
Born at Edinburgh, April 24th, 1825—Died at Rome,
February 8th, 1894
THIS STONE IS ERECTED BY FOUR GENERATIONS OF GRATEFUL
FRIENDS IN SCOTLAND AND ENGLAND

There remains little else to tell.

John Ballantyne died in May 1897, leaving his wife, Teenie, and his remaining child, Edith, in very reduced circumstances, for he had nothing to bequeath them and the pensions on which they had lived for many years ceased with his death.

Within a few years, Jeanie Ballantyne sold the house in Harrow, finding it far too large now that most of her children had left home to make their own way in the world. After her three daughters had married, she made her home first with one and then with another, spending a few months with each, and before long she was surrounded with a growing flock of grandchildren. Her health continued almost perfect until her seventy-ninth year, when she died peacefully while on a visit to her daughter Jane at Swanage.

Their eldest son, Frank, abandoned any idea of becoming a doctor after his father died, and went out to India to plant tea, an occupation at which he seems to have been moderately successful until his retirement on a pension in 1925. Ted Ballantyne rose to the rank of major in the 19th Bengal Lancers, one of the Indian Army's crack regiments, but died of pneumonia at Marseilles at the age of only thirty-five, when on the way home for a spell of leave. Ballantyne's youngest son, Hans, made a fortune. After leaving Harrow School, he too went out to India, having secured a post with a large banking house. The chairman of this company happened to be an Old Harrovian himself, and within a few years Hans was promoted to a seat on the board. At the age of forty-five he gashed his leg on a thorn when on a pig-sticking expedition with the chairman's son, the wound festered and a few days later he died of blood poisoning, but by this time he had become a director of fifteen companies and was the financial adviser to the Viceroy. By his Will, his estate of over one hundred and twenty thousand pounds was divided between his mother and his surviving sisters and brother, thus relieving them of any further financial anxiety for the remainder of their lives.

And what of the man who wrote the hundred or more books that delighted the hearts of tens of thousands of boys of all ages? What literary reputation remains to the Scot who believed so fervently in the civilising influence of the white man and the inevitable triumph of the pure in mind and body over the pagan unbelievers and immoral passions of a very naughty world? The fact that a great number of his stories are still in print today, over one hundred years since they first appeared, is probably the greatest tribute that can be paid to his memory, and one that would no doubt gladden his heart as nothing else could.

Despite his too-good-to-be-true heroes and somewhat threadbare plots, he has earned a place far above the lowly in the annals of English juvenile literature. As the first to allow the youthful heroes of his tales to wander freely far from home, unrestrained by the curbing hands and stifling platitudes of accompanying adults; and as a pioneer of the straightforward adventure story encased in the realism of a factual background, greater recognition should be accorded the author for the influence his works exerted on the many who followed in his footsteps. To dismiss him as one whose popularity stemmed merely from the fact that he happened to be a little less didactic and self-righteous than those who had gone before is to deny him his excellent qualities as a story-teller, one who could hold the attention of his readers through the pages of volume after volume, and keep them waiting impatiently for his next tale to appear. As the reviewer of

The Morning Post put it—'In his tales of the sea, of the forest and the flames, and in all that he wrote, there is a fidelity to nature and a knowledge of many paths of life which were not surpassed by any author in his special field of literature.'

His weakness lay in his being straitjacketed by his puritanism; in being unable to write a romantic and exciting story of adventure that was completely unmoralised and unashamed—as Stevenson did when he enthralled the boys of yesterday, today, and a thousand tomorrows with his immortal *Treasure Island*. Too often the action in Ballantyne's stories is braked by the gum of piety, and the evangelistic soliloquising of the bloodthirsty young characters he made his heroes, who lightheartedly slaughtered the fauna and the natives with impartial vigour, before falling on their knees to thank God for His infinite mercy and a successful day's sport. But, although his pages may have run scarlet, there is no doubt that his books were read, for, from the 'fifties onwards, Ballantyne opened for the sons of the rapidly expanding *literati* of middle- and working-class families an exciting new vista of a world spiced with romance and danger which lay waiting for the young men of Britain to grow up and explore. He projected into lives that were often drab and humdrum a realistically coloured adventure image, mirroring his readers in the figures of his heroes, and leaving them tantalised with the knowledge that they, too, could equally well have overcome the fearful odds against which Ralph, Jack and Peterkin, grappled so bravely. He employed what was soon a well-tried formula, by giving full rein to youthful emotions within the strict bounds set by Christian morality, while leading his readers through dramatically bloody chapters of shipwreck, slaughter, capture and escape, to the inevitable happy ending of a wealthy and pious old age. Boys purchased his annual Christmas book in their thousands and the name of Ballantyne became the best loved of any writer of adventure stories of his day.

It is true that he portrayed a world in which the good were terribly good, and the bad were terribly bad, and the British were terribly British—and worth ten of any foreigners alive, by Jingo! But in the age in which he lived it was not only the young who believed that a benevolent God had arranged things thus, so that Her Imperial Majesty, The Queen, could, with the aid of His occasional intervention (and that of her Army and Navy), more easily hold sway over the coloured masses which peopled her vast dominions. Ballantyne, G. A. Henty and the rest of the boys' authors of the period never for one moment doubted the innate benevolence of British imperialism, coupled, as it always was, with the blessings of Christianity which sooner or later were visited on the conquered. After all—we knew best how to handle the blighters! For any writer to have dared to suggest otherwise would have been considered the blackest heresy by the young men of Victoria's England. For these were the boys who, in their turn, were to become the soldiers and sailors, the explorers and trail-blazers, the missionaries and bishops, the merchant adventurers, the exploiters, the Word-spreaders, the successes and failures of the great British Empire on which the sun would never set.

Index

(The letter 'f' before a page number indicates that the reference will be found in a footnote.)

315